Clearing the Coastline

Matthew McKenzie

Clearing the Coastline

The Nineteenth-Century Ecological & Cultural Transformation of Cape Cod

University Press of New England
Hanover and London

University Press of New England

www.upne.com

© 2010 University Press of New England

All rights reserved

Manufactured in the United States of America

Designed by Katherine B. Kimball

Typeset in Bulmer by Integrated Publishing Solutions

Title page and chapter-opening images: Line drawing by Charles Douglas reproduced from the Canadian Museum of Nature.

Library of Congress Cataloging-in-Publication Data

McKenzie, Matthew G.

   Clearing the coastline : the ninetheenth-century ecological & cultural transformation of Cape Cod / Matthew McKenzie.

      p. cm.

   Includes bibliographical references and index.

   ISBN 978-1-58465-918-1 (cloth : alk paper) — ISBN 978-1-58465-919-8 (pbk. : alk. paper)

   1. Fisheries—Massachusetts—Cape Cod—History—19th century. 2. Fishery resources—Massachusetts—Cape Cod—History—19th century. 3. Marine resources—Massachusetts—Cape Cod—History—19th century. 4. Fisheries—Social aspects—Massachusetts—Cape Cod—History—19th century. 5. Fishers—Massachusetts—Cape Cod—History—19th century. 6. Social change—Massachusetts—Cape Cod—History—19th century. 7. Cape Cod (Mass.)—Environmental conditions. 8. Coastal ecology—Massachusetts—Cape Cod—History—19th century. 9. Cape Cod (Mass.)—Social conditions—19th century. 10. Cape Cod (Mass.)—Economic conditions—19th century. I. Title.

   SH222.M4M275   2010

   333.3'7270974492—dc22   2010035173

5 4 3 2 1

for Shannon and Sam

Contents

List of Tables and Illustrations   ix

Acknowledgments   xi

Introduction   1

1   Wastelands   7

2   Management   28

3   Workspace   54

4   Prosperity   88

5   Abstractions   111

6   Removals   137

Conclusion   174

Notes   181

Bibliography   207

Index   221

Tables and Illustrations

Tables

4.1.	Financial overview of select Barnstable County fisheries, 1865	103
6.1.	Alewife catch, Barnstable County, 1879–86, with Chatham and Harwich catch proportions	143
6.2.	Trophic levels and food consumption rates for select species	147
6.3.	Catch and catch-per-haul figures, Woods Hole area traps, 1886–95, 1898, and 1907–14	148

Figures

1.1.	Moraines and heads of outwash plains	10
2.1.	William Wood, *The South Part of New-England, as It is Planted This Yeare, 1634*	30
3.1.	H. W. Elliott and Capt. J. W. Collins, *Jigging Mackerel over the Vessel's Rail*	58
3.2.	H. W. Elliott and Capt. J. W. Collins, *Jigs and Jig Molds*	59
3.3.	H. W. Elliott and Capt. J. W. Collins, *Old Style Grand Bank Cod Schooner*	62
3.4.	H. W. Elliott and Capt. J. W. Collins, *Hand-Line Dory Cod Fishing on the Grand Bank*	63
3.5.	John Barber, *Eastern View of Edgartown*	75
3.6.	John Barber, *View from the Northeastern Edge of Provincetown*	76
3.7.	John Barber, *Northern View of Wellfleet Harbor*	77
3.8.	John Barber, *Western View of Fairhaven*	78
3.9.	Albert van Beest, *New Bedford from Fairhaven* (1854)	80
3.10.	William Bradford, *Study of Fairhaven Waterfront* (1850s or 1860s)	81

4.1.   "Taking Fish from Pound Net, Cape Cod" [1891]   97
4.2.   Plan of Captain Isaiah Spindle's pound net, Cape Cod, [1891]   99
6.1.   Annual average baitfish catch per weir, Barnstable County,
        1879–86   142
6.2.   Annual average alewife catch per weir, Barnstable County,
        1879–86   142
6.3.   Annual alewife catch per unit of effort (CPUE), 1879–86   144
6.4.   Annual average "food fish" catch per weir, Barnstable County,
        1879–86   144
6.5.   Annual average "food fish" catch per weir, by species,
        Barnstable County, 1879–86   144
6.6.   John Frederick Kensett, *Eaton's Neck* (1872)   162
6.7.   Thomas Worthington Whittredge, *Second Beach at Newport*
        (1878–80)   163

Acknowledgments

No book sees the light of day without the help of numerous friends, family members, colleagues, and professionals whose attention and support give as much life to a book as the author himself. This work is no exception. Throughout the six years I spent researching, conceptualizing, writing, and polishing this study, I have piled up debt upon debt to an army of people whose assistance and guidance proved essential in bringing this work about. In addition, as this project's interdisciplinary approach took me well out of my formal training—sending me to ecologists, fisheries policy professionals, and art historians—I owe even more than had I kept this book's scope within traditional historical fields.

Far from a liability, however, these debts bring me the greatest pleasure to publicly thank those who helped me. To the extent this book is any good, it is because of their assistance; its weaknesses, errors, and other shortcomings are mine alone.

The germ of this project came from my involvement with the History of Marine Animal Population (HMAP) project's 2002 International Summer School hosted by the University of New Hampshire and supported by the Census of Marine Life (CoML) and the Sloane Foundation. Working with marine ecologists from around the globe, who derived very different conclusions from the same sources I was working with, I learned the importance of seeing historical records from a variety of disciplinary perspectives. I continued these studies during a brief collaboration with the Gulf of Maine Cod Project at the University of New Hampshire in 2003. There, conversations with Andy Rosenberg, Jeff Bolster, Andy Cooper, Karen Alexander, Stefan Claesson, and Bill Leavenworth got me thinking about the importance of detailed understandings of marine ecology in interpreting the maritime past. These interests received further nurturing from my involvement with HMAP's World Whaling Project directed by Tim Smith, and through friendships with others from HMAP: Rene Poulsen, Bo Poulsen, and Loren McClenachan. More immediately, however, it was the opportunity Catherine Marzin and Stefan Claesson extended to me to hunt down southern New England fisheries records for the Stellwagen Bank National Marine Sanctuary's Marine Historical Ecology source survey (NOAA Contract/Grant No. NA04NO54290190) in 2004 and 2005 that allowed me to see the wealth of material detailing the southern New England inshore fisheries.

The Sea Education Association (SEA) in Woods Hole, Massachusetts, and the many friends I gained there also helped bring this project along. SEA allowed me, as maritime studies faculty, to work my passage to the 2004 Three Societies' Meeting in Halifax, Nova Scotia. SEA supported trips to the 2004 American Society for Environmental History annual meeting in St. Paul, Minnesota, and, along with the University of New Hampshire, to HMAP's 2004 Oceans Past meeting in Kolding, Denmark. SEA also allowed me the opportunity to visit Cape Cod's many local archives and present findings at the Cape Cod Natural History conference in March 2005 and at the Wellfleet Bay State of the Harbor meeting in the fall of 2006.

Most importantly, SEA encouraged me to bring my research into their unique, motivating, and inspiring classrooms on shore. In addition, Paul Joyce, SEA's academic dean, saw the value of sending me and my work to sea, where trips with Captains Virginia Land-McGuire, Chris McGuire, Steve Tarrant, Beth Doxsee, and Elliot Rappaport taught me much, including the fact that tall-ship sailing, even in a modern context, was work that most professional mariners preferred not to discuss on shore. During these voyages I was fortunate to work alongside Dr. Gary Jarasolow and Dr. Chuck Lea (who have spent more time at sea performing oceanographic research than I think any other oceanographers living or dead).

I also had the pleasure to sail, twice, with Dr. Jeff Schell. Standing at the science-deck rail of the ssv *Corwith Cramer* on the Scotian Shelf, and that of the *Robert C. Seamans* in the Pacific Northwest, he challenged to me to situate my historical findings within a larger marine ecological context. He loaned me lab copies of marine ecology textbooks and took time to explain— to a historian—the different ways of measuring biodiversity, and the value of linking marine animals to one another and to different fishermen through trophic studies. I shared with him literary explorations of the sea, and of

Jack Kerouac, and on the quarterdeck, in the lab, in the aft cabin, and on the rail our conversations over those weeks always reminded me that oceanographers and historians really chase after similar goals.

At the Avery Point campus of the University of Connecticut, I found myself among like-minded researchers and scholars who supported interdisciplinary work even as far-ranging as that presented here. Associate Vice-Provost Joseph Comprone encouraged me to keep my interdisciplinary focus as I took up the coordinatorship of the American studies program there. Furthermore, my friend and colleague Helen Rozwadowski pushed me to think more carefully about the role of the sciences in the history of marine resource use. I did not *want* to "think more carefully about the role of the sciences in the history of marine resource use," but she was right in the end, and I am indebted to her for her help, friendship, and support.

Peter Auster deserves special mention. In him, I found a friend and marine ecologist willing to see what comes up when maritime history and the marine sciences come together. He talked me down from the edge of taxonomic distinctiveness calculations, further coached me on ecological principles, and constantly reminded me that "stuff changes and it doesn't necessarily mean we caused it. What does the data say?" Through our seminar "Historical Marine Ecology / Marine Environmental History" I have had the pleasure working with him in presenting these ideas to students and working through the methodological, interpretive, and epistemological questions this field raises. To the extent any of the ecology in this is right, it is because of him; to the extent the ecology is not right, again, that's my fault.

I need to extend thanks to a number of other University of Connecticut colleagues—friends—who took time to read, comment, and challenge my work. In the History Department, Christopher Clark, Ken Gouwens, Brendan Kane, and Charles Lansing all read portions of the manuscript to its ultimate improvement. Brendan Kane donated hours in reading, evaluating, and constructively critiquing drafts, and his skill in identifying the one key point I had left out of a discussion has improved this manuscript to no end. My thanks go to all my History Department colleagues, but especially to Brendan. Wayne Franklin in the English Department also helped me tighten my argument, as did Kevin McBride in Anthropology, who shared his expertise of Late Woodland southern New England native peoples. A draft of chapter 3 similarly benefited from the insights offered by the University of Connecticut's Humanities Institute's manuscript working group organized by Anna Mae Duane in 2008.

From the broader marine environmental history field, five colleagues have my special thanks and my unending gratitude: mentor Nancy Shoemaker, again Helen Rozwadowski, Lance van Sittert, Matthew Morse Booker, and Katey Anderson all read the complete draft and offered detailed, concise, and constructive commentary. Their gifts of time and feedback helped me transform a very rough manuscript into something better, and I am especially grateful to all of them. I hope this work will speak well of their efforts on my behalf.

The University of Connecticut's Research Foundation and AAUP chapter funded travel to a number of conferences where various elements of this book were presented: the North Atlantic Fisheries History Association's 2007 meeting in Bergen, Norway; the 2009 American Historical Association meeting in New York; HMAP's 2009 Oceans Past II meeting at the University of British Columbia in Vancouver; the North American Society for Oceanic History's 2009 meeting at the California Maritime Academy in Vallejo; and the 2010 meeting of the American Historical Association in San Diego, California. A History Department and University of Connecticut College of Liberal Arts and Sciences junior faculty leave in the spring of 2009 provided me with essential time needed to finish the manuscript.

A number of librarians also helped make this work possible: the staff at the Marine Biological Laboratory Library in Woods Hole; Jan Heckman, Beth Rumery, and Barbara Vizoyen at the Avery Point library; and the people at the National Archives and Records Administration in Waltham, Massachusetts, all helped me greatly. So did Mary Sicchio, of both the Falmouth Historical Society and Cape Cod Community College's Nickerson Room: Mary's knowledge of Cape Cod sources is without parallel, and this work could not have moved forward without her help. I also wish to thank David Starkey, Poul Holm, Michaela Barnard, and the anonymous reviewers for selecting an early draft of these ideas for publication in Starkey, Holm, and Barnard (eds.), *Oceans Past: Management Insights from the History of Marine Animal Populations Project* (London: Earthscan Press, 2007).

At University Press of New England, I had the good fortune to find strong supporters. Phyllis Deutsch early on took an interest in this project, and working with her and Stephen Hull has been a pleasure and an education. Similarly, the editorial attention this work received from Ann Brash, Glenn Novak, and Katy Grabill has also made this work far better than I could ever imagine. In addition, Richard Judd and Tim Smith both offered great advice in improving the manuscript, and while I did not follow all their recommendations, I am grateful for their every word. In addition, I received assistance from my Avery Point colleague Mark Newall in preparing digital files for publication.

In addition to the colleagues on which I relied, I must thank my family and friends—including those listed above—for listening to more about small fish and inshore fishermen than anyone could be humanly expected to tolerate. In particular, I would like to thank Jill and Ken Wilson for their support for Shannon and me, and then Sam. They recognized better than many how much help an extra pair of hands, a wonderfully relaxing holiday, or an unexpectedly free afternoon could be. Thank you.

Ultimately, however, Shannon and Sam deserve my greatest thanks. There simply isn't the space to list all the ways they have helped me. Besides, the three of us know it better than I can put into words, anyway. Thank you both.

Clearing the Coastline

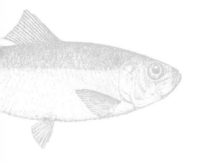

Introduction

In 2005, Connecticut, Rhode Island, and Massachusetts imposed a three-year ban on taking of alewives or blue-black herring. Unlike the reaction to the cod and other fishery cutbacks introduced in the 1990s, no one protested these complete closings of southern New England's centuries-old river herring fisheries. No one yelled. No one called politicians. No one rallied on fishing docks. No one called lobbyists, or the New England Fisheries Management Council, or, for that matter, environmental defense foundations. No one hurled insults. What little response the bans elicited was limited to a handful of local groups and fisheries managers, who reacted approvingly. Aside from those particular folks, however, few cared. For perhaps the first time in the history of New England fisheries management, a whole fishery was closed, and no one screamed.

Just over a century before, however, southern New Englanders *had* screamed about the health of their river herring stocks. Between 1869 and 1872, hook-and-line fishermen avowed that stationary shore-fishing gear (including weirs, pounds, and traps) was destroying stocks of these important fish. In one of the area's largest grassroots movements since the American Revolution, three thousand hook-and-line fishermen and their supporters marshaled economic, political, and even moral arguments to seek an end to what they saw as an abuse of local marine resources. They filed petitions, they testified in hearings, they enlisted the aid of prominent politicians. They, along with their scientific supporters, pitted their claims of ecological change against arguments by the weir fishermen, and their scientific supporters, that people had no influence upon nature's bounty.

In the end, the hook-and-line fishermen lost. The shore gear expanded, and the fish, along with the fishermen, left Cape Cod's coastlines. Even worse, within a generation, few retained any memory of the people and the fish that had, for centuries, shaped, defined, and subsisted on Cape Cod's harsh coasts. By 1900, the fishermen, their knowledge patterns, and their communities lay forgotten, and Cape Cod's once-abundant runs of river herring had all but disappeared. Within two generations, the small fish and the small fishermen that had once defined the Cape had been cleared from its shores, and no one even noticed they were gone.

This book seeks to uncover how Cape Cod went from a place where communities managed their local resources for long-term survival to one where those resources and traditions came to be all but forgotten. On the surface, this transformation could be explained away simply by claiming fishermen took too many fish. That has been the pat explanation for the collapse of numerous fish stocks in the northwest Atlantic throughout the twentieth century and into the twenty-first. Such reductionist views, however, ignore the wider social, ecological, and cultural contexts in which fishing exists. As Arthur McEvoy has argued, fishermen have long found themselves at the intersection of the human and nonhuman worlds, where changes in one affect— through the fishermen—changes in the other.[1] Such a vision also ignores half the equation, which, as Jeff Bolster has recently contended, must include an understanding of the complex dynamism inherent in both human and marine communities.[2] But for too long, however, historians have ignored this dynamism and instead have chosen to see the marine world as a passive recipient of human actions and ambitions. Thus, simply blaming the fishermen for the collapse of fish stocks at once misrepresents the problem and excuses the rest of society for environmental degradation.

Not surprisingly, then, *Clearing the Coastline* argues that the nineteenth-century transformation of Cape Cod was the product of more than fishermen taking too many fish. Rather, the metamorphosed Cape Cod coastal realm represented a complex intersection of changing labor regimes, economic orientations, ecological changes, and cultural representation. Far more than another tale of fishermen taking too many fish, Cape Cod's path from an eighteenth-century backwater to twentieth-century resort destination emerged through a variety of influences found far from the decks of fishing vessels and fish merchants' piers.

At the heart of this study lies people working different types of fishing gear along Cape Cod shores in two different but overlapping fisheries. When most people think of New England's fishing history, they think of the banks fishery, where large, fast, well-built schooners sailed to offshore grounds for days or weeks on end for cod, haddock, pollock, halibut, hake, or other groundfish. This was the fishery that, through its ties to the international Atlantic market, built New England's fortunes and brought in needed cash and credit from the seventeenth through the twentieth century.

Another fishery appears, however, when fishing records are examined more carefully. This one—the inshore fishery—focused on local fish stocks and local markets. It was so ubiquitous that it rarely gained any attention, and it operated along different lines, in providing fresh fish for immediate consumption. The two fisheries were not mutually exclusive: before, during, and after banks-fishing careers, fishermen worked inshore on their own hook when weather, age, or access to good berths prevented them from sailing to the Scotian Shelf or the Grand Banks of Newfoundland. Moreover, the inshore fishery represented an important mainstay for Cape Codders' subsistence and prosperity. It may not have been glamorous, but taking small inshore fish—like river herring—for food, fertilizer, bait, or oil allowed many people living on Cape Cod's sandy soils to survive until spring harvests arrived.

Not all inshore fishing was the same. This study differentiates between the hook-and-line fishermen and the weir fishermen, all of whom worked inshore (though for most of the nineteenth century, banks fishermen also used hook and line almost exclusively). Inshore hook-and-line fishermen, as the name suggests, relied upon baited hooks, small boats, inshore fish, and local markets to make their livings.

Traps, pounds, and weirs, on the other hand, all essentially corralled passing fish into a holding pen, until the crew came out to clear the net. Weirs, most commonly found in Maine's protected coves, were usually made of sticks, slats, or saplings driven into the mud and spaced so tightly as to form a barrier to fish. Pound nets—the most correct term for the southern New England forms—used barriers made from netting, which withstood the storms and weather better than weirs. Traps, commonly used in Rhode Island during the period in question, were shaped differently from pound nets or weirs, but again worked along the same principles. By the end of the nineteenth century, all three forms of fishing were lumped under the heading "weir fishing," although technically, few Cape Codders actually used weirs, strictly defined.

While differences between fishermen may seem minute, how each group fished affected its access to investment capital, markets, influence, and insulation from economic change. Stationary fishing operations had a relationship to markets and capital unlike that of inshore hook-and-line fishing: Weir men looked to more distant markets that could absorb the larger volume of fish they took and shipped by rail to Boston, New York, New Bedford, or Gloucester. They worked on different terms from their hook-and-line colleagues and most likely constituted a separate population. Consequently, such minute categories represented very real differences to those within them, and we can make sense of Cape Cod's nineteenth-century fisheries only when they are viewed through this lens.

While this study will examine the changing labor, scientific, ecological, and economic contexts of Cape fishing that drove much of the region's nineteenth-century transformation, it will also consider the question of how such changes and the conflicts they engendered came to be lost to the region's collective memory. The answer to that question rests far from the working beaches and fish piers lining Cape Cod's coastline. How and why people forgot the fate of their fish can be answered only through examinations of larger cultural visions of the southern New England shore. Consequently, this study must consider the role that changing popular perceptions of coastal spaces—first as places of industrious work and later as places of pristine nature—also influenced the way people changed and understood their coastal environment. Southern New England inshore fishermen took fish for sale, certainly, but they did so within larger, changeable economic, social, scientific, ecological, and cultural milieus that affected how, how much, and for how long they could continue to do so. More than just a story of how changing labor practices led to ecological, social, and scientific changes along the southern New England shore, this work also explores the power of coastal zone representations—scientific, artistic, and literary—in celebrating, and then erasing, southern New England's fish and fishing communities.

While this work focuses on Cape Cod, it does so not from a regional interest. Cape Cod was one of the first areas on the eastern seaboard to find its growing population and commercial development colliding with the region's finite agricultural and inshore maritime resources. Exploring human economic, social, intellectual, cultural, and ecological ties to the marine environment requires a wide array of historical sources. The range of materials used to uncover these nuanced ties also introduces, however, perils of scope and scale, if some boundaries are not imposed. Past works that have examined issues similar to those addressed in this study have embraced conceptual bounds to keep their studies focused and coherent. For example, scholars exploring the management of riparian resources in industrial development have focused on the related social and legal implications. Other scholars have examined coastal fisheries, too, in light of New England's transformation from a "precapitalist" to a capitalist and industrial economy.[3] Similarly, researchers exploring the advent of tourism and the creation of regional identity have included in their work events taking place on Cape Cod.[4]

As insightful and important as these works are, however, something is lost when such a wide range of historical change is pulled apart strand by interpretive strand. As this work will argue, Cape Cod's industrial development (such as it was), the management of its river fisheries, "scientific" understandings of the region's marine environment, and cultural visions of the Cape as a whole, when considered together and folded into an ecological frame, reveal important new insights into how people related to their immediate world. In this work these subjects will not represent ends in and of themselves, but rather part of a larger history of how a people related to their inshore marine resources. That story emerges only when we see these strands laid together.

In addition to weaving together different historical perspectives, this study attempts to situate human history within a larger story of changing marine ecosystems. To do so, it must borrow tools from marine ecology to interpret yet one more rich archive Cape Cod offers for marine environmental history—its century-and-a-half of fisheries data. Since the 1860s, Cape Cod has been the site not only of the development of fisheries science, but also the application of that discipline to political conflicts over the fisheries themselves. Those conflicts left behind comparative troves of catch records. Like a foreign-language grammar system, marine ecology allows us to translate these numerical sources into understandable stories, which when situated within a larger historical context, offer glimpses into how the marine ecosystem responded—if at all—to changing human behaviors. In other words, marine ecology allow us to determine to some degree how Cape Cod's inshore environment responded to changing fishing practices, and how Cape Cod people, in turn, responded to those ecological changes.

Some may take exception to my use of the terms "environment" and "ecosystem" in referring to fishermen's and scientists' understanding of the marine world. Clearly, people from the nineteenth century and earlier did not think of the world in terms of "ecosystems." But they were aware of relationships between animals competing for food and space within the same marine region. In this, "ecosystem" is similar to other interpretive lenses used in historical analysis—gender, race, ethnicity, class, sexuality, just to name a few. While past people may not have thought in these terms as explicitly as we do now, they were aware that constructed differences between men and women, blacks and whites, rich and poor, gay and straight did shape the world they lived in, for better and for worse. They may not have used the technical language we have now, but the same concepts shaped parts of their consciousness, and in this, the Cape Cod fishermen who saw the fates of one fish tied up in the availability of another followed patterns of thought much the same as ours.

Arguably, nowhere else in North America did the finiteness of the local resource base collide so early with human economic systems; and nowhere else can the complex responses—both human and ecological—be traced as clearly as those at work on Cape Cod in the nineteenth century. While this is a story about how people related to, understood, used, and then overused their inshore fisheries, it is also a moral tale about how communities try to look away from the unpleasant and unsettling signs of environmental degradation. Commercial prosperity lulled Cape Codders into allowing laxer management of local inshore fisheries resources, which in turn led to dire consequences for communities of both fish and fishermen. After a long tradition of tight regulation of fisheries based upon local knowledge, that same local knowledge allowed local people to more heavily exploit their fish runs and bring to the Cape a long-sought financial security. That economic success attracted the praise of artists and painters, who contextualized Cape Cod's coastal fisheries development within a larger tableau celebrating Americans' ingenuity in extracting wealth from nature. Praised by outside observers, and now with some financial security, Cape Codders stopped paying close attention to how their resources were managed and began to embrace more intensive forms of coastal fishing that changed coastal life.

As fishing people left, artists, writers, and tourists arrived, and through their embrace of new aesthetic tastes and tourist economies, they erased evidence of the region's social and ecological changes. They recast Cape Cod as pristine nature, untrammeled by industrial development. Thus, as well-heeled tourists arrived on the Cape to buy up abandoned homes and to bask on empty beaches abutting empty waters, they saw such emptiness as a natural state. In doing so, they—and we—have relegated the once-thriving communities of fish and fishermen to distant memory, and severed the line of memory tying past to future.

CHAPTER 1

Wastelands

So, more than 5,000 years ago, Moshup got a glimpse of the coastal plain and told his father that was where he wanted to settle; there was a magical call to him. Everything was perfect there and no one was yet continuously living on the coastal plain; rather, People were coming and going to hunt and fish.

Moshup had lots of cousins and they were all named Moshup too. He gathered them together and told them of the beauty at Aquinnah and the abundance of whales and game meat for food. Moshup was not happy on the mainland. So, after long and careful consideration, he decided he would search out a new place where he and his followers might live in peace. He invited all who wanted to come to follow him to this new home.

Moshup wandered along marshes, over dunes and through the forest. After dragging his huge foot, Moshup paused to look around and the ocean rushed to form a pool behind him. The pool deepened and became a channel; and, the waves, along with the full moon tides, formed the wide opening which now separates the Elizabeth Islands and Cappoaquit/Noman's Island. Still, it was the land ahead where Moshup wished to live in peace. So, he again dragged his great toes, permitting the waters of the ocean to rush in and surround the land we now know as the island of Martha's Vineyard [Noepe]. He dragged his foot once again and the majestic Aquinnah cliffs appeared.

—Helen Vanderhoop Manning, with Jo-Ann Eccher, *Moshup's Footsteps: The Wampanoag Nation Gay Head / Aquinnah, The People of First Light*

Moshup was the first schoolmaster . . . .
—Wampanoag Tribe of Gay Head, "Other Stories and Information"

The Wampanoag creation story of the trickster and teacher Moshup offers important insights into how people viewed, understood, and related to Martha's Vineyard and the larger Cape Cod and Island area of southern New England. The first insight stems from the story's ecological information. As Moshup traveled, he created the key components of the southern New England coastal ecosystem: dunes protected marshes and estuaries; estuaries, fed by forest nutrients, supported marine and terrestrial animal life; and those animals, in turn, supported human life. Tellers of Moshup's tale also acknowledged the important role that marine life played in local subsistence strategies. As he walked across the sands, Moshup's huge foot created shallows, which then, with the aid of currents, created the channels that separated islands from the mainland. Into these waters came fish and whales, which eventually provided a major source of food for the Wampanoag people. Consequently, the elders who passed this story down to the next generation were not just telling a tale of the creation of Noepe—what we now call Martha's Vineyard. Moshup's legend also explains how local people came to understand and live in their local environment. The story highlighted the key components to the success of this local region—shallow waters, marshes, tides and currents, forests, and dunes. As the first teacher, Moshup also taught the Wampanoag people to whale, to fish, and to be generous. Ultimately, the Moshup legends simplified for the Wampanoag people the millennia-long, complex process by which a people came to understand their local environment.

These two elements in the story of Moshup's creation of Noepe, that life relied upon both land and sea, and that the resources of each had to be learned through immediate local experience—that "Moshup was the first schoolmaster"—represent the starting point for this study of how people learned, used, envisioned, and then abused the fisheries resources they found along the southern New England shore. As much as this story is one of social, ecological, and cultural change, at its core rests the fundamental questions of how and why people turned to the inshore fisheries to augment thin and weak soils, what they learned in doing so, and how those lessons shaped the pressure people placed on local inshore resources.

Moshup taught his people to use marine resources to support life on land. Europeans would come to learn this in time, too. Both peoples found marine resources abundant, but soils thin. This stems from Cape Cod's formation, a process the Wampanoag people ascribed to Moshup's feet, but modern scientists ascribe to more complex processes. Contemporary scientific research reveals that at the foundation of Cape Cod life lay its unique combination of glacial soils, seawater, fresh water, sunlit estuaries, and nutrients. Geological evidence shows that Cape Cod's lands were formed twenty-three thousand years ago, when the Laurentide ice sheet reached its southernmost extent, leaving at its base a ridge of dirt, boulders, and rocky debris. As temperatures rose, meltwater pooled on the surface of the glacier until those lakes broke through the glacier's edge and ran off the glacier's surface and into the sea. Cape Cod came into existence as that water cut the glacier's southern edge into three lobes and carried sandy sediments into the ocean in fans of out-washed sand, gravel, and other lightweight sediments. Between the westernmost Buzzards Bay lobe and its eastern neighbor, the Cape Cod lobe, Martha's Vineyard—Noepe—slowly grew from under the waters. A similar process, happening farther east between the Cape Cod lobe and the South Channel lobe, formed the island of Nantucket (Fig 1.1).

For five thousand years, the Laurentide ice sheet retreated. Around eighteen thousand years ago, however, the retreat stalled. Again, moraines formed at the base of the ice lobes, creating the string of hills running from the southwestern end of the Elizabeth Islands northward to the middle of the isthmus between Buzzards Bay and Cape Cod Bay, and then east again to form western and central Cape Cod's backbone. The two valleys between the ice lobes also shifted. The first valley retreated north and a little west, with its outwash plain creating the western portion of the Cape. The second valley shifted farther east, eventually forming the Cape's outer arm and elbow. Between the two valleys, outwash plains joined to form the southern Cape Cod shore. As the ice retreated farther, Cape Cod's outer arm formed as a trail of outwash sands spilled out along the glacier's northern migration.[1]

By 10,000 BCE, Cape Cod's coast stretched southeast to roughly the edge of the Georges Bank's Great South Channel. As glaciers retreated farther, and as sea level consequently rose, the Atlantic crept north and west, breaking into the low-lying areas that would become Muskeget Channel and Nantucket Sound. Two thousand years later, encroaching waters filled in around Moshup's feet (as the Wampanoag envisioned it), isolating Martha's Vineyard and Nantucket. Waters also narrowed the lands that separated Cape Cod Bay from the Nantucket and Vineyard sounds, and filled in Buzzards Bay. By 4,000 BCE, with sea level rising roughly twenty feet (six meters) every thousand years, ocean waters eventually carved out the Elizabeth Islands.

On land, the development of Cape Cod's soils would play an essential role in shaping how human communities survived in the region. Like the rest of New England, Cape Cod developed fertile, nutrient-rich podzol soils on top

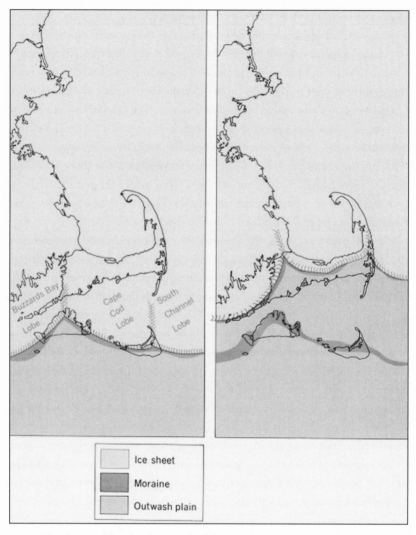

FIG. 1.1 Moraines and heads of outwash plains. Robert N. Oldale, "Geologic History of Cape Cod" (U.S. Geological Survey, http://pubs.usgs.gov/gip/capecod/index.html)

of less-fertile substrates as vegetation decomposed to create topsoils of vary-ing depths. In New England's interior, substrates made of more clay than sand developed, creating a less-permeable barrier for water to drain. This allowed more nutrients to remain and deepened topsoils. On Cape Cod, however, the porous, sandy, glacial moraine substrates allowed water to pass through more quickly.[2] As water flowed into the earth, it carried away with it more of the nutrients and minerals that larger plants needed for growth. This process created soils that favored pitch pines and scrub oaks whose root structures allowed them to survive in thinner soils, but whose acidic leaves and needles further leached out topsoil nutrients. This combination of thin, well-drained soils and acidic plant detritus helped create distinct areas of pines and oaks—called pine barrens—where relatively few other plants could survive. While areas on Cape Cod were certainly more fertile than the more distinctive and expansive New Jersey Pine Barrens, southern New England's soils still remained relatively thin and less fertile than other New England soils.[3]

While topsoils formed, between 7,000 and 4,000 BCE, rising sea levels elevated coastal water tables and pushed dense saltwater lenses through these sandy shores and into coastal ponds. Freshwater pond levels rose and eventually broke free of their basins, creating freshwater streams running to the sea. Where streams met the ocean, the waters filled in coastal estuaries, and as entrained sediments settled where ocean tides halted river currents, sandbars and barrier beaches formed at the river mouths.

Eventually the estuaries' sunlit shallows, well-mixed nutrients, and oxygenated water combined to create ideal conditions for marine plants. Like plants on land, marine plants require light, oxygen, and nutrients to convert solar energy into organic matter. Unlike terrestrial ecosystems, however, oceans provide relatively few nutrients, and for most forms of marine plants, nutrients must come from some other source. Around Cape Cod, numerous freshwater streams brought those necessities from the land, and as nutrients flowed into the shallow, protected estuaries, they mixed with oxygen and sunlight to provide the foundation for phytoplankton to capture and convert nutrients and sunlight into organic matter.[4]

This process—what ecologists call primary production—eventually formed the base of a food web of larger animals. As Cape Cod's estuaries came to host thriving communities of plankton, a wide array of predators, each one occupying its own distinctive niche, formed around estuaries and eventually in all of Cape Cod's coastal waters. Zooplankton fed upon phytoplankton, planktivores fed upon both, small shrimp and crabs fed upon the planktivores— and so on. Each predator in turn attracted other predators. Soon, a large web of predation linked every marine animal to every other, either directly or indirectly. Schooling fish such as alewives and blue-black herring, menhaden, scup, butterfish, and mackerel all came to feed on either the organic detritus, phytoplankton, or zooplankton, or on the smaller animals that fed on single-celled organisms. Of these schooling fish, blue-black herring and alewives also spawned in Cape Cod's protected streams and estuaries. Eventually, larger fish such as mackerel, bluefish, some basses, and even some of the smaller tunas followed the schooling fish inshore.

Some of these migratory species chose to remain. Driven by what ecologists call the marginal value theorem, some fish balanced the lower energy cost of remaining in one place and depleting desired food sources against the higher energy costs of traveling to find another patch of desired food. Around Cape Cod, where so many species of fish came to feed and spawn, it became more energy-efficient for some species to remain in one place.[5] In an area whose primary production attracted a higher concentration of prey species, predators could remain longer, optimizing their time feeding and reducing their time spent traveling to other patches of food. Gadid fish, for example—cod, haddock, pollock, and hake—arrived from Arctic waters but evolved into year-round resident fish that ate any readily available smaller fish (even their own young) or crustaceans, shifting inshore and offshore only as ocean temperatures fluctuated. As a result, some fish did not have to migrate away from preferred depth ranges, ocean temperatures, and bottom conditions to find sufficient food.[6]

Other species, however, chose to travel. Menhaden, mackerels, herrings, scup, bluefish, and tunas all embraced a migratory lifestyle, chasing food and fleeing predators. For these species, changing water temperatures and the behavior of prey—often influenced by temperature change—dictated range of movements. Menhaden, herrings, and shads, for example, opted to migrate south each winter and remain off the mouth of the Chesapeake and Delaware bays, feeding upon the rich flow of nutrients, small fish, and plankton that those estuaries produced. Tunas ranged even farther, along the shore and out to sea, and chased open-ocean stocks of mackerel as they, too, ranged. Each of these species in their turn, however, returned to Cape Cod's waters as water temperatures and prey availability dictated, creating as they did so a parade of fish coming through each spring.

Over time, Cape Cod developed rich communities of fish, divided roughly into those that carved out a local niche that allowed them to reside year-round, and those that passed through in the spring and fall to spawn or feed. Here, marine animals ranging from plankton to small fish and crustaceans thrived because nutrients from the land and the physical shape of the shore allowed smaller marine animals to grow. Consequently, more marine animals came inshore to feed and spawn, and eventually the area supported an abundant and diverse array of marine animals.

In a region marked by marine abundance and weak soils, it is not surprising that Moshup taught his peoples the importance of linking the resources of the land and sea. Harsh terrestrial conditions and rich coastal resources profoundly shaped local peoples' survival strategies, both before and after European settlement. Archaeologists have found that Cape Cod's earliest humans relied heavily upon inshore fish and shellfish species. As early as the Middle Archaic period—between 6,0000 and 4,000 BCE—coastal margins and estuaries emerged as some of first areas to see sustained human settlement. For example, archaeologist Frederick J. Dunford has found thirty-four Middle Archaic sites on Cape Cod; more than half of these sit in two clusters close to rich fishing areas along the Bass and Herring rivers.[7] Other sites reveal that sturgeon, Atlantic salmon, scup, bass, lobsters, white perch, bluefish, cod, and tautog all appeared in southern New England's pre-contact archaeological records, and according to archaeologist Elizabeth Little, Native American diets on Nantucket in the Late Woodland period comprised 15 percent fish and 43 percent shellfish.[8] For as long as people lived in the area, the abundant margin along southern New England's shores and estuaries directed much of the settlement patterns and formed the backbone of local peoples' diets.

The abundance of inshore resources also shaped Native Americans' economic and social development. For most of North America, maize agriculture provided human communities the impetus to shift away from nomadic existences and adopt more sedentary living patterns. In southern New England, however, inshore fish runs played this role. Separate studies by Jordan Kerber, David Bernstein, Mark Treskov, and Kevin McBride exploring Rhode Island and southern Connecticut human communities reveal that regular fish runs allowed people to develop settled life patterns long before the advent of maize agriculture.[9] Little and Schoeninger have shown similar findings for Martha's Vineyard and Nantucket.[10] Ultimately, Kathleen Bragdon argues, Late Woodland southern New England Algonquians used abundant inshore fish stocks to adopt what she calls "an estuarine conditional sedentism based on reliance upon a wide variety of marine and estuarine resources."[11] Such a change profoundly affected the social organization of coastal communities: by about 1,000 CE, coastal Native Americans, with increased population growth, a more sedentary life pattern, increased social hierarchy, and a distinctive political centralization, stood out from neighboring riverine and upland communities.[12] In short, Cape Cod offered distinct challenges to any human or animal living along its shores. With weak soils, unfruitful plants, and few tall trees, life, if limited to the land, promised to be hard. But Moshup ensured, when he dragged his feet and created the shallow waters and calm estuaries, that marine resources could provide for his people what the land could not. Living on the margin of land and sea did not necessarily mean a marginal life: if an animal or a human could draw upon both, life could be quite secure.

Moshup's legendary role as a teacher simplified a long, complex process by which the Wampanoag people observed, understood, and used their local environment. For Europeans coming to the region in the early seventeenth century, however, survival along southern New England's shores presented a steep learning curve. Certainly, New England appeared to offer quantities of animals and plants that amazed European visitors. While those resources may have seemed abundant, getting them, and surviving among them, proved anything but easy. Within a generation, Europeans had to find new ways to survive in what many contemporaries came to view as southern New England's coastal wasteland. Much of this knowledge they learned from native peoples following Moshup's teachings of generosity. Along with instruction from the Wampanoag, however, colonists also learned how their local environment functioned through observation, and through trial and error. In other words, they learned to live in the region though brutal firsthand experience.

Aside from the legendary rich shoals of fish they encountered there, the first wave of European navigators reconnoitering the coastlines for harbors and favorable lands found Cape Cod's sandy promontory at best a nuisance, and at worst a hazard. Unlike the Gulf of Maine, where rocky shores anchored the coastline, and where deep waters tend to run closer inshore, shifting sand shoals and shallow waters imperiled navigation for miles along Cape Cod's coastlines.[13] In 1604, for example, French explorer Samuel de Champlain described what is now Nauset Harbor as "a very dangerous harbor in consequence of the shoals and banks, where we saw breakers in all directions. It was almost low tide when we entered, and there were only four feet of water in the northern passage." While he found the interior "very spacious" and home to a broad meadow watered by two or three brooks, the location ultimately represented a mixed blessing: "It would be a fine place if the harbor were good."[14] Based on these impressions, Champlain named the area Cape Mallebar, to warn future explorers to avoid the area altogether.

Nor did the Frenchman find Cape Cod's weather particularly inviting. "While we were [at Mallebar], there was a northeast storm, which lasted four days: the sky being so overcast that the sun hardly shone at all." Even though it was the middle of July, Champlain noted "It was very cold and we were obliged to put on our great coats, which we had entirely left off." Unlike the treacherous harbor mouth, however, the inclement weather was something Champlain was willing to overlook: "I think the cold was accidental, as it is often elsewhere out of season."[15] Ultimately, however, the combination of moving sands and weather powerful enough to shift them posed too great a challenge to be brushed off.

> In consequence of the fogs and storms, we had not been able to go farther than Cape Mallebarre, where we waited several days for fair weather, in order to sail.... Accordingly, on the 25th [of July], we set out from this harbor, in order to make observations elsewhere. In going out, we came near being lost on the bar at the entrances, from the mistake of our pilots . . . who had imperfectly marked out the entrance of the channel on the southern side, where we were to go.[16]

Champlain may have been unfair in blaming his pilots. Cape Cod's southeastern corner is notoriously changeable, as storms and currents shift sand and carve entirely new channels every year. And, as John Stilgoe has pointed out, physical forces have even erased islands and created new ones for as long as people have charted the area.[17] Cape Cod's shifting coasts proved so notorious to early explorers that later attempts to change the name faced uphill battles against Cape Cod's navigational reputation. After Gosnold named the peninsula "Cape Cod" for the abundant stocks of fish he found nearby—again in an attempt to inform future voyagers—and after John Smith named it Cape James to curry favor with the English king, it was Champlain's Cape Mallebar that stuck until Europeans had more familiarity with navigating along the New England shore. As late as 1628, eight years after Plymouth's settlement, the Dutch agent in North America, Isaack des Rasieres, reported back to a business partner that "because [Plymouth's settlers] are afraid to pass Cape Mallabaer, and in order to avoid the length of the way," their traders had built a house and a shallop at a site called Aptuxcet on Buzzards

Bay's eastern headwaters.[18] In the 1630s William Bradford stated that the "point which first showed those dangerous shoals unto [sailors], they call Pointe Care, & Tuckers Terror; but [the] French & Dutch to this day call [Cape Cod] Malabar, by reason of those perilous shoals, and [the] losses they have suffered there."[19] Fish may have been abundant, but so, too, were the dangers to be faced in simply navigating along the southern New England shore. And before Europeans could ever consider harnessing Cape Cod's natural resources, they had to survive traveling along its coasts.[20]

Navigational hazards aside, European visitors to southern New England immediately believed they saw the region's commercial prospects. John Brereton, for example, traveling with Bartholomew Gosnold in 1602, described Cuttyhunk island as hosting "many plain places of grass, abundance of strawberries and other berries before mentioned." The mainland struck the European even more powerfully. Traveling by boat to a small inlet on the coast, Brereton wrote, "Coming ashore, we stood a while like men ravished at the beauty and delicacy of this sweet soil. . . . [there were] Meadows very large and full of green grass; even the most woody places (I speak only of such as I saw) do grow so distinct and apart, one tree from another, upon green grassy ground, somewhat higher than the plains, as if Nature would show herself above her power, artificial."[21] The following year, Martin Pring voyaged to the same area to explore and gather sassafras to sell on European medicinal markets. The land impressed him as much as it had Brereton the year before. Pring commented that it offered "vines, cedars, oaks, ashes, beeches, birch trees, cherry trees bearing fruit whereof we did eat, hazels, witch-hazels, the best wood of all other to make soap withal, walnut-trees, maples, holly to make bird-lime with, and a kind of tree bearing a fruit like a small red pear-plum with a crown or kno[t] on the top."[22] Descriptions such as these flowed from other explorers' pens, as Europeans encountered a natural world almost wholly unimaginable to Old World denizens. For sailors who had been at sea for months, American vegetation grew more lush; exotic fruits and nuts outshone European varieties; and abundant fish and game promised an easy life to those willing to uproot, cross the Atlantic, and establish colonial settlements.[23]

Such beauty, in and of itself, would not satisfy commercial backers, however, and consequently early explorers sought to test the region's apparent abundance. Gosnold's party, for example, "did sow on the island (as for trial) in sundry places, wheat, barley, oats, and peas, which in fourteen days were sprung up nine inches or more." Brereton concluded that "the soil is fat and lusty; the upper crust, of gray color; but a foot or less in depth, of the color of our hemp lands in England; and being thus apt for these and the like grains." Ultimately, the island represented a land where "the sowing or setting (after the ground is cleansed) is not greater labor, than if you should set or sow in one of our best prepared gardens in England."[24] Pring also sought to verify the suitability of this abundance for European needs. While at camp for a few weeks, Pring reported that

> we pared and [dug] up the Earth with shovels, and sowed wheat, barley, oats, peas, and sundry sorts of garden seeds, which for the time of our abode there, being about seven weeks, although they were late sown, came up very well, giving certain testimony to the goodness of the climate and of the soil. And it seemeth that oade, hemp, flax, rape-seed and such like which require a rich and fat ground, would prosper excellently in these parts. For in diverse places here we found grass about knee deep.[25]

Other European surveyors reported equally promising commercial prospects. Before he faced the shifting sands off Chatham and Nantucket shoals, Champlain reported that Cape Cod shores offered "woods, which are attractive and beautiful."[26] Around what would become Nauset, he noted, "The woods are filled with oaks, nut-trees, and beautiful cypresses [junipers] which are reddish in color and have a very pleasant odor."[27] John Smith, in 1614, wrote, "By reason of those sandy cliffs and cliffs of rock, both which we saw planted with gardens and cornfields . . . [the area was] well inhabited with a goodly, strong and well proportioned people." Ignorant of how native peoples fertilized and augmented the soils, Smith wondered that the rocky and sandy cliffs could support such magnificent people: "Who can but approve this a most excellent place for both health and fertility?"[28] Most of these early descriptions of the Cape's bountiful lands carry a hollow ring, however: overwrought, too good to be true, and certainly produced by men with great stakes riding on developing New World resources. Future settlers would find out that whatever bounty was to be had from the soil of southeastern New England would not last long.

Early descriptions of marine abundance, however, fell closer to the mark. Gosnold and almost all his successors commented on the rich stocks of commercially valuable codfish found in southern New England and Gulf of Maine offshore waters, so much so that these accounts have become a staple in colonial economic history and American environmental history alike.[29] Yet early explorers also commented on how many species of marine animals could be found inshore; and for the first wave of settlers, the abundance and utility of inshore species played as important a role as more commercially valuable species, like cod, that lived farther out to sea. For example, inshore species provided both food and raw materials that could be caught or collected with little investment and little skill. Martin Pring recorded in 1603, for example, "And as the land is full of God's good blessings, so is the Sea replenished with great abundance of fish, as Cods . . . seals to make oil withal, mullets, turbots, mackerels, herrings, crabs, lobsters, Creuises, and mussels with ragged pearls inside them."[30] James Rosier, accompanying George Weymouth to Maine in May 1605, commented, "While we were at shore, our men aboord with a few hooks got above thirty great Cods and Hadocks." The next month, he noted more species that Weymouth's men had found desirable: cod, haddock, thornback, lobsters, rockfish, plaice (flounders most likely), and lumps. Many of these species Weymouth took in nearshore waters with little difficulty: "Our Captaine . . . caused a hook or two to be cast out at the mouth of the harbour, not above half a league from our ship, where in small time only, with the baits which they cut from the fish and three hooks, we got fish enough for the whole Company."[31] And for Smith, looking to send settlers in 1614, the ease with which nutritious and useful inshore species could be caught represented an important feature to New England's prospects, not as exports, but as locally useful food sources.

> You shall scarce find any bay, shallow shore or cone of land where you may not rake many clams, or lobsters, or both at your pleasure, and in many places load your boat if you please; Nor lies where you find not fruits, birds, crabs, and mussels, or all of them, for taking, at low water. And in the harbors we frequented, a little boy might take of cunners, and pinacks, and such delicate fish, at the ship's stern [while moored], more than six or ten can eat in a day, but with a casting net, thousands when we pleased: and scarce any place but Cod, Cusk, Halibut, Mackerel, Skate, or such, a man may take with a hook or line what he will. And in diverse sandy bays, a man may draw with a net great store of mullets, basses, and diverse other sorts of such excellent fish as many as his net can draw on shore: no river where there is not plenty of sturgeon, or salmon, or both, all which are to be had in abundance in their season.[32]

As much as Europeans found the numbers of fish incredible, the large variety of different species of fish filled them with equal wonder.

If early explorers had been interested only in commodities, they would have identified only those species that could be caught, cured, and packaged for sale six months or more into the future at European markets. Instead, early explorers took keen interest in the most readily caught inshore fish species they could identify. In this light, the lists of species that these explorers detailed—often with little context—take on more significance. Not exclusively a list of possible exports, these lists represented a catalog of resources that future settlers might draw from to augment their tables. Furthermore, these observations of inshore marine resources represented an important first step in a process by which Europeans came to better understand the world into which they were venturing. More than just evidence of European desires to identify profitable commodities in the New World, their catalogs of species, the locations where they could be found, and the means by which they could be taken represented an initial effort to understand their New World home.

For example, Rosier cataloged nineteen species of inshore fish and shellfish, very few of which could possibly be salt cured for commercial success in European markets. John Smith followed suit, including in his materials a list of twenty-four species that included both commercial and domestically useful species: whales, grampuses, porpoises, turbot, sturgeon, cod, hake, haddock, cole, cusk, shark, mackerel, herring, mullet, bass, "pinacks," cunners, perch, eel, crab, lobsters, mussels, whelks, and oysters. By the time Smith wrote, however, Europeans were sufficiently familiar with the New England shore to also present the calendar of species that migrated through the region each year. Smith noted, "In March, April, May and half June, here is Cod in abundance: In May, June, July, and August, mullet and sturgeon. . . . In the end of August, September, October, and November, you may have Cod againe to make Core-fish or Poore-John. Hake you have when the cod fails in the summer."[33] Smith was interested in exportable commodities, to be sure; his mention of the commercial name for dried cod—cor fish—shows that clearly. But he was also interested in presenting to settlers a calendar showing when commercially and domestically useful inshore fish species arrived along the coast. In this vein, Smith unknowingly played a similar role to would-be English settlers that Moshup had played for the Wampanoag people. In teaching people about the local marine life, both were providing their respective constituents with the tools needed to survive southern New England's challenging coastal environment.

No settlers came to New England at Smith's behest. But the first settlers that did arrive on southern New England's coast faced a far more challenging life than the one pitched by early colonial promoters. Evidence from Bradford and Edward Winslow's *Mourt's Relation*, published in 1622 and before it was clear that Plymouth would survive, suggests that the challenges the Pilgrims faced were not just zealous hyperbole. As the first English to establish permanent settlements in New England, Pilgrims faced the immediate challenge of translating the descriptions penned by colonial boosters into community subsistence. Early Pilgrim sources covering the establishment of the Plymouth colony need to be read with caution. Both *Mourt's Relation* and Bradford's *Of Plimoth Plantation* were produced to contextualize, celebrate, and commemorate Pilgrims' actions to backers in England, future émigrés, and ultimately to fellow worshipers looking back at the genesis of an experiment in religious living.[34] To accomplish this, Bradford and Winslow may have stretched the challenges their people faced and exaggerated the area's hospitality or hostility. While Winslow and Bradford viewed these challenges through their religion, underneath rested the impressions, landscape, and concerns that Plymouth's settlers faced in coming ashore in the winter of 1620. And these observations further reveal an important ecological education. Far from a "park-like Eden," as one historian has claimed, southern New England's environment forced Englishmen to think differently about how they were going to secure livings in southern New England's thin soils and rich seas.[35] In the wastelands of southern New England, Pilgrims learned with difficulty that their survival required them to look to inshore waters.

Naturally, the writers expressed relief upon seeing land after almost two months at sea: indeed any land they sighted might have appeared "so goodly a land" that "caused us to rejoice, and praise God."[36] After raising land, the *Mayflower* tried to head southwest toward the Hudson River. In *Mourt's Relation*, only contrary winds turned the vessel back to Cape Cod. Writing ten years later, however, Bradford recalled a more challenging situation, similar to that experienced by Champlain a decade and a half earlier.

> But after they had sailed the course about half the day, they fell amongst dangerous shoals and roaring breakers, and they were so far entangled therewith as they conceived themselves in great danger; and the wind shrinking upon them withal, they resolved to bear up again for the Cape [Cod], and thought

them selves happy to get out of those dangers before night overtook them, as by God's providence they did.[37]

Once anchored in Cape Cod Bay, the voyagers faced more challenges that they had not anticipated. Getting to land, for example, posed a logistical problem. "We could not come near the shore by three quarters of an English mile, because of shallow water, which was a great prejudice to us, for our people going on shore were forced to wade a bow shot or two in going a land, which caused many to get colds and coughs, for it was nigh times freezing cold weather."[38] Cape Cod's broad shallows, so good for schooling fish, hindered later efforts in assembling the settlers' shallop; as Winslow and Bradford recounted: "The discommodiousness of the harbor did much hinder us for we could neither go to nor come from the shore, but at high water."[39] Nor did the coast offer much to refresh the travelers once they landed. "We found great mussels, and very fat and full of sea-pearl, but we cannot eat them, for they made us all sick that did eat, as well sailors and passengers."[40]

Despite these challenges, however, Winslow and Bradford tried to put Cape Cod's soils in the best light possible.[41] Rather than making an unfavorable comparison to better-known agricultural lands in England and the Netherlands, Winslow and Bradford stated, "The ground or earth, sand hills, [is] much like the downs in Holland, but much better; the crust of the earth a [spade's] depth excellent black earth."[42] This is thin praise. Compared to sandy stretches along a windswept coastline, Cape Cod soils were indeed likely to be more fertile. But with topsoil only a shovel-blade deep, readers back in England could judge for themselves how productive that soil could be and for how long. Furthermore, while in places Pilgrims noted open and inviting woods, exploration revealed a less hospitable landscape. Apart from lands cleared by local native peoples, which the party perceived as evidence of divine welcome, the English "marched through boughs and bushes, and under hills and valleys, which tore our very armor to pieces, and yet we could not meet with none of [the local Indians], nor their houses, nor find any fresh water, which we greatly desired."[43] Eventually, Cape Cod's dunes, shoaling harbors, and thin soils compelled the *Mayflower* to move on.

In contrast to the bleak landscape, the plentiful—and familiar—fish readily found alongshore provided some solace. When the Pilgrims landed at what would become Provincetown, for example, they quickly identified many fish species similar to those from Europe. This diversity and familiarity, as much as the abundance, shaped their choice of settlement location. "[Plymouth Bay] is a bay greater than Cape Cod [that is, Provincetown Harbor], compassed with goodly land . . . and cannot but be full of fish in their season: skate, cod, turbot, and herring, we have tasted of, abundance of mussels the greatest and best that we ever saw; crabs, and lobsters, in their time infinite." Indeed, Plymouth Bay's bounty relied heavily upon the complementary seasonality of different species appearing along the coastline: "Fresh cod in the summer is but coarse meat with us; our bay is full of lobsters all the summer and affordeth [a] variety of other fish; in September we can take a hogshead of eels in a night, with small labor, and can dig them out of their beds in winter."[44]

As Pilgrims settled at Plymouth and the surrounding areas, however, they realized that others' initial impressions of terrestrial fertility fell short of their own experience. Besides experiencing the winters, which Bradford called "sharp and violent, and subject to cruel and fierce storms," Europeans learned early that southern New England soils were not the rich loams Gosnold and Pring had related.[45] Bradford recalled that "Some English seed they sew, as wheat and peas, but it came not to good, either by the badness of the seed, or lateness of the season, or both, or some other defect."[46] Indeed, given southern New England's thin, sandy topsoils, crops would grow only modestly. Consequently, as farmers and husbandmen equipped with only agricultural skills, Pilgrims—and other European immigrants—faced a dual challenge. At the same time as they needed to be building their future farms and communities, they also needed to fish to survive. Certainly, the labor demands of farm building would become a defining feature of New England social, cultural, and economic life throughout the seventeenth century.[47] Before these challenges could be faced, however, Europeans needed to learn how to best adapt their expectations to the ecology of their marginal location.

Because the region's weak soils prevented any reliable agriculture, Pilgrim settlers had to turn to the seas for survival. To do so, however, required that they learn how to read the coastal environment and use that knowledge to blend the resources of land and sea, as their Native American neighbors had learned to do centuries before. The famous story of Tisquantum's instructions to the Pilgrims highlights their precarious position. According to Bradford, Tisquantum (Squanto) taught the English that crops without fish fertilizer "would come to nothing."[48] To ensure a good crop in the fall, the English needed to look to the seas in the spring. "He showed them that in the middle of April they should have stored enough [of manure fish that] come up the brooks, by which they began to build, and taught them how to - take it, and where to get other provisions necessary for them; all which they found true by trial and experience."[49] By sheer necessity, Europeans momentarily abandoned—or at least held in check—earlier conceptions of Native American savagery and learned how Native Americans bridged the marine and terrestrial ecosystem.

Recalling the events of 1620 over a decade later, and in a conscious effort to show providential salvation for a godly people, Bradford focused on the environmental conditions as the source of his people's trials:

> Besides, what could they see but a hideous & desolate wilderness, full of wild beasts and wild men, and what multitudes there might be of them they knew not. Neither could they, as it were, go up to the top of Pisgah, to view from this wilderness a more goodly county to feed their hopes; for which way so ever they turned their eyes (save upwards to the heavens) they could have little solace or content in respect of outward objects. For summer being done, all things stand upon them with a weather beaten face; and the whole county, full of woods and thickets, represented a wild and savage hew.[50]

When the next boatload of Pilgrims arrived at Plymouth in 1621, Bradford recalled, the landscape presented equally grim prospects to the uncertain newcomers. They included "lusty young men, and many of them wild enough," Bradford remembered, people "who little considered whither or about what they went, till they came to the harbor at Cape Cod, and there saw nothing [but] a naked and barren place." Uncertain whether the Plymouth settlers were still alive and fearing abandonment, passengers aboard the ship considered the capital offense of mutiny when "they began to consult (upon some speeches that some of the seamen had cast out) to take the sails from the yard lest the ship should get away and leave them there."[51]

For the Europeans who followed the Pilgrims to New England throughout the seventeenth century, the need to survive forced them to develop very quickly fundamental understandings of their local environment. Limited agricultural prospects meant that marine resources, easily taken at the water's edge, played important roles in feeding the English even after the first years of settlement. As Edward Johnson recalled in his 1653 history of English settlement in New England, the variety of easily obtainable inshore fish allowed settlers to see God's desire for their success. "In the absence of Bread [settlers] feasted themselves with fish, the women once a day, as the tide gave way, resorted to the mussels, and clambanks, which are fish as big as horse mussels, where they daily gathered their Families food with much heavenly discourse of the provisions Christ had formerly made for many thousands of his followers in the wilderness." As settlers adapted to their new settings, "Christ caused the abundance of very good fish to come to their nets and hooks, and as for such want as were unprovided with these means, they caught them with their hands, and so with fish and onions and other herbs were sweetly satisfied till other provisions came in." As a result of God's blessings, and the availability of food fish inshore, Johnson claimed, "Me-thinks our children are as cheerful, fat, and lusty with feeding upon those mussels, clambanks, and other fishes as they were in England, with their fill of bread, which make me cheerful in the Lord's providing for us."[52]

As more Europeans settled in New England, the descriptions of the region's wide array of food fishes gained greater attention back in London. William Morrell's 1625 poem *New-England, or a Briefe Narration of the Ayre, Earth, Water, Fish and Fowles of that Country* listed ten species waiting for settlers to "Man forth each Shallop with three men to sea / Which oft return with wondrous store of prey."[53] The Council for New England's 1627 *An Historicall Discoverie and Relation of the English Plantations in New England* listed "fish of several sorts" as one of the key commodities of "that country."[54] Other writers, too, soon after arriving in New England, began to pay close attention to local natural cycles and applied that knowledge to annual subsistence strategies. As early as 1624, for example, Edward Winslow pointed out that natural cycles on land and in coastal waters were related: "As the fowl decrease [in the fall], so fish increase."[55]

In 1634 William Wood also acknowledged that the seasonal variety of species, as well as their abundance, was an important asset for communities' year-round subsistence. For Wood, the variety of food fish was worthy of poetic celebration: he cataloged no fewer than thirty-five different species in only twenty-four lines of verse. "The scale fenc'd sturgeon, wry-mouth halibut / The flouncing salmon, codfish, greedigut / Cole, haddock, hake, the thornback and the skate / Whose slimey outside makes him sold in date." While Wood placed cod in its usual prominent place as chief export commodity, the variety of other fishes also offered an array of readily available food fish year-round. Bass, for example, "is one of the best fishes of the country," not only because people never tired of their taste, but also because they were available during different seasons. "[Bass] are at one time (when Ale-wives pass up the rivers) to be [caught] in rivers; in Lobster time at the rocks, at mackerel time in the bays, at Michaelmas in the seas." Mackerel made their entrance twice a year: "[These fish] be of two sorts, in the beginning of the year are great ones, which be upon the coast; some 18 inches long. In summer as in May, June, July, and August, come in a smaller kind of them."[56]

Writings by Thomas Morton also revealed how quickly English settlers were learning that their survival depended upon their understanding New England's natural cycles. In 1632 Morton listed thirteen marine species of fish (and more shellfish and freshwater fish) that prospective settlers could rely on for subsistence: cod, bass, mackerel, sturgeon, salmon, herring, eels, smelt, shads or alewives, turbot or halibut, plaice, hake, and "pilchers." Morton also identified which fish can be taken during which times of year.[57] He listed year-round resident species, such as cod and sturgeon, which southern New Englanders caught and exported. In addition, however, he included a number of fish that arrive in early spring (salmon, herrings, shads), late spring (mackerel), and species that arrive and remain throughout the summer (basses). In listing plaices, Morton also included fish that could be caught in the depths of winter. A right-eyed flatfish, plaice share similar sizes and characteristics of other flounder species commonly found in New England waters. One of these species, winter flounder, derives its common name from its tendency to come inshore as waters begin to cool in the late fall and early winter. Unlike other fish that tend to leave New England waters at that time of year, winter flounders represented one of the few options available for settlers seeking fresh protein in the early winter while minimizing the risks of winter seafaring. Taken as a whole, Morton's list—and those of other promoters, too—not only celebrated an array of food fish on which early settlers could rely, but also revealed the extent to which early English settlers had studied their coastal resources.

Observations by early promoters show that the first settlers early understood the annual migration behaviors of useful fish. Those uses, however, represented more than just settlers' cravings for export commodities. As early as 1634, William Wood's treatise showed that settlers weighed choices in disposing of their fish as food or as export products: "There is no country known, that yields more variety of fish winter and summer; and that not only for the present spending and sustentation of the plantations, but likewise for trade into other countries." While some marine animals represented possible export, others were more useful in the home. For example, seals filled "diverse uses," even though "his body being between fish and flesh . . . is not very delectable to the palate." Seal oil, however, "is very good to burn in lamps." Sharks "are often taken, being good for nothing but to put on the ground for manuring the land." Skate "is given to the dogs, not counted being worth the dressing in many places." Mussels, "in great plenty," were "left only for the hogs, which if they were in England would be more esteemed of the poorer sort." Clams provided livestock feed, conveniently without requiring human tenders: "These fishes be in great plenty in most places of the country, which is a great commodity for the feeding of swine, both in winter, and summer; for being once used to those places, they will repair to them as duely every ebb, as if driven to them by keepers."[58]

Thomas Morton similarly differentiated between domestic and commercial uses. Among the nineteen species he cataloged, Morton explicitly identified five fish as holding some potential value as an export. Cod, sturgeon, herring, eels, and halibut represented prized fish, which, based on his assessment, prospective settlers might find valuable in the transatlantic market.[59] For the remaining fourteen, Morton's use of the term "commodity" reflected a contemporary definition of the term referring to an item's ability to accommodate its owner's needs.[60] Lobsters, for example, represented a commodity only in a local sense. "The most use that I made of them, in 5 years after I came there was but to bait my hook for to catch bass, I had been so cloyed with them the first day I went ashore. This being known, they shall pass for a commodity to the inhabitants." Mackerel also held value only for their local utility: not only "bait for the bass," they were also "good, salted, for store against the winter, as well as fresh, and to be accounted a good commodity." Similarly, New England eels—which Morton claims a London fishmonger judged "the best he had found in his life"—were more valuable as food at home. "I have with [eel] pots found my house hold, (being nine persons, without dogs) with them, taking them . . . and preserving them for winter store: and these therefore may prove a good commodity." Shads and alewives (what Morton calls "allizes") also represented a commodity, but only because of the region's weak soils. "You may see in one township a hundred acres together, set with these fish, every acre taking 1,000 of them: and an acre thus dressed will produce and yield so much corn, as 3 acres without fish . . . and this [fish] is therefore a commodity there." Morton is more explicit about how he viewed "commodities" in discussing the eight species of freshwater fish he also included. "Now that I have showed you what commodities are there to be had in the sea, for a market, I will show what is in the land also, for the comfort of the inhabitants, wherein it doth abound."[61]

Settling in sandy wastelands, Europeans learned quickly that marine fish represented the key to anything more than a marginal existence. Unable to replicate, initially, the agricultural economies they had left behind, early settlers reveal in their accounts that in addition to learning from local Indians about how to mix the resources of land and sea, they also developed complex and detailed understandings of their new environment on their own. Forty years before John Josseleyn published what many see as the first systematic overview of New World plants and animals, sheer necessity compelled English settlers to pay close attention to how New England's coastal environment functioned.[62] Especially in southern New England, where Moshup had to teach his people how to survive on Cape Cod's thin coastal wastelands, English settlers faced the same challenge. In the first ten years of settlement, southern New England settlers recognized that the environmental understanding they brought with them from Europe needed to adapt to New World circumstances. And when it became clear that standard European farming practices would not suffice—as it had with Plymouth's settlers after 1620—settlers did what people had always done when facing similar challenges to their survival. They paid attention, and made the best of what was available.

Squanto taught English how to
fertilize & fish

CHAPTER 2

Management

The country from Sandwich to Barnstable is hilly and in a great degree bare, bleak, and desolate: the inhabitants having universally cut down their forests and groves and taken no measures to renew them. The soil is thin and unproductive and furnishes very little that is sprightly to enliven the scene. . . . At Yarmouth also may be said to commerce the general addiction of the people on this peninsula to fishing. Born and bred at the verge of the water, they are naturally tempted to seek for plenty and prosperity on the waves, rather than glean a pittance from the field. From this source is derived their wealth and much of their subsistence.
—Timothy Dwight, *Travels in New York and New England*

Timothy Dwight was well prepared to make such a harsh assessment of Cape Cod lands, for by 1800 the Yale College president had toured much of the Northeast, taking stock of the new nation and its people at the turn of the nineteenth century. What he failed to realize, however, was that fishing, and Cape Codders' "addiction" to it, represented one of the few ways local communities sustained themselves. In fact, by the mid-seventeenth century, Cape Cod's first settlers recognized that fishing represented an essential crutch for local subsistence. Within two decades of the arrival of the *Mayflower*, Cape Cod's weakening soils forced settlers to balance the commercial development of a variety of resources against long-term community survival. Between 1650 and 1800, settlers realized how precarious their situation was and extended that balancing act to stocks of inshore fish. In short, as Cape Codders expanded their use of inshore fisheries, they did not do so in a rush to produce commodities for export. Instead, they tried to balance immediate use with long-term resource—and community— survival. To do that, Cape Codders looked to their understandings of local ecosystem function to best use and protect what few resources they enjoyed.

While Plymouth's soil may have been healthy when they arrived, the English émigrés soon discovered they could push the sandy glacial moraine only so far. By the 1640s, weakening soils compelled a group of Plymouth residents to campaign to relocate the entire colony to Cape Cod lands that they believed—erroneously—could sustain them longer.[1] The small group of Plymouth residents who did relocate to Eastham soon found, however, that even these most healthy of Cape Cod soils failed to provide the security they sought. Similar experiences awaited those settlers venturing along Cape Cod's coasts from Plymouth and from Massachusetts Bay. As they surveyed Cape Cod's southern shore, settlers encountered a new range of resources that, while providing them with good food and fertilizer, also presented them with new challenges in their efforts both to survive and to engage in the Atlantic market.

After initial settlement of the northern shore of Cape Cod at Sandwich, Eastham, and Barnstable in the 1630s and 1640s, those still wanting land looked to Cape Cod's southern shore. While land was still available there, the region offered little to compete with the better lands available elsewhere. This kept many away, as can be seen in William Wood's 1634 map of New England, which provided almost no coastal details or features from Provincetown to Buzzards Bay (Fig 2.1). Even after a decade and a half of travel, trade, and navigation, European settlers entertained little interest in southern Cape Cod's rivers, harbors, or other features.[2] Eventually the need for open lands drew settlers into the area after better lands on Cape Cod's north shore had been taken. Only then did Europeans settle Chatham (1656), Falmouth (1661), and Harwich (1688), long after northern shore towns had been established. Even then, new southern shore towns struggled for years after settlement. Not until after 1690 were these towns sufficiently established for formal political incorporation.

Unlike residents of Salem and Boston, by the end of the seventeenth century Cape Cod settlers faced no struggle between worldly wealth and spiritual purity. Cape Cod's wasteland offered few prospects for material gain, leaving people with only spiritual pursuits. Sandy outwash soils, shallow coastal waters, few good harbors, and strong coastal currents prevented these communities from establishing either an agricultural or a commercial economy.[3] Furthermore, unlike areas surrounding the Gulf of Maine, southern

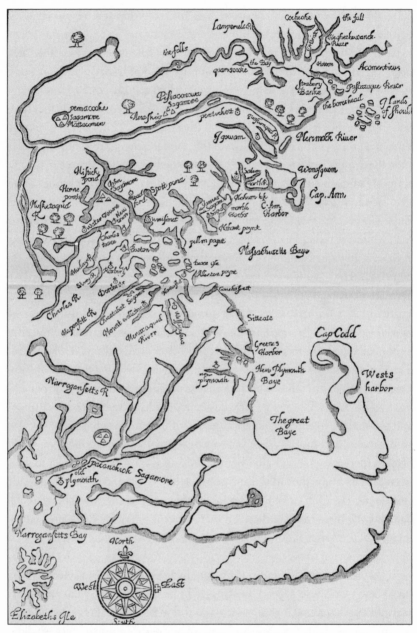

FIG. 2.1 William Wood, *The South Part of New-England, as It is Planted This Yeare,*
1634. Note Wood's lack of information about Cape Cod. Wood, *New England's*
Prospect (1634)

New England's shallow inshore waters failed to support any extensive and lucrative inshore cod fishery. Instead, Cape Codders found a different variety of inshore fish, few if any of which could have been turned into export commodities.

Recent ecological findings have shown that Cape Cod represents an important boundary between the Middle Atlantic and the Gulf of Maine biogeographic provinces.[4] In the Gulf of Maine, as many fisheries histories have shown, cod—with its preference for water between about 30 feet (roughly 10 meters) and 450 feet (135 meters) in depth—dominated the marine ecosystem even inshore, allowing Europeans to take fish for export close to home with small boats year-round.[5] Surrounded by broad, shallow waters, Cape Cod fishermen had to venture farther from shore to find commercially exportable cod. They did, to be sure, but they also took advantage of the seasonal arrivals of highly abundant migratory species that came close inshore. River herring, mackerel, basses, menhaden, bluefish, scup, and weakfish all arrived in the spring just as winter larders were running low and crop fields needed fertilizing. Like the native peoples before them, Cape Cod settlers soon looked to these fish as a mainstay of their annual survival.

As bountiful as runs of small schooling fish were for settlers, however, they also presented unique challenges. In particular, while some fishermen tried, few of these species lent themselves well to salt preservation and long-distance transport. The challenges faced by Cape Cod fishermen hoping to export highly abundant migratory species emerge most clearly by first understanding how readily codfish could be turned into a transatlantic commodity. Cod emerged as the premier export commodity for the early modern northwest Atlantic not only because of its flavor and the cultural tastes in Europe, but also because the biology and behavior of the fish itself simplified the work fishermen needed to undertake to catch, cure, and ship these fish to European markets. Cod can grow to tremendously large sizes: even as late as 1953, Bigelow and Schroeder reported that cod typically grew to fifty and sixty pounds, with the occasional individual breaking one hundred pounds. In the 1850s the average fish landed by the Salem and Beverly fleet was over twenty-five pounds, and in the seventeenth century the average was almost certainly even higher.[6] This wide morphological range meant that if fishermen could target larger fish—which they could with larger hooks and skill—they could fill their holds with fewer fish. Larger fish also meant fewer fish to head, gut, split, salt, and dry. Given that cod was sold by the quintal—112 pounds dry weight—more-skilled and more-efficient fishermen could produce the same amount of dry weight as a competitor by targeting fewer but larger fish and thus reducing the work needed to process them.

Species found along the southern New England shore were very different from cod, however. Cape Cod's inshore fish were smaller and had oilier flesh. Both these characteristics affected the ease with which these fish could be turned into export commodities. Blue-black herring, mackerel, alewives, and scup all grow to only twelve to twenty-four ounces. As a result, fishermen had to catch and prepare many more fish to make up a cargo, which in turn represented a significant additional labor cost.[7] In newly formed, labor-strapped communities, such a cost was significant.

The higher oil content in the flesh of these schooling fish also affected how easily they could be exported. Cod house much of their bodies' oil in the livers, while herrings, mackerels, bluefish, scup, basses, and menhaden all host higher fat contents in the muscle tissue. Before the widespread use of ice and railroads in the 1830s, preserving fish required some form of salting. This could happen in many ways: packed in salt, air dried and lightly salted, or submerged in a high-salt solution in a watertight cask. In all these preparations, salt removes sufficient moisture from tissues to prevent bacteria and enzymes from decomposing cells. Generally, this takes place when salt content rises to about 6 percent, but a number of factors also influence this process. The thickness of the cuts and the oil content of the flesh both slow the speed with which salt content rises, allowing more time for decomposition.[8] Codfish, with a fat content of less than 2.5 percent, are one of the leanest fish found in the North Atlantic fisheries and therefore required less salt to effect a cure. Other species, like those that Cape Codders were forced to live with, were not so easily cured. For example, mackerel and alewives have fat contents of over 6.5 percent.[9] To cure these oilier fish for export, settlers had to prepare a brine and pickle them in watertight barrels, which had to be carefully built. Again, such increased preparations added overhead costs to labor- and cash-strapped settlements. Furthermore, even when processed, packed, and shipped, American herring products still faced stiff competition from the Dutch product that dominated European markets for pickled herring in the seventeenth century.[10]

In short, the additional steps needed to catch, prepare, preserve, and package Cape Cod's inshore fish simply made exporting them too expensive for labor-strapped colonists. Certainly some tried: sturgeon, long highly prized in Europe, quickly became a valued export along with cod, but just as quickly were fished out.[11] For the most part, however, the combination of urgent local need and the added expense of processing meant that fish other than cod were kept for domestic and local use.

As a result, in the seventeenth, eighteenth, and nineteenth centuries, two overlapping but distinct fisheries operated in southern New England. First and foremost, the cod fishery emerged as the backbone of New England's export sector, with ties to capital and international markets that allowed fishermen and merchants to send large vessels to offshore banks near Nova Scotia and Newfoundland and, to a lesser extent, to Georges Bank. This "banks fishery" far and away dominated coastal New England's economy, and ports all along the coast, including Cape Cod, sent vessels and fishermen offshore to take advantage of those resources.

Alongside the banks fishery, however, emerged a much smaller inshore fishery that targeted a variety of inshore fish for either subsistence use or immediate local sale. For the most part, this was a casual day fishery, manned by boys or old men, who used small boats to fish grounds no more than a day's row or sail away. The limited, intensely local market allowed its workers to profitably take the oilier inshore fish readily found along the southern New England shore. Smaller in scale, the inshore fishery emerged in southern New England as an important part of local community survival.

The inshore fishery required little to enter and dealt mostly in cash or by barter. As a result, it also produced few records, presenting a challenge for historians. Glimpses do emerge, however. Accounts by William Wood and Morton, along with John Josseleyn's *New England's Rarities Discovered* (1675), indicate that seventeenth-century settlers used a wide array of fish species for food, fertilizer, and, as in Josseleyn's case, a variety of other household uses.[12]

Yet the fishery comes into clearest focus as visitors to North American colonies throughout the colonial period took note of how their fellow Europeans lived in the New World. Frequently, these visitors noted the variety of fresh fish available in local fish markets. One visitor to Boston in 1740 remarked on the cheap and fresh fish he found in the colonial city. "They sell fine fresh cod . . . just taken from the sea. . . . They have smelts. . . . Salmon they have. . . . They have flounders and plaice, too, and eels, and likewise mackerel in their season, and several other sorts of fish not known in England—all of which are good and cheap."[13] Another observer, a French captive held in Newport in 1745, also recounted how local tables offered bass, tautog, sheepshead, mackerel, horse mackerel, menhaden, herring, and alewives. Of these, however, the observer mentioned that only menhaden carried export value as food for slaves: "[Menhaden] they export many hundred barrels [of] to the West Indies."[14] As late as 1797, François, duc de La Rochefoucauld, observed in Stonington, Connecticut, that "blackfish [tautog or sea bass], bass, and crab, being in great abundance on this coast, a considerable number of small craft is engaged in that fishery. The fish are kept in ponds along the shore and are generally shipped to New York."[15] While these accounts date from later periods, they do suggest that local fishermen took what was available for local fresh-fish markets and as a result offered a much wider array of fish species than export markets could.

Timothy Dwight saw this quite clearly as he traveled in 1800, en route to the barren wastes that awaited him on Cape Cod. In Newport, home to one of the largest fresh-fish markets in southern New England, he made special note of the variety of species available. Of the 112 species listed, local residents deemed 66 "fit for a table." Some of these did enjoy export markets by then: bass, codfish, sturgeon, salmon, halibut, alewives, and menhaden. For the rest of the table fish, however, no export value has been documented, suggesting that species such as tautog, grunts, mullet, bonito, bluefish, and scup may have been consumed locally. Newport fishermen in the seventeenth and eighteenth centuries sold most of these fish as fresh, and processed few, if any, for export. For the remaining forty-six species, Dwight made no mention of their use, but presumably southern New Englanders found them of sufficient domestic utility to encourage local fishermen to take them.[16]

The scant records of this local fishery also offer us a glimpse of how it functioned. One of the few records that shed some light on the inshore fishery comes from the late eighteenth-century journal of Rhode Island blacksmith Thomas Hazard. Beginning in 1780, the journal reveals a rural craftsman relying upon a variety of coastal resources, as settlers had done for the previous century. Terse and to the point, Hazard recorded how fishing represented a casual, even spontaneous activity that targeted whichever species happened to be available. In May 1780, for example, he "made an eel spear [and] went eeling"; in April of 1782 he went fishing for flatfish; and two years later he landed 135 pounds of bass. In 1794 alone Hazard took clams, perch, rockfish, and one "mudtorkle." Hazard's journal also shows that good hauls of fresh fish allowed residents to barter with neighbors. In November 1785

Hazard noted, "Brian Carpenter brought me a mess of Bass and I paid him in nails"; and in April 1806 a friend of Hazard's "sent me a mess of fresh codfish [as] a present." Between 1780 and the War of 1812, Hazard indicated only once, in February of 1795, that he sought preserved fish: "I went to the pier after salt fish." Such a trip represented an aberration, however; for the rest of his fishing before the War of 1812, the blacksmith targeted only currently available fish species for food or barter.[17]

Hazard's journal demonstrates a different intensity between inshore fishing and banks fishing. Casual day-fishermen, taking locally available fish, solely for local markets, represent an approach to marine resources fundamentally different from that of the highly capitalized, internationally oriented banks fleet that was compelled to take as many fish as possible, as efficiently as possible, even as early as the seventeenth century.[18] Inshore fishermen, on the other hand, drawing upon what Europeans had learned about the inshore ecosystem, used local knowledge to harvest local resources in a relatively tight balance between local demand and local supply. Neither idealized subsistence fishers, nor grasping capitalists, inshore fishermen filled a local niche where immediate needs could be met with little cost, effort, or overhead.

Not surprisingly, settlers who viewed inshore fisheries as essential elements to long-term subsistence took different approaches to the development, exploitation, and conservation of those resources. Throughout the seventeenth and eighteenth centuries, Cape Cod communities struggled over how to manage terrestrial resources in the face of soil depletion and resource overuse. Town records, in particular, show recurring debates over how best to manage local soils, common lands, grazing animals and fence maintenance, meadows and beach lands, and local forest resources. As more and more people came to Cape Cod to build farms, towns faced the immediate political exigencies generated by commercial development in a region with finite terrestrial resources to support such growth. They tried, however. Initially, Cape Cod's Puritan communities sought to preserve common resources as a protection against an uncertain world and as another arena where the commonwealth could be served.[19]

This was especially true for their inshore marine resources, on which whole communities relied. As early as the seventeenth century, settlers recognized that because inshore fish stocks were intimately tied to the local area, and because of the relative ease by which these fish could be taken, inshore fisheries use and development required careful and informed regulation. This was the only way that these essential stores of fish would remain large enough, for long enough, to continue to support communities built on southern New England's thin and mean soils.

Several inshore fisheries came under close management almost as soon as Plymouth was founded. In 1623 Plymouth legislated that fishing and fowling were to be free to all inhabitants, but only with the proviso that "all orders from time to time made by this General Court for the due regulating of fishing and fowling be observed."[20] Reaffirmed in 1633, 1636, and 1658, these regulations made sense in a colony still struggling to feed its people and develop its economic base.[21] At the same time as lands began to weaken in the 1640s, however, Plymouth's leaders enacted laws aimed at securing local fisheries resources exclusively for local benefit. In 1646 the Plymouth General Court required that Massachusetts Bay fishermen, previously permitted to fish freely around Cape Cod, had to obtain licenses. Four years later, citing conflict between Massachusetts fishermen and Plymouth settlers, the court excluded Massachusetts fishermen altogether by replacing the licensing system with a monopoly fishery owned by such prominent Plymouth leaders as Myles Standish, Thomas Prence, and, in 1652, William Bradford.[22] In 1661, in another attempt to limit and profit from foreign fishing, Plymouth's court required all foreign fishermen to secure permissions and pay fees on their catches. By 1670, however, the monopoly system had proved a failure, and the General Court returned Cape Cod fishing to governmental control. While the court did allow Hull fishermen to continue to fish along Cape Cod in 1671, they reined in Hull fishermen in 1677, mandating that they hire Plymouth residents when available.[23]

While the rest of New England embarked upon a dramatic expansion in cod fishing, Plymouth's tightening regulations on the inshore fishery revealed not only a desire to preserve local resources, but also a marked awareness of how those fish populations behaved. For example, in 1670 the court enacted another lease system by which Cape Cod fishing could be periodically evaluated and controlled. At the same time, the colony still issued regulations aimed at maintaining healthy fish stocks. Claiming to have seen "great inconvenience of taking mackerel at unseasonable times, whereby their increase is greatly diminished," Plymouth's leaders limited the season and catches of mackerel. Not only did these regulations protect mackerel from fishing during the spawning seasons; they also clearly privileged local consumption: "No mackerel shall be caught, except for spending while fresh, before the first of July annually."[24] In 1682 the Plymouth General Court renewed the protective regulations, so that these important food fish "be not wholly destroyed or driven off the shore."[25] In addition, "forasmuch as the lands where such benefit is made by fishing with seines or nets hath been purchased by the Colony and are truly theirs," no foreigner could seine without paying a license fee and abiding by other regulations.[26] These protective regulations clearly reveal that Plymouth's leaders linked the long-term survival of local human communities with long-term preservation of local fish.

To pass laws protecting a fishery during spawning seasons required that Plymouth's legislators understand—or at least be accepted by the rest of the community as understanding—when and where those fish spawn. Other regulations suggest that Plymouth's settlers also developed understandings of other elements of the local inshore marine ecosystem. In 1684, for example, Plymouth resident William Clark offered to lease the right to Cape Cod bass fishing for thirty pounds sterling, provided that the General Court also banned mackerel seining for the same term. One of the most plausible explanations for Clark's provision was that he understood that striped bass feed upon almost any smaller fish—including mackerel—they encountered.[27] It would make very little sense to pay for the privilege to take bass at a time when others were taking the food that bass chased inshore. More significantly, despite the commercial value of the mackerel fishery to the colony, the court initially agreed with Clark's request. Only after a suit by mackerel fishermen did the court revoke the ban on mackerel seining. Without some assurance that mackerel would be left to feed bass, Clark recognized that he was not getting his money's worth. He reneged on the deal, and the lease was prorated and canceled.[28] Plymouth's regulations through the 1670s and the colony's dealings with William Clark clearly demonstrate that Plymouth's leaders and settlers alike drew upon their accumulated understandings of the local coastal ecosystem in developing fisheries regulations.

In fact, Plymouth's early regulatory efforts reveal three important themes that would come to define how southern New Englanders managed their inshore resources over the next century and a half. First was the need for regulation itself: with so many fish coming inshore, and so easily taken, the fear of overexploitation was almost a mainstay of Plymouth's fisheries management.

Second, regulation clearly privileged local fishermen over outsiders, implicitly linking the survival of the local community to the survival of the local fisheries. By banning, and then licensing foreign fishermen, and exempting local subsistence fishing from regulations, Plymouth made a clear distinction between fishing for use and fishing for export, and in doing so acknowledged that those most reliant upon local fish were also more likely to protect them. Finally, in order to effect regulations, and to optimize money spent on monopoly privileges, Plymouth's settlers had to draw upon the knowledge of the marine environment that they had been developing since they first stepped off the boat. Beginning with the sheer need for survival, the sophisticated understandings indicated in early fishing regulations suggest that Plymouth's settlers used what they knew of the inshore environment to balance commercial and subsistence uses of commercially valuable fisheries. Unlike the banks fisheries, where limits on catch would not come into effect until the twentieth century, the seventeenth-century inshore fishery represented an instance where local ecological knowledge laid the foundation for balancing resource conservation, local subsistence, and commercial development.

Of all the inshore fisheries resources upon which southern New England towns relied, however, few were as important and as heavily managed throughout the colonial period as the river herring fishery. For Cape Cod towns, the easily caught and plentiful spring runs of alewives and blue-black herring represented one of the most important elements in people's efforts to combine resources of the land and sea in order to survive Cape Cod's harsh environment. Looking to return to the small, freshwater streams and rivers where they were born, every spring spawning river herring choked the many tributaries that defined southern New England's coastlines. With thousands of fish passing upriver through narrow streams—sometimes as narrow as two feet—river herring represented some of the easiest fish to catch for people and animals alike. With a net and some creative use of stones to funnel running fish through even narrower gaps, settlers—even children—could take barrels of these fish in just a matter of hours.

The timing of river herring runs also made the fishery an important element to southern New England survival. Not only were they abundant, but river herring also arrived during the hungriest time of year, when winter larders were running low, spring crops had yet to be harvested, and summer fields needed fertilizing. Alewives arrive on southern New England shores first, in March or April, as ocean temperatures warm to between about forty and fifty degrees Fahrenheit (5–10°C). Blue-black herring closely follow, when water temperatures reach between about fifty and sixty degrees Fahrenheit (10–15°C). For Massachusetts this usually means that blue-backs arrive in April or early May, though it is not uncommon for both fish to spawn at the same time in the same stream.[29]

The ease by which these fish could be caught, and their value to farmers and fishermen alike, represented both a blessing and a curse. For a struggling colony, or later as farmlands grew increasing hungry for fertilizer, river herring offered Cape Cod's settlers one of the strongest temptations to overuse a plentiful resource. Since river herring return to their natal streams every three years to spawn, large catches in any single stream one year could seriously undermine catches, but not for another three years.

All these factors explain why river herring became one of the most carefully managed resources in the seventeenth and eighteenth centuries. Town records detail the care with which southern New England settlers balanced needs for fish and the long-term health of the fishery. Sandwich, for example, was managing river herring catches as early as March 1651, when the town meeting consciously limited who could take alewives running up local streams. To prevent overfishing, the town contracted with Daniel Wing and Michael Blackwell "for to catch fish at Herring [River weir] for three years for [nine pence] a thousand for the town." In 1681 the town contracted with another Blackwell to serve as town fish catcher for five seasons. Once caught, the fish were distributed to residents for their own domestic use, and to ensure that distribution, in 1687 fish catcher William Hunter was required to "give timely notice to such persons that is to have fish, and to keep each man's shares two days, and if such fish be not fetched away within two days, the said Hunter may put them to others."[30] Sandwich residents also privileged the fishery over other internal economic developments.[31] In 1717, for example, the town granted residents permission to set up a sawmill across the Herring River, provided that its operation did not prevent the spring and fall runs of fish. By 1728, mills on the Herring River were ordered to cease grinding "in order for the herring to go up."[32] Similar ordinances were passed again in 1734, 1740, and 1741.[33]

In fact, Sandwich's desires to preserve local fisheries countered increasing demands for all fish exports. By the early eighteenth century, West Indian planters sought fish—any fish, in any condition—to feed growing slave populations. As early as 1686, Samuel Sewall of Boston, for example, exported mackerel and cod; he also experimented exporting pickled bass and far less desirable alewives. The last he sent to West Indian merchants, who sold them to plantation owners to feed slaves.[34] West Indian demand for alewives may have been inconsistent, however, as William Douglass noted in 1755 that alewives were "a very mean, dry and insipid fish; some of them are cured . . . and sent to the sugar islands for the slaves, but because of their bad quality, they are not in request."[35] Regardless, the West Indies became such an important market for all New England trash fish that, in 1768, a Boston customs officer observed, "On this West India trade not only the improvement and cultivation of the lands in this country depends, but even the cod fishery could not be carried on if it was not for this vent of such defective fish as happens not to be fit for the European market, which is generally a very large proportion of the whole."[36]

In the face of such market demand, Sandwich cautiously flirted with open-market herring fishing. In 1734 the town meeting agreed that in exchange for a fee, permission would be granted "to any person in this Town to catch herrings at the Herring River for sale as they go up the stream this Spring."[37] Apparently such changes were well received: by 1740 enough residents had taken fish under these auspices that the town appointed Samuel Tupper to collect back fees. In opening the fishery, however, the town still retained tight controls over when and where fish could be caught, and in May 1743 the town voted to prosecute anyone who fished at illegal places and times.[38]

In 1744 town residents differentiated between subsistence and commercial fishing by imposing different regulations upon each. Stating that "no person or persons do take more of said fish than they shall judge to be necessary for the use of the family or families of those that take them," new regulations limited subsistence fishers' total catches, means, places, and times. Commercial fishers faced additional restrictions: those seeking to "to pickle and send fish to market" were required to post a bond, provide an accurate tally of their catch, and pay a fee for every barrel of fish taken. In creating these two categories, Sandwich residents sought to balance the needs of local residents reliant upon subsistence fishing, town needs to raise revenues through fish exports, and the long-term health of the fishery itself. To better ensure that balance was maintained, the town elected a committee in 1745 to petition the Massachusetts General Court for greater regulatory powers "to preserve the Herring Rivers on this town from being ruined."[39] Even with a growing West Indian market for fish, preservation and profit needed to walk hand in hand in Sandwich.

Almost all New England towns strictly managed river herring. The farming town of Rochester, situated at the headwaters of Buzzards Bay, also restrained fishing pressure as early as 1734 by banning weirs and traps that
blocked herring from running up the Weweantic and Mattapoisett rivers.[40]
The town also elected annually herring inspectors to keep runs clear and to
pull down illegal fishing weirs. By 1742, when the Massachusetts General
Court passed its laws regulating fish runs and mill operations, Rochester had
already collaborated with neighboring Middleborough to coordinate fishing
policies on streams that ran through both towns. At some point before 1763—
town records give no indication of precisely when—Rochester also experimented with liberalized fishing by granting a group of local proprietors the
right to free fishing on the Mattapoisett River.

By midcentury, however, both Rochester and Sandwich drew back from
the previous decade's experiment with open fishing. In 1752 Sandwich ended
export fishing from its streams, and to show this was no empty letter, it pros-
ecuted Jonathan Bourn for violating the law the following year.[41] Nine years
later the Rochester town meeting also withdrew the liberties granted to individuals to freely take river herring. Stating that "the Authority of the town is
needful for the ~~prosecution of~~ preservation of the fish," the town reclaimed
rights to the profits, management, and protection of local river fisheries.[42]
Even as demand for Cape Cod fish grew overseas, towns on and near Cape
Cod jealously guarded the long-term health of their inshore fisheries.

Town experiments with open fishing coincided not only with increasing
West Indian demand, but also with regional economic fluctuations brought
on by war. Again, Sandwich's detailed records offer the best insights into
these decisions. In May of 1764 the Sandwich town meeting looked to local
fish to offset some of the French and Indian War's economic legacies. The
committee recommended that "the remainder [of the herring profits] be divided equally between the ratable polls . . . and those widows who have or-
phans under their care and charge for a maintenance[,] except the polls of
those persons who are under warning."[43] To further benefit local residents, in
March 1765 Sandwich voted, for the first time, to take and sell "at vendue,"
outside Sandwich town bounds, four hundred barrels of fish from the Herring River, with the proceeds also deposited into town coffers. In 1767 the
take rose to five hundred barrels; in 1773 and 1777 the town elected to take six
hundred barrels each year. Not until 1779, after the outbreak of the American
Revolution and the advent of France's alliance, did Sandwich reduce to three

hundred barrels the amount it would sell for town revenue. These acts reveal that Sandwich was willing to use its fishery to offset unforeseen economic hardships. From the town's perspective, it was far less painful to catch and sell more fish to offset town costs than it was to try to pull more money from residents' pockets in a region already marked by poor soils and poor people.

But even here Sandwich maintained limits to the extent to which it would turn its fish into cash. By the 1780s, pressures from competing towns, wartime shortages caused by the Revolution, and the desire to preserve the long-term viability of the fisheries led Sandwich to re-impose heavy restrictions on the fishery. In March 1780 a committee convened to revise town regulations, recommending that, in an effort to curb demand, no more fish were to be sold to markets outside town, and only those fish taken and sold by the town were to be used for domestic consumption. Prices for town-caught herring were fixed, and residents were not allowed more than two barrels of fish. Still needing funds, however, Sandwich continued to allow nonresidents to purchase up to thirty barrels—no more than two to any one household—but only at the inflated price of thirty dollars per barrel. Finally, in what can only be seen as an ironic act of largesse, Native Americans and mulattoes were allowed to catch for themselves up to two barrels per day.[44]

By the 1780s, other southern New England towns, too, embraced similar means to ensure the long-term health of their fisheries. In Harwich, for example, the owners of a herring stream agreed to sell the run to the town, provided that the town sought protective legislation for the stream from the state government.[45] Similarly, in 1788 Falmouth banned its residents from exporting any alewives to neighboring towns, allowed only taxpaying residents to take fish, and required that on any given day, all male inhabitants at the river receive an equal share of the day's catch.[46] More broadly, the first two decades of independence witnessed an expansion of town-controlled river fisheries across southern New England. Newly established town fisheries were created in Falmouth's Coonamessett River in 1798, the abovementioned Herring River in Harwich in 1787, in Edgartown's Great Pond on Martha's Vineyard in 1783, the Mattapoisett River in 1788, in Brewster's Stony Brook in 1787, and along the various tributaries of the Taunton River before 1792. Wareham established a town fishery in the Weweantic in 1798.[47] In a republican-spirited effort to ensure that the public interest was best preserved against individuals seeking private gain, towns pulled under their jurisdiction those resources on which the community most relied.

Early river herring regulations and the expansion of town-controlled fisheries reveal the complex relationships between Cape Cod settlers, their understandings of the inshore environment, local subsistence, and a larger commercial market. First, at the very foundation of river herring regulation lay the knowledge of where, when, and how frequently these fish returned to spawn in local streams. While this knowledge rarely emerges in town records, it formed the foundation for fishing regulations and catch limits. With such knowledge in hand, towns enacted regulations that, like Plymouth's in the seventeenth century, privileged local subsistence use over export sales. Towns freely imposed barriers on trade and markets, even at times when external demand richly rewarded communities that opened their public runs to commercial development. Finally, towns actively sought to ensure the continued public benefit of these fisheries by assuming control of the various rivers and streams that provided such important resources. Ultimately, town herring regulations reveal the importance that those resources played in a region with little else to rely upon. In that light, the long-term viability of local herring runs represented an essential component in the long-term survival of communities. Far from extracting as much profit as possible from these fisheries, towns used what they knew about them to ensure those fish would always return in the spring.

Through the seventeenth and eighteenth centuries, Cape Cod towns had come to closely monitor and regulate the abundant alewives and other inshore fish that augmented waning local agricultural production. And at the core of those regulations lay understandings about how local fisheries behaved. But where those understandings came from, how they developed, and who had the right to speak for the fish fails to emerge from the town records detailing a century of fisheries management. Falmouth's "Herring War" of 1802, however, lays clear the mechanisms by which early settlers came to understand how local ecosystems worked, and to whom towns turned when they needed information about the local marine environment. In fact, the controversy focused almost entirely on the epistemological questions of who knew what about fish behavior and how they knew it, rather than on any breach of the law.

Since 1794, mill owner Barnabas Hinckley had worked with the town of Falmouth to reconcile alewives' need to swim above his dam to spawn with his need to preserve water to run his mill later in the summer. While the town wanted the mill and valued it as a source of income and employment, it also needed the river to run freely during the spring rains, to allow alewives to run upstream to spawn. Herein lay the conflict: to keep his mill running through the late-summer dry period, Hinckley needed to dam the stream and store the spring rains. And for eight years, the two parties worked to resolve the seemingly mutually exclusive needs of milling and fish spawning. In April 1802, however, Hinckley was tired of this annual negotiation and closed the sluice gate in his mill dam.[48] Immediately, the town arrested him, fined him three dollars, and mandated that he post bond until sentencing.[49]

While Hinckley awaited sentencing, his son, James, enlisted the lawyer William Holmes of Rochester, Massachusetts, for his father's legal defense. On initial review, Holmes identified a number of procedural technicalities that compromised the town's case. Those questions aside, however, Holmes saw a more fundamental problem for the town's case against Hinckley. Holmes wrote, "If I understand the law of 1798 [which Hinckley was accused of violating] the penalty is for obstructing the herring ways when opened between the sea and the [natural] *ponds* where fish *usually* cast their spawn. Now if I understand your statement[,] there was no [natural] pond above your father's mill dam where the fish USUALLY cast their spawn; and if that is the case the Law could not be broken there." Given this, then, the case distilled down to a seemingly simple question: "Does your father's mill stand on a River, between the sea and the ponds, where the fish generally and commonly cast their spawn[?]" That question directed attention away from Hinckley's actions and onto those of the fish themselves: "As it is a mere question of fact whether the fish do usually cast their spawn in a pond above your father's dam[,] you can [tell] as well as any Lawyer on Earth whether they have a right of action or not."[50] With this keen observation, Holmes replaced Hinckley with herring in the defendant's seat.

In shifting his case in this direction, Holmes took advantage of the difficulty that people in early nineteenth-century America had in assessing the behavior of marine animals. Historians of science, in particular Helen Rozwadowski, have made compelling arguments about the difficulties nineteenth- and twentieth-century people—from naturalists to budding oceanographers— encountered when looking below the water's surface.[51] Forced by the simple fact that humans cannot exist underwater without some technological support, inquiries into the state of marine resources always relied upon indirect representations—often derived through some intervening piece of technology—to gain any understanding of what was happening in the marine realm. And, as D. Graham Burnett has shown, such secondhand understandings frequently became apparent through legal disputes.[52] Similar circumstances challenged Falmouth's residents in trying Hinckley's case. If the case hinged on questions concerning fish behavior, to whom should those questions be directed, and how would their answers be evaluated? In Falmouth's case, the court looked to townspeople whose day-to-day work allowed them to develop long-term, in-depth knowledge about the local environment and how it functioned to assess how fish behaved in the stream where Hinckley's mill stood. Before the establishment of university-trained experts, before the creation of the very word "scientist" itself, Hinckley's case reveals that people turned to local knowledge to answer questions about the environment.

The case wound through legal and political channels for two years, sometimes causing sharp conflicts to emerge within town. Finally, in May 1804, the court convened to settle Hinckley's case. At issue were two fundamental questions: Were there natural ponds above the stream on which Hinckley's mill sat? And if so, did fish usually swim past the mill to spawn? Testimonies ran all day, as even the first question proved more complicated than immediately apparent. Hinckley supporters claimed that the Coonamessett River stemmed from springs and not the nearby Coonamessett Pond, and no fish had ever run up past the mill. Opponents countered that, if one looked carefully enough, it was clear that a dry ditch connected the headwaters of the stream to the pond, and artificial as it may have been, it allowed fish to run up to the pond to spawn.

To settle the issue, both sides looked to fishermen, neighbors, and local workers to inform the court about whether alewives did indeed spawn above Hinckley's dam. It became clear that age, experience, and physical proximity to the streams were the criteria by which both sides granted credibility to different witnesses. When Malachi Davis gave his testimony, for example, his age, knowledge of local fishing customs, and his proximity to the stream underlay his credibility as a witness. After asking his age, court officers then asked the sixty-seven-year-old Davis, "Was it ever considered a usual place for the alewives to cast their spawn above [Hinckley's] mill?" He replied, "[I] never knew or heard of such a thing." Town selectmen continued, "Should you know if large quantities of said fish was taken?" to which Davis replied,

"I live so near I think I should know." "How often do you pass the river?" "Frequently to my house back and forward."

David Crowell's age and familiarity with the river also made him an important witness. He testified that "I have been acquainted ever since I was six years of age with the mill called [Hinckley's] Lower Mill & never was knowing the Town claiming any [fishing] privilege to the stream on which the said mill stands & never knew it to be a place to catch alewives." Again, the town's first question established the witness's age, and therefore the credibility of his testimony. "How old are you?" "In my eighty-fourth year." As familiar as Crowell was with the river and the mill, he made it a point to indicate that others living closer could provide better information. "Did you ever know of any communication between [Coonamesset] Pond and the head of [Coonamesset] River?" "I never did, but I am not so well acquainted there as men that live close by." James Jenkins's accounts indicated that during his sixty-nine years, he "lived near the mill river until I was eleven years of age and since [then] have lived about four miles from said River . . . and I never see Alewives above the lower mills although I have frequented going to said mills every year." Eighty-five-year-old William Swift stated, "I tended to the lower mills for twenty years and never saw any water run from the Coonamesset Pond into [the] river . . . and never knew the dams being opened for the purpose of taking alewives." In total, five of the nine people giving depositions were older than sixty-five, and most lived near the stream. For both prosecution and defense, the combination of age and familiarity with the Coonamesset River served as the best credentials, providing the best information available from which to establish fish behavior.[53]

For this study's purpose, Hinckley's guilt or innocence is not really the issue; and after a fatal accident during a protest over the court battle, Hinckley and the town settled.[54] From our perspective, perhaps the most interesting aspect of Falmouth's Herring War was how the larger community assessed ecosystem function. While Hinckley's mill brought employment and income to a region wanting reliable economic foundations, the mill also threatened inshore public resources that the town had so carefully preserved for over a century. Falmouth's struggle between common good and private development was far from unique: communities across Massachusetts hammered out how to ensure river fisheries while also allowing the construction of water-powered industries.[55] In Falmouth, however, Holmes's defense strategy pushed questions about the role of the environment onto center stage. Falmouth's reliance on local residents to attempt to answer those questions highlights how local ecological knowledge represented the best source of information about how ecosystems functioned.

By the late eighteenth century, local residents and visitors alike looked upon Cape Cod's overused soils, cleared forests, and struggling communities and asked two questions: how could anyone survive in such a locale, and why would anyone want to remain when better lands lay available elsewhere? After a century and a half of settlement, weakening soils had forced Cape Cod people to rely increasingly heavily upon their marine resources. The important roles those soils played in supporting what little Cape Cod could produce meant that towns had to manage them carefully, limiting their use and commercial development in favor of the long-term health of the entire community. Such restrictions—either natural or managerial—hardly made Cape Cod appear ripe with prospects for the future. As the people of the struggling new United States began to take stock of the country's future, Cape residents were hard pressed to show how their region could continue to survive.

In 1791, for example, a correspondent for the *Massachusetts Magazine* described Falmouth's soil as "thin" and Yarmouth soils as "sandy and barren." The paucity of Cape Cod's agriculture emerged most clearly, however, in the author's description of Eastham. There, while "the sands move swiftly with the wind, and constantly roving," the writer still noted, perhaps sardonically, that "this town is the granary of the Cape." Even land ownership proved challenging under such conditions. "Many fields, have here [in Eastham] become so wandering, that the possessors have removed their fences, they be insufficient to keep them within due limits."[56] After a century and three quarters of settlement, many Cape Cod lands had been used up.

There were some bright spots, however. In 1794 one Massachusetts Historical Society correspondent, for example, found Sandwich pleasantly surprising in its ability to accommodate guests: "It may be said that the appearance and accommodation [found in Sandwich] will rather exceed than disappoint the expectations formed from their outward appearance." Even here, however, the land alone could not provide for farmers, and instead, as people had done for centuries, local planters made good livings by combining land and sea resources. "Their extensive salt meadows enable them to keep large stocks in proportion to their pasture grounds; and the severity of a drought is mitigated by cutting the coarser kind of salt grass, and giving it green to the cattle as the occasion may require."[57] Still, local farmers worked their fields too hard. "Almost all of the land goes through a course of tillage once in the space of six or seven years; which, by the way, may have led the people here into an instance of bad husbandry, in leaving so few trees upon their cultivated lands." Even for what farmers could grow well—onions sold to Boston, in this case—the drive for a marketable commodity butted up against the limits of the soil. "Although good ground, improved for onions, yields a great profit; yet as it requires a large quantity of manure, it has been thought that the inhabitants of this town devote too much of their land to this article, for the general advantage of their farms." Even abundant marine resources also showed signs of degradation. Whereas Oyster Bay and Lewis Bay "in years past produced a great quantity of excellent oysters . . . now they are very much reduced." Even whaling had passed Barnstable by. "Seventy or eighty years ago, the whale fishery was carried on in boats from the shore, to great advantage. . . . But few whales now come into the bay, and this kind of fishery has for along time (by this town at least) been given up." As a sign of times to come, only the fisheries appeared to thrive. "A hundred men or upwards, are employed by the fisheries, which is yearly increasing."[58]

These observations reveal that local residents were not ignorant of how deteriorating lands were forcing people to rely more heavily upon marine resources. On the outer Cape this was especially true. A resident of Truro, by 1800, saw the deeper danger that lurked behind his contemporaries' observations: "A traveler from the interior part of the country, where the soil is fertile, upon observing the barrenness of Truro would wonder what could induce any person to remain in such a place. . . . The soil in every part of the township is continually depreciating, little pains being taken to manure it." Here, where once the Pilgrims found abundant land to grow grains and corn, a century and a half of overuse and shortsighted farming practices had undermined what little agricultural foundation the town's farming people had once depended on. Only the emerging fisheries offered Truro a brighter future. "[The inland visitor's] wonder would cease, when he was informed that the subsistence of the inhabitants is derived chiefly from the sea. The bay and ocean abound with excellent fish and with crabs and lobsters. . . . A subsistence easily obtained [from fishing], the young people are induced to marry at an early age. . . . Though Truro in respect of soil is inferior to every other township in the county, except Wellfleet and Province town . . . [and] in spite of every disadvantage, it has become full of inhabitants." If Cape lands were weak, its fisheries were strong, and therein lay the region's future.

Reliance upon fishing for survival, however, represented a double-edged sword. Quite simply, with so many pulling their livings from the sea, few residents were interested in developing the land for agricultural production. "Not much attention is paid to agriculture, as the young men are sent to sea very early in life." As a result, "The elderly men and small boys remain at home to cultivate the ground: the rest are at sea, except occasionally, two thirds of the year." Truro's reliance upon fishing to the detriment of agriculture even appeared to affect the landscape. "Few trees are planted, so that the orchards as well as the forests are continually lessening, and probably in a few years, will disappear." After a century of such dynamics, the consequences for Truro—though apparently still less pronounced than elsewhere on the Cape—lay bare for visitors and locals to see: "There are however no such appearances of desolation as are exhibited on the plains of Eastham where an extensive and what was once fertile spot, has become a prey to the winds and lies buried under a heap of barren sand."[59]

Wellfleet resident Levi Whitman observed a similar pattern. "Since the war, the whale and cod fisheries have revived, people's circumstances are mended, and the number of their vessels has been increased." Such growth was good, given how little else Wellfleet could look to. "The land is barren. The growth of wood is small pitch pine and oak." Even Wellfleet's famous shellfish threatened to give out. "No part of the world has better oysters than the harbour of Wellfleet. Time was when they were to be found in greatest plenty, but in 1773, a mortality from an unknown cause carried off the most of them." For a town in such otherwise dire straits, seafaring seemed the only logical, and only profitable, course for the future. Yet even here, Whitman, like other observers, was aware of the costs. "It may be noted that many of the people of this town spend more than half their lives at sea and on ship board. Navigation engrosses their whole attention, otherwise excellent gardens might be made in swamps, near ponds and marshes where the tide might be dyked out. . . . The inhabitants do not raise grain sufficient for the town. The common method is to import it from the southern states."[60] For Whitman, overused terrestrial resources and abundant marine resources charted only one possible course for local residents, but such a course closed off other routes and represented a one-way path of economic development.

Yale College president and traveler Timothy Dwight agreed with local residents' assessment of Cape Cod's grim prospects. For him, coastal areas were of little use. In a letter discussing the development of sea-salt manufacture, Dwight noted that "The American coast, as you know, is chiefly barren, and of course thinly inhabited. It is almost everywhere low and level; and therefore, while it is unsuited to most other employments, is remarkably fitted to this."[61] Cape Cod was particularly useless. "To my own fancy it appeared as the eternal boundary of a region, wild, dreary, and inhospitable, where no human being could dwell, and into which every human foot was forbidden to enter."[62] The Cape was far from a pit of despondency, however, and Dwight recognized, perhaps even rationalized, that the unique local circumstances required observers to rethink conventional understandings of happiness.

> A stranger born and educated in the interior of New England, amid the varied beauties of its surface and the luxuriant succession of its produce, naturally concludes when he visits Provincetown that the inhabitants and the neighbors also must possess a very limited share of enjoyment. Facts, however, refute this conclusion. For aught we could discern, they were as cheerful and appear to enjoy life as well as any equal number of their countrymen. This indeed is easily explicable. Food and clothing, houses, lodging, and fuel, they possess of such a quality and with so much ease in the acquisition as to satisfy all the demands of that middle state in life which wise men of every age dignified with the name *golden.*

Provincetown's people, living in a barren place, forced to go to sea for their living, and lacking the outward appearance of wealth evident in other American towns in the early republic, in fact offered Dwight an opportunity to question the meanings of wealth and poverty. "The truth is, a great part of human happiness or misery arises from comparison only. Our misfortunes spring not from our poverty, for we are rarely poor in such a sense as to suffer, but from a perception that we are not so rich as others. . . . Such in a good degree is the situation of these people. Their lot is the lot of all around them. They have little to covet, because they possess most of what is seen and known."[63] For Dwight, local people's adaptations to Cape Cod's harsh environment allowed him see a brighter future for his young nation. More virtuous for their poverty, and happier in their ignorance, Cape Cod people showed Dwight how resourceful and creative his fellow countrymen could be.

In most respects, however, Dwight's assessments of Cape Cod's ideal life and honest people represent a romanticization of a land that he found harsh and barren, and one filled with people unwilling or unable to move. In light of his early harsh words about life on Cape Cod, the people he later describes come across as too virtuous, the bounty of their local seas too convenient, and their harsh landscape too rationalized to ring true. A short conversation with a Harwich man, as Dwight was leaving the Cape, best revealed his more honest impressions: "We lodged at Harwich with Captain A. This man had been thirty years at sea and, as he informed us with emphasis, had seen the world. Now he was the principal farmer in Harwich, and cut annually from four to eight loads of English hay, a greater quantity, as he told us, than was cut by any single farmer further down the Cape. A farmer in the interior, who cuts annually from one or two hundred tons, may perhaps smile at this story."[64]

If Dwight hedged his condemnation of his fellow countrymen, Englishman Edward Augustus Kendall, who visited the Cape in 1809, was appalled at the poverty, isolation, and cyclical desperation that residents lived in even after almost two centuries of settlement. Kendall was most struck with how Cape Cod's weak soils and subsequent reliance upon fishing created a cycle of what he saw as laziness and endemic poverty. Like Dwight, Kendall noted locals' needs to combine resources of both land and sea to eke out their meager agriculture. "The favourite manure is the king or horseshoe crab, of which there are great numbers on the coast. . . . The sand, thus nourished, yields an adequate return for their labours of the husbandman."[65] But where Dwight and the Truro resident saw fishing as compensating Cape Codders for their poor soils, Kendall entertained no delusions as to how much support Cape people received from the seas. "In every account of the fisheries, great profits are represented as accruing; but, if the happiness of the bulk of the people, in all this country, depend upon the profits of their toil, it is, like their profits, both precarious and little."[66]

In fact, Kendall saw that the abundant sea and the thin soil created an ironic state of destitution, easily overlooked by romantic visions of provident nature. "One of those visionary writers, of whom we are acquainted with so many . . . might say, that the youth and strength of the country are employed, for two-thirds of the year, in obtaining, by hardy and audacious toil, the wealth of the seas beyond the line . . . [while] their blooming wives and daughters might be exhibited as deriving an easy subsistence from the bounteous hand of nature." But from Kendall's perspective, a harsher reality existed onshore.

> The truth is, that early habits of life, and the lure of voyages occasionally prosperous, induce the male population to devote themselves to the fisheries. . . . Meanwhile, their daily subsistence, and the subsistence of all the family, young and old, depends almost exclusively on fish taken with a line, or on shell-fish raked out of the sand. . . . Their persons are frequently squalid; their hair hangs often in dirt over their eyes, and their dress is marked by poverty. And how can it be otherwise, among a race that depends for its subsistence upon a search after food, directed almost by the immediate cravings of the stomach; and whom a stormy day may deprive of a dinner, or send [a person out] shivering, when the tide is out, to prowl upon the beach for food?[67]

In short, the ease by which food could be taken from the sea undermined any ambition to develop other resources. "It is certainly in their power to do better; but, for the poor and destitute, the temptation is strong to seek food at free cost to-day, and, having found it, to seek it so again to-morrow. The facility encourages the practice, and encourages indolence; and, indolence once become habitual, it is easier to suffer than to labour."[68] As Kendall left Cape Cod, he took with him little love for the destitute region. Poor soils and the need for fishing left the people, in Kendall's eyes, stuck in such a grind of poverty and subsistence living that he could understand no reason why anyone would want to settle there.

In fact, Cape Cod attracted few seeking prosperity, whether they were Puritan immigrants, American travelers, or foreign correspondents. Overtaxed soils and an abundant and heavily relied-upon marine environment defined how people survived on Cape Cod through the early nineteenth century. Ironically, however, the wastelands that residents, fellow countrymen, and foreign visitors universally perceived along Cape Cod's shores, and the endemic poverty that the exigency of fishing generated, helped local residents develop the ecological knowledge on which to base management regimes that encouraged the long-term health of their inshore resources. Poor soils and poor prospects also offered a silver lining. With so little to attract outsiders, Cape Cod towns did not have to face two important pressures. First, they did not need to support a large or rapidly growing population—with fewer people, fewer resources from both land and sea were needed to support them. The second reprieve was less tangible, but equally important. Perceived as it was by residents and visitors alike, Cape Cod was not viewed as a place ripe with economic opportunities. With better lands and better fishing elsewhere, developmental pressure from business investors and merchants bypassed Cape Cod, looking instead to interior lands and fishing operations elsewhere on the New England shore. Cape Codders, far from eschewing such pressures, would have welcomed the opportunity to secure more stable existences for themselves and their families—and in the nineteenth century, they would indeed seize the opportunity. For the first century and a half of settlement however, Cape Cod suffered from an underdevelopment that, while painful, forced its human population to learn about, manage, and cherish what natural resources they enjoyed.

CHAPTER 3

Workspace

In the early part of the season the vessels trawling on the Western Bank bait with frozen herring . . . and later in the year use herring and mackerel. . . . Vessels going to the Grand Bank in April usually carry a few barrels of salted clams, but rely chiefly upon herring . . . in spring and capelin in June and the early part of July, and squid, which are used for the remainder of the season.
    —G. Brown Goode and J. W. Collins, "The Bank Trawl-Line Cod Fishery" (1887)

Instead of the sublime and beautiful; the near, the low, the common, was explored and poetized. That, which had been negligently trodden under foot by those who were harnessing and provisioning themselves for long journeys into far countries, is suddenly found to be richer than all foreign parts.
    —Ralph Waldo Emerson, "The American Scholar" (1837)

Attitudes toward Cape Cod's wastelands would change dramatically in the first half of the nineteenth century. Initially viewed as a backwater, with ignorant and isolated people unable to grow their own food and forced to send their men off to distant fishing grounds for most of the year, after 1820 Cape Cod began to be seen in a different light. Two important trends caused people to recast their views. First, through local creativity and knowledge of the local marine ecosystem, Cape Cod fishermen reoriented their banks fisheries from export production to a far more profitable business serving growing domestic markets. In doing so, they appeared to secure the lives and the futures of Cape Cod's previously precarious communities. Secondly, as Cape Cod fishermen turned their coastal wasteland into an economically thriving region, they attracted the attention of painters and writers seeking to moralize on a new nation nurtured by an ever-abundant nature. For those watching fishermen find wealth in a previously barren space, the expansion of Cape Cod's fisheries provided an ideal pastoral image of how society, nature, and work fit neatly together. Both these forces—the development of Cape Cod's fisheries and their celebration in art and literature—transformed Cape Cod's shores after 1820 from wastelands into productive workspaces where an American narrative of national development through abundant natural resources played out most dramatically. If turn-of-the-century travelers spurned Cape Cod, their midcentury successors idealized the region as an iconic American workspace where natural (marine) bounty, human ingenuity, and commerce overcame the limits of an erstwhile wasteland.

At the foundation of Cape Codders' ability to turn their wastelands into prosperous and celebrated workspaces lay their fishermen's skills, natural knowledge, and ingenuity. Fishermen's knowledge of the marine environment and of the behavior of the fish they sought allowed them to modify fishing processes and gear to meet the demand for fish then growing along the American seaboard. Other factors played equally important roles: the spread of rail lines and the use of ice preservation allowed a fisherman's catch to arrive at market in a salable condition, while growing urban centers increased demand for all forms of fresh, cheap fish.[1] To attribute the improved efficiency of the fisheries solely to improved technology, however, would be to separate the inanimate implements of fishing from the people who designed, refined, and used them.[2] Behind every technological improvement stood people whose knowledge of fishing's work, workspaces, and environments allowed them to make the modifications that improved catches and generated more profit. This was clear on Cape Cod, where changes in fishing gear—from hooks to vessels and most importantly to bait—brought a prosperity to towns such as never before experienced. If local natural knowledge allowed Cape towns to better manage their inshore fisheries during the seventeenth and eighteenth centuries, that same knowledge allowed them in the nineteenth century to better exploit the offshore fisheries.

As had earlier colonial wars, the American Revolution crippled American fisheries. Peace in 1783 allowed Cape Cod ports to rebound quickly. According to Massachusetts merchant, politician, and shipmaster Stephen Higginson in 1790, "Those, who live beyond Cape Cod, and along the south Shore [of Boston] . . . have much extended their fishery, and will continue to thrive; while the others are declining, and will not recover. . . . There is a strong probability . . . [fishing wealth will] be in good degree transferred from the north [of Boston] to the south shore."[3]

While the embargo from 1807 to 1809, and war again between 1812 and 1815, crippled the American fisheries once more, the arrival of peace spurred the rapid growth of Cape Cod fleets. After 1815, moreover, Cape Cod fishermen experienced two more particular boosts to their fisheries. First, they benefited from their proximity to new fishing grounds, such as Georges Bank and Nantucket shoals, whose currents had kept most fishing vessels away until the late 1820s.[4] After 1820, Cape Cod fishermen increasingly fished Georges Bank, and success there helped expand the banks fleets that had long operated out of Cape Cod ports such as Provincetown and Chatham. As Higginson predicted, those fleets expanded and would continue to do so for much of the antebellum period.

In addition, a new banks fishery for offshore mackerel developed as fishermen applied their natural knowledge to meet an expanding urban demand for fresh and pickled fish. Mackerel fishing's success best represents how fishermen used their knowledge to transform the coasts into workspaces. No other fishery, new or established, underwent such dramatic expansion in such a short time as Cape Cod's mackerel fishery in the first half of the nineteenth century.[5] While cod fishing retained its position as the largest banks fishery, mackerel fishing emerged as a highly capitalized, highly profitable business. By midcentury, this mackerel fishery had come to rival, if not surpass, the profitability of Cape Cod's cod fishery.

Throughout the seventeenth and eighteenth centuries, fishermen had hand-lined or beach-seined for mackerel. Because of the fish's erratic behavior, however, these methods resulted in relatively small catches. Like their tuna relatives, mackerel require tremendous amounts of oxygen to live. When mackerel find themselves in the warm, relatively oxygen-poor waters of the summer, they have to constantly swim to bring enough oxygen into their systems. As a result, mackerel schools swim at about 1.5 miles per hour (2.4 km per hour) when they arrive in New England in the spring. This mobility made them difficult for fishermen to find, and even more difficult to catch. Their feeding habits offered fishermen few opportunities, too. Mackerel feed in two ways: as they travel they can filter out small, single-celled organisms such as zooplankton, or they can actively pursue almost any swimming animal they see and that can fit into their mouths. Consequently, mackerel only need to surface when prey species or bait draws them into feeding frenzies— called spurts—where their desire for food trumps their desire to remain in deeper, safer waters between 150 feet and 180 feet (46–55 meters). For fishermen, this meant they had only limited time to catch mackerel.[6]

Hence, mackerels' speed and aversion to surface feeding made increasing catches of these fish no small task. Traditionally, the growth of New England's antebellum mackerel fisheries has been attributed to growing urban markets, expanding rail lines, and new material technologies that provided the means and motivation for fishermen to take and sell more fish.[7] Certainly, these technological factors played significant, if not prominent, roles. Before any of those forces came into play, however, fishermen needed to develop new ways to catch more mackerel, and this task relied upon fishermen's skill, knowledge, and their ability to develop new gear that would best match mackerel feeding behaviors. In short, before the advent of net fishing, increased mackerel catches resulted from fishermen using their knowledge about these elusive fish and applying it to new gear, vessel design, and bait selection.

For fishermen working hooks and lines, mackerels' short feeding spurts meant that fishermen needed skill and technique to land the hooked fish, clear them off the hook, rebait the hook, and set it out again as many times as the school allowed. One quick way fishermen developed to clear fish was to "slat" the fish from the hook (Fig 3.1). According to one observer, "A barrel is placed behind each man, in which the fish are snapped [or slatted] as fast as they are caught, the jaw tearing out as easily as though made of paper. Owing to this tenderness of the jaw, the fish must be hauled very carefully, though with great rapidity."[8]

Before 1815, fishermen used simple and light iron hooks that tangled easily and broke when slatting fish, which resulted in lost time and added expense.[9] In response, some fishermen redesigned hooks to reduce tangling and to strengthen the hook's shank. In making these new "mackerel jigs," fishermen soldered a tapered, three-quarter-ounce to three-ounce mass of lead, pewter, or tin to the hook's shank (Fig 3.2).

The added weight solved many problems fishermen faced with light iron hooks. First, the additional metal reinforced the hook where it faced the greatest stress when slatting fish. Second, when fishermen swung hooked fish into their catch buckets, the added weight gave more momentum—and

FIG. 3.1 H. W. Elliott and Capt. J. W. Collins, *Jigging Mackerel over the Vessel's Rail.*
George Brown Goode, ed., *The Fisheries and Fishery Industries of the United States, Section V: History and Methods of the Fisheries,* II (Washington, D.C.: Government Printing Office, 1887), Image ID figboo71, NOAA's Historic Fisheries Collection, National Marine Fisheries Service

hence more force—to help rip the fish's jaw free from the hook. Finally, weighted jigs kept fishing lines straighter when set over the side, reducing tangles and snares. Lighter versions could be used more quickly in calmer conditions, but in heavier weather, fishermen could deploy heavier models. It is uncertain whether inventors of this new "mackerel jig" hailed from Pigeon Cove, Cape Ann, or Hingham, Massachusetts. In any case, fishermen started using the jigs around 1815, and soon fishermen were designing and casting their own unique models to best suit their immediate conditions. Ultimately, jigs made the fishing process more efficient and allowed fishermen to keep pace during the brief window when mackerel fed at the surface.

Fishermen also shortened the amount of time a hook was out of water by selecting baits that could withstand multiple strikes. Fishermen realized that by using tougher cuts of meat from baitfish, they would not have to rebait their hooks every time a mackerel took a bite. Using flesh cut from around a baitfish's belly or anal fin, fishermen stacked cuts onto the bend of the hook and then scraped the pile of strips to help the bait distend into a pulpy mass. When the fish took the bait, the pulp compressed, setting the hook deeper. The benefit of this baiting technique lay in its time savings: tougher cuts held to the hook better, so hooked fish were less likely to take the bait with

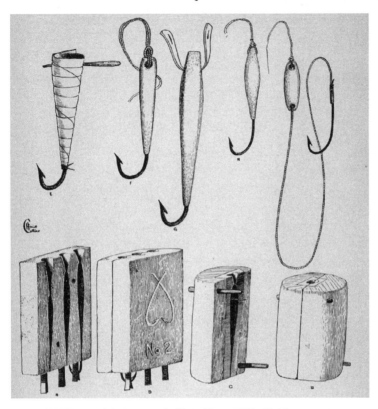

FIG. 3.2 H. W. Elliott and Capt. J. W. Collins, *Jigs and Jig Molds*. George Brown Goode, ed., *The Fisheries and Fishery Industries of the United States, Section V: History and Methods of the Fisheries*, II (Washington, D.C.: Government Printing Office, 1887), Image ID figb0070, NOAA's Historic Fisheries Collection, National Marine Fisheries Service

them, and fishermen could reset the hook without taking the time to rebait it. As a result, fishermen could work the same bait for an hour or more— even when the fish hit hard—and in lighter spurts a single bait could last an entire day.[10]

As the mackerel fishery developed, and as fishermen and investors began to realize the fishery's long-run viability, fishermen began building dedicated mackerel schooners that had the speed and maneuverability needed to chase down and remain on top of mackerel schools. Before 1848, mackerel vessels typically measured between twenty-five and ninety tons. Many of these were slower square-sterned or pinky schooners that were not dramatically different from vessels that had dominated the cod fishery since the colonial period. By

1855, however, owners and captains launched new mackerel vessels built along more aggressive lines. Dubbed "sharpshooters," or "file form," to describe the vessels' V-shaped cross section beneath the waterline, these vessels had a significantly deeper stern than stem, which favored speed and nimbleness over stability and "weatherliness." Though it has not been confirmed, tradition alleges that the crew of the first sharpshooter, *Romp*, built in Essex, Massachusetts, in 1847, refused to sail in the vessel because her hull was so aggressively designed for speed over stability. Despite these alleged misgivings, however, sharpshooters soon dominated not only the mackerel fishery, but also the fresh codfish fishery, where speed and maneuverability were similarly valued.[11]

As a result of fishermen taking what they knew about mackerel and applying it to new gear and vessels, Massachusetts and Cape Cod fishermen increased their catches several times over. Between 1805 and 1818, Massachusetts mackerel inspectors never saw more than fifty thousand barrels landed annually. In 1820, however, shortly after widespread adoption of mackerel jigs, Massachusetts' annual take of mackerel rose to one hundred thousand barrels, and by the early 1830s production peaked at just under four hundred thousand barrels. In just twenty years, mackerel landings in Massachusetts rose almost tenfold.[12]

While Massachusetts as a whole saw a marked expansion of the mackerel fishery, Cape Cod witnessed some of the fishery's most dramatic growth. Wellfleet, for example, took to mackereling by 1826, and between 1845 and 1865 the town claimed over one hundred vessels in the mackerel fishery alone. It lagged behind only Gloucester and Boston in landings. By the mid-1830s and 1840s, other Cape towns hosted mackerel fleets as well. Dennis started mackerel fishing in 1836 and within nine years hosted between fifty and seventy vessels in the fishery. Provincetown added a mackerel fleet to its cod and whaling fleet and landed over 31,000 barrels in 1848 alone. Harwich, too, prospered in mackereling between 1846 and 1866.[13] Thus, within a single generation, Cape Cod mackereling—driven by fishermen's understanding of their prey—emerged as one way by which Cape Codders could wrest wealth from the oceanic wilderness and ensure what many thought would be long-term prosperity.

Cape towns also prospered from a growing cod fishery that benefited from newly identified, unfished stocks close to home. Before the 1830s most fishermen avoided Georges Bank because the bad weather, strong currents, and heavy seas threatened to sink their vessels. In the 1830s, however, Gloucester fishermen developed new anchoring gear that allowed them to hold position on those grounds, and as they pulled up larger and larger codfish, the financial benefits of risking Georges Bank became clear to all. Soon, larger vessels came from Gloucester and elsewhere to fish the waters off Cape Cod year-round. Many of these vessels came from Cape Cod ports, whose relative proximity to Georges Bank allowed Cape fishermen to make short trips, from three days to two weeks, all year long. As Cape Cod expanded its Georges Bank fleet, local support industries also thrived, as business expanded to take up the entire calendar year. Flake yards—where codfish were dried and salted—carters, merchants, chandlers, dealers, and brokers all along the Cape Cod coast soon benefited from this expanded business, while Cape towns added more cod vessels and fishermen to their rolls.[14]

In addition to profiting from new fishing grounds, the Cape's codfish fishery, like its mackerel fishery, also benefited from new gear developed as fishermen applied their understandings of the marine environment to improve catches. Traditionally, cod fishermen anchored on the banks and worked hand lines from the rail of the fishing schooner itself (Fig 3.3). Spread along both sides of the vessel, fishermen worked two hand-lines apiece, targeting the waters and ocean floor immediately beneath the vessel.

Beginning in the mid 1850s, banks fishermen—mostly on the Grand Banks and the Scotian Shelf—began expanding their "hook footprint" by sending crews out to hand-line from dories (Fig 3.4). Dory hand-lining allowed a vessel's crew to leave their vessel and cover more bottom, with more hooks.[15]

Dory hand-lining translated quickly into larger catches. Data from voyages in the 1830s and 1840s is scarce, but Wayne O'Leary's study of Maine's Grand Banks fishery perhaps best documents this new gear's increased efficiency. In 1853, for example, the *Martha Burgess* from Penobscot Bay, using hand lines, took 31,000 cod in the three trips or "fares" that made up a five-month season. The hand-liners aboard the *Black Hawk* of Bucksport averaged 22,000 fish per season between 1848 and 1852, and the *Mirror* out of Vinalhaven landed 33,000 cod in their fares to Banquereau and the Scotian Shelf in 1851. On all these voyages, fishermen worked hand lines from the vessel's rail. By contrast, the crew of the *Gertie Lewis* from Portland, using dory hand lines, took 52,000 fish in a single fare alone on Western Bank in 1879. Similarly, the *Lady Elgin* took 64,000 cod in two months in 1886 also hand-lining from dories. According to O'Leary, Maine fishing schooners that

FIG. 3.3 H. W. Elliott and Capt. J. W. Collins, *Old Style Grand Bank Cod Schooner; Crew at Rail Hand-line Fishing*. Note the working positions of the fishermen along the vessel's rail and the tight clustering of hand lines surrounding the fishing vessel. George Brown Goode, ed., *The Fisheries and Fishery Industries of the United States, Section V: History and Methods of the Fisheries,* II (Washington, D.C.: Government Printing Office, 1887), Image ID figb0024, NOAA's Historic Fisheries Collection, National Marine Fisheries Service

had averaged 30,000 fish per season with deck hand lines in the 1850s took almost 50,000 fish per season using dory hand lines by the 1880s.[16]

In the late 1850s, banks cod fishermen adopted another new technology to increase their catches. As early as 1815, the French banks fleet began using tub trawls or bultows (what are now called longlines). Tub trawls were composed of a set line, sometimes hundreds of yards long, with short lines, called gangings, attached at roughly six-foot intervals. A baited hooked was attached to the end of each ganging. To set this gear, fishermen in dories anchored and buoyed one end of the set-line and then paid out the line and the baited hooks as the dory drifted downwind. When they reached the end of the line, they set another anchor and buoy and rowed off to be picked up by the schooner. After beating back to windward in the night, schooners launched their dories again, whose crews cleared their trawls' catch and rebaited the hooks. This new technology allowed fewer fishermen to catch far more fish than ever before. For example, in 1858 an American hand-line fishing captain visited a French vessel that was using tub trawls. The French captain complained that he had only 160,000 fish in his hold; the stunned American captain had caught only 15,671 fish in that entire year using hand

FIG. 3.4 H. W. Elliott and Capt. J. W. Collins, *Hand-Line Dory Cod Fishing on the Grand Bank*. Note how the use of dories allowed fishermen's hand lines to cover more area—and hence catch more fish—than the techniques shown in fig. 3.3. George Brown Goode, ed., *The Fisheries and Fishery Industries of the United States, Section V: History and Methods of the Fisheries*, II (Washington, D.C.: Government Printing Office, 1887), Image ID figb0025, NOAA's Historic Fisheries Collection. National Marine Fisheries Service

lines. After the mid-1850s, and despite resistance from fishermen to being sent out in dories on the high seas, American fishing schooners began using more dory hand lines and tub trawls than ever before.[17]

Onshore, new gear aboard cod and mackerel vessels allowed banks fleets, including Cape Cod's, to expand. As early as 1837, gazetteer compiler John Hayward claimed that Cape Cod had over four hundred vessels in the cod and mackerel fisheries. These vessels employed 2,385 men and earned $571,521 per year. Based on these numbers and census figures, the fisheries employed directly a full 7 percent of Barnstable County's 31,109 people, and ancillary industries supporting fishing voyages employed even more. For towns with large mackerel and cod fleets, such as Truro and Wellfleet, a greater proportion found work. In those towns, mackerel fleets landed 33,250 barrels of mackerel, representing almost a full quarter of the 138,157 barrels inspected in all of Massachusetts for the year.[18] As early as the 1830s, Cape Cod banks fishing was bringing new prosperity to the land of barren sands.

In the years following Hayward's profile, the fisheries continued to grow, as expanding northeastern cities demanded more and more inexpensive protein. Federal census records reveal that in 1840 Cape Cod fisheries employed 2,474 men, produced over 100,000 quintals of dried cod and 38,000 barrels of pickled fish, and used almost $740,000 in invested capital.[19] By 1851, Lorenzo Sabine reported that in the Cape's mackerel fleet alone, 4,044 men found work aboard 350 vessels of about seventy tons apiece.[20] Indeed, one correspondent reported that on Cape Cod, "scarcely aught else is heard of than the prospect for fish and the state of the markets. Children scarcely large enough to walk, discourse upon the relative merits of codfish, halibut, mackerel, &c., with a knowing air, and the male members look forward with joyous eagerness to the time when, as 'skipper' of some bonnie craft, they shall carry death and destruction to the finny tribes of the great waters."[21]

Not surprisingly, between 1810 and 1860 Cape Cod's population grew markedly. After the Revolution, Cape Cod claimed only 17,354 people, with another 7,000 residents living there by 1820. During the next forty years, however, as the banks fleet grew at unprecedented rates, the Cape's population grew along with it. Between 1830 and 1860, Barnstable County experienced a growth that averaged more than 10 percent per decade: in 1840 about 29,000 people lived on Cape Cod, and in 1850 just over 36,000 people called the region home. By 1860, the Cape supported more than 35,000 residents— more than double from 1790.[22]

Expanding banks cod and mackerel fishing brought to the Cape the wealth and prosperity that allowed the region to overcome its terrestrial limitations. Driven by the Cape fishermen's understanding of their prey and their marine environment, that prosperity delivered Cape Codders from their earlier penury in ways never before imagined. Within a decade and a half from the end of the War of 1812, it looked like Cape Cod, finally, was enjoying the commercial growth that other areas had experienced long before.

If expanded cod and mackerel fishing helped bring prosperity to Cape Cod communities, it was another application of fishermen's ecological understanding to the fishing process that most definitively and visibly transformed Cape Cod from a wasteland to a workspace. Along with new gear and new vessels, bait—its use, selection, and deployment in the fishing process— represented one of the most important technological innovations in the New England fisheries before 1865. Like changes in gear design and work processes, bait selection represented fishermen's expanding understandings of how their prey species interacted with the larger marine world. As all the new gear relied upon inducing a fish to take a baited hook, a fishermen's ability to select and obtain the best baits represented a key point in the fishing process—a point that could make or break a voyage. Not surprisingly, therefore, as they developed and deployed new gear, fishermen also developed increasingly sophisticated understandings of the best baits and baiting methods for each species. Knowing which bait species best attracted which target species at which time of year was as important a change in the nineteenth-century New England fishery as was new gear or new fishing grounds or new ships.

Again, fishermen in the competitive mackerel fishery demonstrated innovation in selecting and deploying bait to increase catches. As jigging voyages got longer and more competitive, fishermen soon realized they could not afford to rely upon sporadically available supplies of bait taken on the banks.[23] True, forage fish—such as herring, capelin, menhaden, and smaller mackerel—taken from the same region occupied by mackerel schools were a source of fresh, free, and attractive bait. Economically, however, time spent catching bait represented time lost catching mackerel, and if fishermen could have on-board bait that was good enough to induce mackerel to bite, more time could be spent making money.

Consequently, fishermen developed new ways to obtain and use bait to improve catches. In 1804, Rockport, Massachusetts, mackerel schooner captain Epes W. Merchant first used "toll" or "chum" bait to draw mackerel to the surface during a banks voyage. Shore fishermen had long tolled mackerel to the surface by casting fish offal overboard around their lines, or by crushing smaller fish under their boots and casting the pulp over the side. For larger vessels, however, tolling required far more bait than crews could catch from the banks themselves. If sufficient quantities of bait could be shipped aboard, however, then mackerel schooners could also use this inshore tactic to induce a school to feed and to keep mackerel biting hooks longer.

The problem was that larger vessels required more toll bait than inshore boats did, and after Merchant's trip, mackerel vessels began sailing with barrels of bait specifically designated for tolling. Preparing toll bait also became part of the daily watch routine while fishing, and crews soon fined fellow fishermen who failed to chop sufficient quantities of toll bait to keep mackerel feeding at the surface. In response, beginning in the late 1810s, fishermen developed bait mills to speed up the processing of toll bait. Consisting of two cylinders with interfacing lines of sharpened nails, the early design shredded fish much faster than a fisherman could chop it by hand.

In 1823, however, a merchant on Cape Ann named Burnham replaced the nails with small, spirally positioned knives, which markedly improved mill performance.[24] Now armed with mills that could process bait more efficiently, fishermen started using toll bait in greater quantities, and in more wasteful ways. In a practice called "lee-bowing," for example, one schooner took station downwind of another already working a school of mackerel. Once in position, the leeward schooner, in an attempt to lure the fish away from the vessel already working, cast toll bait between the two vessels, and as both vessels drifted downwind, the bait created a trail that, in theory, attracted the feeding school from the windward vessel to the newcomer. To counter, the crew of the windward vessel cast out even more—and "better"—toll bait to keep the mackerel under them.[25] In these wasteful tugs of war, the quantities of baitfish caught, chopped, and cast out onto the water increased dramatically, and eventually, by the 1830s and 1840s, mackerel vessels shipped as much as twenty-five to forty barrels of fish bait, along with ten barrels of salt clams, for just one fare in a single season.[26]

Nor was the mackerel fishery alone in its increased hunger for baitfish. In the cod fishery, too, bait emerged as an important variable in increasing catches. In the Grand Banks and Scotian Shelf cod fisheries, increased demand for bait was driven by fishermen's transition to tub trawling. Like mackerel vessels, early nineteenth-century cod hand-lining vessels could afford to spend time securing bait simply because they required relatively little. With only eight men fishing two or four hooks each during the day, hand-liners could take in one night most of the bait they would need for the next day's fishing.[27] As a result, banks hand-lining vessels, until the early 1850s, carried relatively little bait. Vessels either shipped with fifty barrels of salt clams for the entire ten-to-twelve-week trip to the Scotian Shelf or the Grand Banks, or carried about five hundred individual herring to get started fishing, and then shifted to locally available fish on which cod were already feeding.[28] Again, collecting bait on-site meant lost time taking commercially valuable fish, and sometimes bait collecting represented a significant effort. In the Georges Bank fishery, for example, a vessel spent up to two to three days of a two-week trip chasing around for bait.[29] And when no bait was left, fishermen had to stop working in order to find and catch a sufficient supply. As long as little bait was needed, though, such costs were bearable.

New tub trawls required much more bait, however, and as a result on-site bait collecting became all but impossible. Unlike hand-liners, who needed little bait to work two lines per fisherman, tub trawlers prebaited hundreds of hooks every night before the following day's set. Consequently, they required far greater amounts of bait than hand-lining vessels.[30] For example, if a typical hand-liner used 500 individual herring to start fishing, tub trawling vessels working Georges Bank in the late 1850s shipped between 18,000 and 20,000 herring.[31] Trawlers heading to the Grand Banks and Scotian Shelf typically used between 150 and 200 barrels of prepackaged bait each season, and sometimes as much as 300 to 350 barrels. Bait became so important to trawlers that voyages out to the banks came to be broken up into shorter "baitings," when vessels tucked into convenient ports closer to the fishing grounds to refresh bait supplies. Furthermore, by the 1870s bait was being built into fishing vessels' very architecture, with bait rooms specifically designed to keep bait as long as possible and to facilitate the baiting of trawls.[32]

For both the cod and mackerel fleets, then, as fishermen began to ship more prepackaged bait, they created new complications for the fishing process. As long as they obtained bait on the fishing grounds they worked, they remained within the "logic" of the marine ecosystem—that is, they used for bait those species on which their prey was already feeding. This allowed the ecosystem's internal function to tell them how best to take fish. These new, bait-intensive technologies, however, introduced new variables into the fishing process that simpler technologies did not face. By shipping prepackaged bait from afar, fishermen stepped out of the local ecosystem and as a result had to develop their own understandings of which fish desired which kind of bait. In addition, packaged bait altered the lure's texture and taste and ran the risk of not appealing to fish-feeding preferences by the time it arrived on the fishing grounds. Thus, prepackaged bait created new challenges as new fishing gear forced fishermen to use bait from outside the ecosystem.

To meet this challenge, fishermen applied what they knew about the marine ecosystem to select those baitfish that would best fit into the place, season, and tastes of their target species. Generally, they tried to mimic with bait whichever forage fish were currently present on the banks. For example, cod vessels on the Scotian Shelf and Grand Banks used frozen herring in the spring and then followed with fresh herring and mackerel as those fish migrated north onto the banks. By June, many shifted over to capelin when that fish made its annual appearance on the grounds. Finally, for the remainder of

the summer, fishermen turned to squid.[33] On Georges Bank, fishermen similarly used frozen herring in winter and then shifted over to fresh herring,
alewives, mackerel, and menhaden as those fish came available during each
species' regular migration.[34] Fishermen also speculated on what appealed
most to a given prey's tastes. Haddock fishermen preferred to use menhaden
baits, believing that haddock would bite at those when nothing else would
tempt them.[35] Mackerel fishermen, on the other hand, believed that clam bait
better "held" mackerel alongside, and they kept reserves of this choice bait to
induce mackerel to start biting, or to thwart lee-bowing competitors' attempts
to lure fish away.[36]

Fishermen's abilities to match prepackaged bait from one ecosystem to
the prey's food desires in another represented no small feat. Fishermen
needed to note how and what their targeted species ate at what time of year,
and how to obtain and preserve that bait to ensure it would attract fish once
deployed. That fishermen were able to do so highlights their keen observations of how fish and other marine animals interacted on a given fishing
ground. Thus, as much as jigging, tolling, and tub trawling represented technological revolutions in the fisheries, so too did fishermen's abilities to identify, obtain, and transport bait species from one marine ecosystem to another.

Fishermen's expertise was not lost on the academicians beginning to investigate the region's fisheries resources. In fact, by the 1830s, when nascent
ichthyologists and naturalists began their surveys of New England's marine
resources, fishermen and working watermen were the first sources to which
these researchers turned to collect information about the marine environment. For example, in 1839, Humphrey Storer, tasked by the Boston Society
for Natural History with cataloging Massachusetts fish, turned to fishermen
and fishmongers for information. "I at once commenced my labors, by writing to all parts of the State from whence I could hope for the slightest aid, and
by engaging upon the spot the services of intelligent fishermen."[37] Such information, Storer claimed, was essential, for "Not knowing a single ichthy-
ologist in New England, to whom, in cases of doubt, I could refer for advice
and instruction, I have been compelled to rely wholly upon myself."[38] Storer
also collected many of his specimens from local fish markets and commonly
referred to names used by fishermen. Furthermore, Storer presented important ecological conclusions based on fishermen's testimony. For example,
"The squeteague, or weak fish, have disappeared since the return of the bluefish, who are their avowed enemy. I have conversed with our fishermen, they

say they have scarce seen one for six years. . . . Thus it appears that while the blue fish was absent, [squeteagues] were abundant—and at the appearance of the blue-fish, they left us."[39] As in the previous century, the larger public in the early nineteenth century still looked to fishermen to provide the foundational knowledge of local marine ecosystem function.

One such "intelligent fisherman" Storer encountered was Provincetown captain Nathaniel E. Atwood. In 1843 the thirty-seven-year-old fisherman's observations and assistance impressed Storer, who in 1847 sponsored Atwood for election to the Boston Society of Natural History. In 1852 the famed naturalist and Harvard professor Louis Agassiz also sought information from this Cape Cod fisherman when he visited Atwood at his home during a trip to Provincetown. In 1856 state fish commissioner Theodore Lyman hired Atwood, and not another naturalist, to investigate the feasibility of artificial fish propagation. Ultimately, Atwood's work in the fisheries, and then in fisheries science, so impressed Agassiz that he recommended the Lowell Institute hire him to offer a series of lectures on food fishes, which Atwood ultimately delivered in 1868 and 1869.[40]

Certainly Atwood was not representative, for as we will see, his future career reveals a fisherman with a keen political sense and an ability to steer proceedings according to his own interests. More important, however, was the fact that it was his and other fishermen's understandings of the marine environment that attracted the attention of the naturalists Storer and Agassiz in their attempts to catalog Massachusetts fishes. Through observing the marine environment, and through applying those observations to redesign gear and select bait, fishermen not only caught more fish, but emerged before the Civil War as the most important center of information about the marine ecosystem.

Fishermen's knowledge transformed Cape Cod's economy as much as it transformed the effectiveness and efficiency of banks fishing. As the Cape's population began to grow along with the area's new prosperity, fishing became even more important, as increased numbers of people mounted more formidable ecological challenges to Cape Cod's thin, degraded soil. With cash flowing in from the fisheries, however, Cape Codders could overcome the region's environmental limitations through regional trade—an adaptation that seemed to overcome earlier visions of the region's poverty. For example, Hayward commented in the 1839 gazetteer, "Below the town of Barnstable the county is quite sandy, [and] much of the people are generally dependent on Boston and other towns for a large proportion of their meats and breadstuffs. . . . This deficit is amply compensated by the unrivalled privileges enjoyed, and well improved by them, in the cod, mackerel, and other fisheries."[41] Indeed, Cape Cod's involvement in the new cash economy was a marked point of pride. Hayward not only listed the size of each town's fishing fleet and the size of the workforce, but also made sure to include the amount of local capital invested in the fishery. For him, Cape Codders' ability to use market earnings to overcome immediate terrestrial limitations represented a model for other areas. "Although there is but little vegetation at Truro, and the people are dependent almost entirely for their fuel, and most of their food, on other places, yet there are but few towns in the state where the people are more flourishing and independent in their circumstances. . . . To such towns as this old Massachusetts looks with pride for one of their chief resources of wealth—the fishery; and men of noble daring in all her enterprises on the ocean."[42] Nor was this view fleeting. Six years later, William B. Fowle and Asa Fitz also presented the Cape as an example of New England virtue: "The inhabitants in a great measure depend upon commerce and fishing, and are a hardy race, frugal and moral, and not unworthy of their Pilgrim ancestors."[43] If in the seventeenth and eighteenth centuries fishing put food on Cape Codders' tables, in the nineteenth century it put cash in people's pockets in ways that attracted the attention of the whole state.

With distant banks fleets employing local fishermen and purchasing locally caught baitfish, Cape Cod fit neatly within romantic pastoral images of an abundant nature nurturing the new American republic. For indeed, fishermen, like the celebrated yeoman American farmers, brought to market those products desired by a whole nation. Beginning in the early nineteenth century, painters and writers used their canvases and pages to celebrate these industries by constructing allegorical images of how human energy and natural bounty would allow Americans to create an ideal—or at least an idealized—republic.[44] Similar to other pastoral images, representations of southern New England people working along the shore carried equally didactic, rather than documentary, messages, as painters, engravers, and writers imbued coastal laborers with value-laden, iconographical significance. Painters and engravers on the southern New England shore "selected the most picturesque and evocative episodes of rural labor . . . in which [workers] literally reaped the rewards of their virtuous and noble vocation."[45] Like the contemporary pastoral images of rural workers in the interior, southern New England's coastal workspaces were presented as places where nature rewarded the simple and pure labor of those securing honest livelihoods.

More than just romantic visions of a simpler life, these images had at their heart the relationships between people and their local resources. As Sarah Burns argues, "The language of such images constitutes an iconography of abundance and natural wealth."[46] For inland areas, painters used bountiful harvests to highlight the virtue of free labor and moral living. And yet, as Barbara Novak has illustrated, many such representations included ambiguous statements about the costs to nature of an expanding American society. Disorderly fields of stumps, mud-track roads, and symbols of human destruction of nature such as axes all appear regularly in the antebellum landscape vistas at once celebrating and questioning American westward expansion.[47] Coastal painters, engravers, and writers offered little such ambiguity, however. Their images of storms, wrecks, and sublime maritime environments may have questioned the human costs of maritime industry, but they never questioned its affect on nature itself.[48] Given that the ecological consequences of fishing, whaling, and overseas trade could never be seen above water, those representing the seaside towns could look upon developing coastal workspaces as ideal places where the abundance of the marine world would forever support the unconstrained commercial development of American natural resources. In this, images of coastal workspaces represented another version of what Roger B. Stein has called "the domestication of the seascape," wherein the power of the sea as a sublime place where man met the gods was replaced by an everyday world marked by commercial activity and human relationships.[49]

With their unequivocal representations of the coastal workspace, painters and writers played an important if indirect role in driving the coastal fisheries. For at the same time that Cape Codders were transforming their coastal wastelands into workspaces, painters and writers were celebrating such transformations as idealized examples of how American nature nurtured the American nation. Settlers in the New World, tied to their home countries by water, had painted maritime subjects since the seventeenth century. Initially, these tended to be restricted to elements in paintings such as portraits or port town panoramas. After the Revolution, however, as Europeans and Americans alike took an interest in the powerlessness of man in the face of God's nature—the sublime—or in romantic visions of the wilderness, seascapes developed into forms of their own.[50] Despite this allegorical turn, however, these earlier seascapes tended to omit detailed images of the working waterfront. For the most part, these painters used working watermen and mariners iconographically to represent all mankind, rather than as depictions of individual workers in and of themselves. Much of this new appreciation stemmed from larger intellectual and aesthetic interests in everyday life. Some saw such interests as a means by which Americans could establish new cultural motifs best suited to the new republic. In his 1837 essay, "The American Scholar," for example, Ralph Waldo Emerson charged his listeners to produce something new to distinguish American works: "I ask not for the great, the remote, the romantic; what is doing in Italy or Arabia; what is Greek art, or Provencal minstrelsy; I embrace the common, I explore and sit at the feet of the familiar, the low. Give me insight in to-day, and you may have the antique and future worlds."[51]

Such calls echoed through the Atlantic world, as transatlantic observers also compelled local artists to see the coasts in new lights. In Great Britain, renowned art critic John Ruskin in 1855 challenged painters to see in coastal workspaces the broader themes that Emerson challenged Americans to pursue in their scholarship a decade and half earlier. For Ruskin, the beauty and aesthetic sensibility of everyday life was best manifested in the tools, boats, and activities of coastal working scenes. In his opening comments in J. M. W. Turner's *The Harbours of England*, for example, Ruskin wrote: "One object there is still, which I never pass without the renewed wonder of childhood, and that is the bow of a Boat." No yacht, however, generated this wonder, but rather "the blunt head of a common, bluff, undecked sea-boat, lying alongside in its furrow of beach sand." Workboats, in their strength and utility, brought together man, nature, and the wonderful: "The rude simplicity of the bent plank, that can breast its way through the death that is in the deep sea, has in it the soul of shipping. Beyond this, we may have more work, more men, more money; we cannot have more miracle."[52]

Ruskin's wonder lay in the perfection of function and utility residing within working vessels. For him a boat's bow was "naively perfect: complete without an effort. The man who made it knew not he was making anything beautiful, as he bent its planks into those mysterious curves." Those unfamiliar with the sea found the common boat even more remarkable, and therefore exotically appealing: "To all landsmen, from youth upwards, the boat remains a piece of enchantment." Surrounded by such works of everyday art, it is not surprising that Ruskin also found inspiration in fishing itself. In Ruskin's first draft of his essay, however, he explored those perceptions more deeply. In a passage edited from earlier versions, Ruskin wrote, "two black, steep, overhanging sides of fishing boats basking in the beach sun; scenting that beach aether, partly salt, partly embittered by the fresh sea-weed, with vague additions from fish cooked, or uncookable, and noble prevalence of tar, and slight film of smoke from the deck chimney, and a dash of the downs brought through the hollow of the cliffs, even to the very beach."[53] Thus, for even an English art critic—whose views defined artistic expression across the Atlantic in the 1840s and 1850s—coastal workspaces represented places of inspiration and celebration, if only to remind the viewer of the art of everyday life.

Ultimately for Ruskin, like Emerson, it was everyday life—in particular fishing—that brought together the power of nature and the energy of man in ways worthy of celebration: "Any ship, from the lowest to the proudest, has due place in that architecture of the sea . . . yet among them, the fisher-boat, corresponding to the cottage on land (only far more sublime than a cottage can ever be), is on the whole the thing most venerable. I doubt if ever academic grove were half so fit for profitable meditation as the little strip of shingle between two black, steep, overhanging sides of stranded fishing-boats."[54]

Evoking a message so compelling to American aesthetic sensibilities, Ruskin's writings from *The Harbours of England* rapidly appeared in redacted form in the United States. Almost immediately upon the book's publication in England in 1856, the editors of the New York art journal *The Crayon* reprinted portions of Ruskin's introduction for the journal's American readership, under the title "On Boats."[55] This, combined with Emerson's 1837 address and similar calls, encouraged painters and the art-inclined public alike to see coastal workspaces as places where nature and the new nation harmoniously combined.

American painters responding to these calls sought scenes of American expansion, virtue, industry, and activity. Nation and industry carried important themes in these works, for many pictured a young nation on the move, bringing settlements and markets to the wilderness. Indeed, as Angela Miller has argued, "Nationalist aesthetics fostered a new set of associations based not on the traditional litany of European cultural riches, but on a distinctly American inventory of natural resources. . . . This led to a celebration of the

wilderness as a stage, necessarily incomplete, in a process of cultural coloni-
zation. The theme of nature's transformations was deeply rooted in popular
rhetoric."[56] The desire to celebrate ties between nature and society was no
less prevalent in seascape painters' representations of coastal fishing communities. Like scenes of western farms pushing back the frontier, the subjects
depicted by the northeastern painters concentrated on the industry, prosperity, and harmony they saw as the relationship between the community and
nature's resources.

Unlike depictions of an agricultural expansion that visibly destroyed the
very nature that Americans so deeply celebrated, however, seascape paintings raised no such troubling questions about the cost of development.[57]
Some of the earliest pictorial representations of these relationships between
nature and society in southern New England appeared in John Barber's *Historical Collections of Massachusetts* (1839 and 1841). Both writer and engraver,
Barber produced some of the first, and most popular, books describing the
towns and communities of New England and used new developments in
printing to portray images of growing communities in the new republic. Unlike his images of interior New England towns, however, where Barber imposed a visual order by highlighting town greens, church steeples, and neat
stone walls, his images of southern New England fishing towns center the
viewer's attention upon the less orderly activity animating a busy working
port. Instead of a town center, with a green and a church spire, Barber used
middle-distance panoramic views to show the harbor as the center of coastal
communities.[58]

This technique is easily seen in Barber's image of the Martha's Vineyard
town of Edgartown, where the church spire is marginalized to the left of the
image (Fig 3.5). Instead, Barber featured gentlemanly figures in the foreground pointing to a departing fishing schooner, to highlight the town's
maritime focus. Sheep, positioned in the foreground, further suggest the
town's other economic pursuits.

His etching of Provincetown also centers the viewer's attention on the
port's fishing operations (Fig 3.6). Featuring a panoramic view of what could
only be regarded as a small city, Barber conspicuously highlighted the larger
fishing vessels, including a traditional fishing vessel called a chebacco boat in
the lower left, carrying out the town's most important industry. In addition he
also paid close attention to inshore fishing vessels and the ancillary industries
that arose with the fisheries. For example, in front of two arriving figures, a

FIG. 3.5 John Barber, *Eastern View of Edgartown.* Barber, *Historical Collections of Massachusetts* (1841), NOAA Photo Library, Image ID line0993, NOAA's America's Coastlines Collection

dozen or more small inshore fishing boats sit moored close to the beach, while off in the distance windmills used for making salt line the shores, further demonstrating the town's reliance upon fishing. Unlike his depictions of the orderly agricultural communities found inland, Barber's views of Provincetown and Edgartown show busy workspaces centered on the harbor and the industries carried on there.

Even Barber's vision of smaller Cape Cod towns celebrated southern New England's coastal workspaces. The view of Wellfleet Harbor, for example, hardly shows the activity that Barber depicted in Provincetown, but the windmills, wharves, and square-rigged ships in the harbor indicate that even this small port holds ties to the larger commercial world beyond (Fig 3.7).

Perhaps best representing the development of southern New England's coastal workspaces, however, is Barber's image of Fairhaven, Massachusetts, across the river from New Bedford (Fig 3.8). Again replacing the town green with the port's harbor, Barber's view of this whaling community leaves no doubt about its working energy. As he did in his view of Provincetown, Barber prominently featured figures and symbols of the local economy: in the foreground, on the New Bedford side of the river, a coastal worker or sailor stands among a disorderly collection of oil casks and randomly strewn boards.

FIG. 3.6 John Barber, *View from the Northeastern Edge of Provincetown*. Barber, *Historical Collections of Massachusetts* (1841), NOAA Photo Library, Image ID line0998, NOAA's America's Coastlines Collection

Small craft ply the waters between the two towns, as two distant top-hatted figures point to the arriving boats. Across the river, two church towers mark the skyline to the left, but no more so than a cluster of masts and spars that blocks the view of the right side of the city.

Barber's images of southern New England port communities revealed not the wastelands and hardscrabble existences described by Dwight and Kendall, but rather southern New England people using their knowledge to actively and successfully pull wealth from the seas. In contrast to his staid, orderly, village-green-centered views of interior towns, Barber's southern New England engravings celebrated the energy and newfound wealth in what had been one of New England's most impoverished regions. Barber's images also showed how much the coasts, no longer wastelands, had become workspaces, and his work suggested that the development of those workspaces—along with other New England towns—was worthy of attention.

Cape Cod's antebellum prosperity—wrenched from the jaws of endemic poverty—attracted the attention of other observers. Like Barber, painters coming to southern New England sought to celebrate Americans' ingenuity and energy. Unlike Barber, however, whose focus was regional, these celebrants situated the southern New England coastal workspace into a larger romantic national narrative, one that constructed a vision of American prosperity as part of a harmonious relationship between American nature and the new American nation. In prominent fishing towns such as Gloucester and

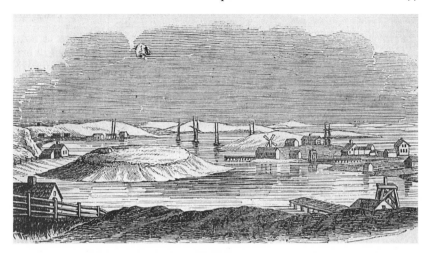

FIG. 3.7 John Barber, *Northern View of Wellfleet Harbor*. Barber, *Historical Collections of Massachusetts* (1841), NOAA Photo Library, Image ID line0997, NOAA's America's Coastlines Collection

New Bedford, painters looked to their local communities for material to celebrate American's energy and industry. In this, these marine painters shared interests with their contemporaries painting inland subjects. Yet unlike those painters representing the power and beauty of the terrestrial wilderness, maritime painters found inspiration where humanity and nature came together in everyday life.

Painters of coastal work scenes, such as Fitz Henry Lane, Albert van Beest, Robert Swain Gifford, and William Bradford, saw none of the tension that their more famous contemporaries Thomas Cole or Asher B. Durand brought into their constructions of American settlement. In fact, Gloucester native Fitz Henry Lane pictured the ties between man and nature on the coastline as harmonious and tension-free. Beginning in the 1830s, Lane frequently painted working coastal scenes readily available in his neighborhood around Cape Ann and along the Maine coast. In these works, Lane focused intently on work processes themselves—whether they were fishing, shipbuilding, fish drying, or marine railway work. As portrayed by Lane, an everabundant sea provided the foundation for harmonious maritime communities, whose livings left no impact on nature.[59] Of all the antebellum American seascape painters, Lane most readily saw Emerson's vision in the working waterfront.

FIG. 3.8 John Barber, *Western View of Fairhaven*. Barber, *Historical Collections of Massachusetts* (1841), NOAA Photo Library, Image ID line0996, NOAA's America's Coastlines Collection

As Lane worked on the New England shore north of Boston, on the southern New England coast, New Bedford supported a number of nascent artists who also found inspiration in the working waterfront. Drawn to the city by whaling wealth in the 1850s and 1860s, Albert van Beest, William Bradford, and Robert Swain Gifford—to name just one cluster of painters—all painted inshore scenes that included shore fishing as part of the natural landscape. Though similar to the pastoral images produced by Barber and his imitators, these painters' works were situated more within American and European landscape painting traditions. In addition, unlike the popular landscape paintings of Niagara Falls, the Catskills, or the White Mountains that helped create tourist industries in those areas, these paintings were not produced for would-be tourists. Instead, these works celebrated the courage, bravery, and energy of fishermen and coastal workers. The appeal of southern New England's vistas rested more in their celebration of American society and natural resource wealth than it did with tourists' encounters with American nature.

Albert van Beest's work clearly revealed this desire to include working people within the maritime landscape. Van Beest arrived in New Bedford in 1854 on the invitation of local painter and collaborator William Bradford, and once settled, he adapted his Dutch painting style to the relatively flat sandy coasts of southeastern Massachusetts. The artist found both inspiration and sustenance from the busy fishing and whaling port, as he painted scenes around the harbor for clients and patrons whose wealth came largely from the burgeoning whaling industry. As much as the physical coast intrigued him, however, van Beest persistently included working watermen in his scenes, suggesting that inshore fishing and fishermen were as fundamental an element to the coastal zone for him as was water or sky. His watercolor *New Bedford from Fairhaven* demonstrates most clearly this desire to mix the human and the natural (Fig 3.9). Van Beest sought to show a stability between the city and its natural surroundings, which, not surprisingly, he defined almost exclusively as water. Viewed from sea level looking across the mouth of the Acushnet River, New Bedford seems to rise from the river, alluding to the town's wealth garnered from the sea. The painting also draws the viewer's eye first and foremost to a small fishing vessel riding at anchor. Other fishing schooners and their small boats fill the image's right side, while a ship surrounded by more small vessels works its way upriver. Centered on the canvas, the smudge from a smokestack curves around a church tower on the opposite shore, dividing the canvas and completing the triangulation between the small fishing vessel in the foreground and the figures awaiting its return. Leo Marx has argued that in the antebellum period, artists' inclusion of machinery in an otherwise unmechanized world represented a means by which Americans acknowledged the reality of history and came to terms with how their world was changing.[60] The figure of the steam vessel in this canvas, however, surrounded by fishing vessels working local waters, makes a pictorial argument about the prosperity of coastal workspaces: while unmechanized, whaling and fishing industries promised as much prosperity as industries where machines redefined people's relationships to the land and each other.

Van Beest's friend William Bradford concentrated more intently on how the work of harvesting nature combined seemingly opposite aesthetics of strength and grace along the shore. In his *Study of Fairhaven Waterfront* (1850s or 1860s), for example, Bradford featured a down-rigged sloop as the centerpiece of the image, highlighting Ruskin's aesthetic of form and function that even a simple fishing vessel embodied (Fig 3.10). The sloop is careened over on its side in the low tide, revealing to the viewer the smooth taper from the bow to the transom. The curvature of the hull and stem carves a strong, graceful line across the canvas and contrasts with the angularity of the dock. In the foreground, as if to complement the skill apparent in fishing-vessel construction, is a figure hauling in a shore-seining net, while others

FIG. 3.9 Albert van Beest, *New Bedford from Fairhaven* (1854). Museum of Fine Arts, Boston (55.709). Gift of Maxim Karolik for the M. and M. Karolik Collection of American Watercolors and Drawings, 1800–1875, Museum of Fine Arts, Boston. Photograph © 2010 Museum of Fine Arts, Boston

lounge and smoke on flotsam washed ashore. By featuring the leaning vessel and the small dory, and by surrounding these shapes with lounging figures, Bradford at once characterized the working waterfront as a place of strength, bounty, skill, and ease. Pulling wealth from the inshore waters required skills and strength, but its challenges generated a beauty, while its bounty also provided ease for those who were daring enough.

Robert Swain Gifford also painted coastal work scenes out of New Bedford in the 1850s. A student of van Beest's, Gifford had begun sketching the waterfront as a child, and then under van Beest's direction, developing his skills with watercolors and oils by the early 1860s. After a brief attempt at establishing himself in New York with van Beest in 1857, Gifford returned to New Bedford, where he painted coastal working scenes he saw locally. He also made trips to Maine (1858) and Martha's Vineyard (1865). Like Lane before him, Gifford focused on the working waterfront; but unlike his North Shore predecessor, Gifford paid less attention to docks, wharves, and ports, focusing instead upon work areas on beaches. His *Beach and Cliffs at Nonquitt* (1863), *Boat on a Beach* (1862), *Two Figures and Boat on a Beach* (1863), and *Pinky off Grand Manan* (1864) prominently feature people working along the shore or inshore waters.[61]

It is not surprising that this first generation of southern New England marine landscape painters looked to the working waterfront for inspiration. Many had close personal ties to the maritime workforce and as a result saw the coastal

FIG. 3.10 William Bradford, *Study of the Fairhaven Waterfront* (1850s or 1860s). Museum of Fine Arts, Boston (64.2382). Gift of Maxim Karolik for the M. and M. Karolik Collection of American Watercolors and Drawings, 1800–1875, Museum of Fine Arts, Boston. Photograph © 2010 Museum of Fine Arts, Boston

workspace as a place worth celebrating. Gifford, for example, was the son of a fisherman on Nonamesset Island in the Elizabeth Island chain off Cape Cod. Born in 1840, Gifford moved two years later with his family to New Bedford, where his father hoped to find more steady earnings. There the young Gifford worked along the waterfront before beginning his studies in painting. His early ties to the working waterfront would define much of his future work. During his tutelage with van Beest, Gifford took his teacher out on his father's fishing boat to help the Dutch painter better understand waves and oceans.[62]

Other painters enjoyed similar ties between art and working waterfronts. Van Beest himself grew up on Rotterdam's shipping wharves, where he was noticed by P. J. Schotel, a Dutch marine artist, who invited van Beest to accompany him on an expedition to the Mediterranean with Prince Hendrik of the Netherlands from 1843 to 1846. During that expedition, van Beest refined his skills painting waterfront scenes, and when he arrived in New York in the early 1850s, he took rooms in the Battery overlooking the harbor to continue his work.[63] Similarly, Bradford was born in Fairhaven, Massachusetts, and after failing as a clerk and as a farmer, he embarked on a career painting ship portraits for local vessel owners and masters. By 1854, Bradford's skills at painting the details of ships' rigging helped persuade van Beest to share a studio with him in New Bedford.

Taken together, the images by these and other artists depicting the southern New England coast before the Civil War played an important role in the transformation of the region from wastelands to workspaces. Supported by the wealth garnered from whaling and fishing, these artists validated, legitimized, and even encouraged the transformation of coastlines into productive centers of industry by painting them and thus situating them within the larger narrative of American national progress. In other parts of the country, such pastoral representations of commercial and industrial development attracted tourists eager to see firsthand new directions in American development.[64] As tourism developed on Cape Cod and along most of the southern New England shore relatively late (the case of Newport excepted),[65] clearly the appeal of these painting did not rest among tourists. Rather, the popularity of coastal working scenes rested among those interested and involved in the conversion of southern New England coastal wastes into productive work sites. Here, where an ever-abundant nature and expanding commerce rewarded the knowledge, daring, and ingenuity of Americans developing their natural resources, southern New England residents buying these works could situate their role in this effort within a grand American narrative of natural resource development and commercial expansion. And in this narrative, there was no ambiguity as to such expansion's effect on nature. Such a context not only popularized and celebrated fishing and coastal work, but also legitimated it and gave it cultural and national sanction.

Far from celebrating an allegedly harmonious relationship between Americans and their natural world, one Cape Cod visitor came with a markedly different agenda. Instead of reveling in pastoral constructions, when Henry David Thoreau took three trips to Cape Cod between 1849 and 1857, he sought a place where the power of nature humbled—rather than harbored—humanity's commercial efforts. But he, too, sought to use the Cape and its people for didactic, even moralizing, purposes. His early descriptions and caricatures reveal someone seeking a symbol, a metaphor, or an ideal, that while inspired by the Cape, more represented what Thoreau wanted the region to be: "I wished to see that seashore where man's works are wrecks; to put up at the true Atlantic House, where the ocean is land-lord as well as sea-lord, and comes ashore without a wharf for the landing; where the crumbling land is the only invalid, or at best is but dry land, and that is all you can say of it."[66] With this preconception, Thoreau viewed all he encountered with an eye for how nature undermined human pretension. Rejecting the more idyllic visions represented on canvas, Thoreau returned to critiques presented by Dwight, Kendall, and others before as he sought to level an equally moralizing argument about material wealth. In short, Thoreau looked to Cape Cod's spartan lands and presumably poor communities to serve as iconic symbols for nonconformity in an increasingly commercialized age.

Like most others traveling to the Cape, Thoreau came by land, stopping first at Sandwich, where he commented on the veneer of respectability he found. "The green and white houses of the gentry, drawn up in rows, front on a street of which it would be difficult to tell whether it is most like a desert or a long stable yard. Such spots can only be beautiful to the weary traveler, or the returning native,—or, perchance, the repentant misanthrope; not to him who, with unprejudiced senses, has just come out of the woods . . . through a succession of straggling homesteads where he cannot tell which is the almshouse."[67] For a people living in such a harsh environment—where nature humbled man—any efforts for material comfort sat out of place. In Brewster, Thoreau complained, "There are many of the modern American houses here, such as they turn out at Cambridgeport, standing on the sand; you could almost swear that they had been floated down the Charles River, and drifted across the Bay."[68] To this Concord resident, seafaring folk should have more distinctive lodgings: "Sea-captains do not employ a Cambridgeport carpenter to build their floating houses, and for their houses on shore, if they must copy any, it would be more agreeable to the imagination to see one of their vessels turned bottom upward, in the Numidian fashion."[69] Thoreau also derided Cape Codders' demonstrations of new wealth and prosperity, as to him they represented a fleeting and foreign corruption of what he perceived to be local traditions of self-sufficiency. "Generally, the old-fashioned and unpainted house on the Cape looked more comfortable, as well as picturesque, than the modern and more pretending ones, which were less in harmony with the scenery, and less firmly planted."[70] In a place that was supposed to represent a wasteland, with all its spiritual lessons, local residents' desires for modern comforts appeared senseless.

Thoreau also initially avoided those people who would challenge his vision, and when that proved impossible, he recast the Cape people to fit into his vision of what Cape people should be. For example, on the stagecoach to Dennis, Thoreau romanticized how nature—and the coastline—defined the characters of his fellow travelers.

> It was evident that the same foolish respect was not here claimed for mere wealth and station that is in many parts of New England; yet some of them were the "first people," as they are called, of the various towns through which we passed. Retired sea-captains, in easy circumstances[;] . . . some of the salt of the earth, who had formerly been the salt of the sea; . . . or a broad, red-faced Cape Cod man, who had seen too many storms to be easily irritated; or a fisherman's wife, who had been waiting for a week for a coaster to leave Boston, and had at length come by the cars.[71]

Thoreau offers nothing to suggest that he actually spoke to these people before imposing upon them histories, sentiments, and situations. In meeting a wrecker farther down the Cape, Thoreau similarly denied the man an individuality and even human features, and instead imposed upon him a caricature of Cape Cod's hardscrabble existence and personality that Thoreau believed such a life created. "We soon met one of these wreckers,—a regular Cape Cod man . . . with a bleached and weather beaten face, within whose wrinkles I distinguished no particular feature. It was like an old sail endowed with life,—a hanging cliff of weather-beaten flesh,—like one of the clay boulders which occurred in that sand bank."[72]

Thoreau looked to Cape Cod's people, as he did to the landscape, to issue an anti-pastoral critique that, ironically, imposed as idyllic an image upon the places and people he saw as did the painters portraying them on canvas. Whether Thoreau's ideas were reflected in the people he met early in his travels was not important to the writer: to him they were just grist for a critical mill that allowed him to view Cape Cod people as specimens or characters he could pick up and put down at will, to mock or critique to entertain his audience.

Eventually, however, Thoreau realized that beneath Cape Codders' seemingly mean and desperate conditions lay a prosperity, spirit, and adaptability that forced him to reconsider his initial assumptions. One evening he came upon the house of a Wellfleet oysterman. Experiencing the old fisherman's hospitality, openness, and willingness to speak and listen, Thoreau realized there was much more to the Cape than he had initially imagined. For the first time in his narrative, Thoreau acknowledged that this local resident had a name and, even more remarkably, a name the writer would not reveal to the reader out of respect. A veteran of the Revolution who had once seen George

Washington, the aged oysterman impressed Thoreau with his knowledge of local weather patterns, plants, and birds. Thoreau was equally impressed by the fact the man had served as a pilot in his youth, directing vessels along the coast to the relief of foreign sailors. Thoreau also, in his caustic but caring way, brought the old man's family into the narrative. Thoreau noted how he had mocked the oysterman's wife's advice about eating a clam unselectively, and then, after a night of stomach pains, gastrointestinally regretted such smugness. He commented on the old man's insane but generally gentle son, and ultimately upon the natural, scriptural, and practical intelligence that the old man had gained through his life. And while the host told Thoreau he "never had any learning, only what I got by natur," Thoreau parted the oysterman's company with doughnuts in his pocket and an openness he had previously avoided.[73]

After the encounter, Thoreau's outlook on the Cape changed. He began noticing local people as individuals, and he listened to their stories in more detail. In Pamet River, for example, he came across a recently erected monument memorializing Truro's fifty-seven fishermen who had drowned the October Gale of 1841.

> Their names and ages by families were recorded on different sides of the stone. They are said to have been lost on George's Bank, and I was told that only one vessel drifted ashore on the backside of the Cape, with boys locked into the cabin and drowned. It is said that the homes of all were "within a circuit of two miles." Twenty-eight inhabitants of Dennis were lost in the same gale; and I read that "in one day, immediately after this storm, nearly or quite one hundred bodies were taken up and buried on Cape Cod."[74]

The monument at once reinforced and refuted Thoreau's understandings of human frailty and natural power. Yes, nature had taken its toll on humanity, but the monument also demonstrated people's ability to continue in the face of adversity. Combined with his experiences with the oysterman's family, it changed the way Thoreau saw Cape Cod residents and their lives. Far from a philosophical metaphor, or a sardonic source of humor, Thoreau found instead the human consequences of his philosophical quest for a space where "men's works were wrecks." Such an existence had profound effects upon people, their community, and, in Thoreau's case, the sensibilities of visitors. "I found that it would not do to speak of shipwrecks there, for almost every family has lost some of its members at sea."[75]

Ultimately, this realization forced Thoreau to see Cape Cod and its people

differently and to recognize that his own perspective derived from very
different experiences.

> The stranger and the inhabitant view the shore with very different eyes. The
> former have come to see and admire the ocean in a storm; but the latter looks
> on it as the scene where his nearest relatives were wrecked. When I remarked
> to an old wrecker partially blind, who was sitting on the edge of the bank
> smoking a pipe, which he had just lit with a match of dried beach grass, that I
> supposed he liked to hear the sound of the surf, he answered: "No, I do not
> like to hear the sound of the surf." He had lost at least one son in the "memo-
> rable gale," and could tell many a tale of the shipwrecks which he had wit-
> nessed there.[76]

After Pamet, Thoreau's criticism of Cape Cod's affluence ebbed, tem-
pered by the difficulty and danger that he realized purchased what little
wealth and pretense Cape Cod people displayed. By the time he arrived at
Provincetown, Thoreau's reactions to Cape people and communities stood
in marked contrast to his earlier criticisms and suggest that the writer looked
at local people as people, and not icons. Tellingly, his description of Provincetown houses revealed his appreciation not only of the exterior conditions,
but the interiors as well. "The outward aspect of the houses and shops
frequently suggest a poverty which their interior comfort and even richness
disprove."[77]

By the end of Thoreau's voyages to Cape Cod (he traveled there four
times), he approached life along the beach in a different way. Far from discovering his critical, antimaterialistic, and anticonventional foil, Thoreau instead
recognized a fundamental truth about the coastal workspace: that living on
the beach put people face to face with their mortality in ways many people
living in the interior could never imagine. "It is a wild, rank place and there is
no flattery in it. [A] vast morgue, where . . . [t]he carcasses of men and beasts
lie stately up upon its shelf, rotting and bleaching in the sun and waves, and
each tide turns them in their beds, and tucks fresh sand under them. There is
naked Nature, inhumanly sincere, wasting no thought on man, nibbling at
the cliffy shore where gulls wheel amid the spray."[78] The shore was not just a
place that merely destroyed man's works: it destroyed men, too, and anyone
surviving there was entitled to whatever comforts he or she could accrue.

Thoreau the social critic may have found some grist for his literary mill,
but his experiences on Cape Cod forced him to change his attitudes about

the place in the face of the people, places, and subsistence strategies locals developed to survive—in short, how Cape people had learned to live in the workspace that Thoreau expected to see as a wasteland. Certainly, as he lectured to audiences at the Concord Lyceum, and later, as he wrote up his travel notes for *Putnam's Monthly* in 1855, Thoreau drew upon humor and even mockery to weave an engaging and entertaining narrative (though one that, once published, so offended Barnstable County residents that *Putnam's* dropped the series, citing his rude comments about the appearance of Cape Cod women and the coarseness of Cape Cod manners).[79] As Robert Pinsky has argued, however, what Thoreau came to mock was not just the people of the Cape, "but himself and the reader and the traveler—the greedy, naïve appetite for 'beauty' and 'interest' and eloquent 'reflections,' the questioning enterprise of moving to and through places in the world."[80] As a traveler himself, whose own appetites for such rhetorical fruit came to be replaced with the more substantive meat of Cape Cod's coastal workspace, Thoreau brought his audiences along on a similar journey of discovery, where what one wanted to find, and what one did find, failed to match up.

Ultimately, Cape Cod's transformation from a wasteland to a workspace relied upon far more than just an expanded fishery. Fishermen's ingenuity and their knowledge of the marine environment—especially their ability to effectively select and deploy bait—allowed that fishery to expand, bringing wealth and prosperity to the Cape for the first time. Like the images presented by those with personal ties to the working waterfront, Cape Codders' new uses for the seacoast—as a place where not just subsistence but prosperity, too, could be won—challenged older views of the Cape as a wasteland, views still retained by outsiders such as Thoreau. Thoreau realized that life was more complex, more rewarding, and more prosperous along Cape Cod's sandy shores than he had originally believed. In realizing this, he not only changed his own assumptions of the region, but as he published his articles (and as his literary executors, Sophie Thoreau and William Ellery Channing, published them posthumously in 1865), Thoreau also laid the foundations for others to change their opinions as well. For the first time since European settlement, Cape Codders found themselves celebrated for their ability to pull wealth and security from the sea—to create a coastal workspace out of a wasteland.

CHAPTER 4

Prosperity

The gradual failure of the fish, and the somewhat rapid increase of the population of the Cape, caused a good deal of uneasiness to the people of that thrifty region. . . . Hitherto there had been abundance for all, according to their frugal expectations; but now the prospect grew dark.
    —Charles Nordhoff, "Mehetabel Rogers's Cranberry Swamp"

In February 1864 journalist Charles Nordhoff published a story about the changing times on Cape Cod. In "Mehetabel Rogers's Cranberry Swamp," appearing in *Harper's New Weekly Magazine*, Nordhoff examined how Cape communities, now thriving in their coastal workspaces, survived Cape Cod's interrelated ecological, economic, and social challenges.[1] Nordhoff's theme was the social and demographic consequences of economic prosperity in a land of limited resources. In a barren region like Cape Cod, economic and then demographic growth put undue pressure on the local environment, and Nordhoff used this story to speculate about what would happen when the region's growing communities came into conflict with their declining natural resource base. Rather than focusing solely on the economic consequences of resource decline, however, Nordhoff was most interested in how human adaptations to terrestrial limitations changed social relationships. This theme emerged in the main plotline, where Mehetabel Rogers tries to convince stubborn fishermen to invest in a radical agricultural scheme of turning marshes into cranberry bogs. But new agricultural developments played only a minor role in Nordhoff's story. Most of the action takes place out on those offshore fishing banks that Cape Cod relied upon heavily for its wealth and community survival; there Nordhoff placed a graver threat to Cape communities. His story presents a vision of how brothers, lovers, and neighbors can turn on one another in their efforts to profit as resources decline and a community scrambles to stay afloat. Far more than just a quaint tale of fishermen, their wives, and their villages, Nordhoff's story foreshadowed a tension between ecology, economy, and community that would grip Cape towns within five years of the piece's publication.

On the surface this was a tale of how Mehetabel Rogers, an independent-minded fisherman's wife, tried to grow a crop on Cape Cod—cranberries—despite generations of tradition that linked prosperity to fish and the men who went fishing. Not only was Rogers's plan for commercial agriculture a departure from Cape Cod's traditional reliance upon the fisheries, but it was a plan presented by a *woman*—a fact that threatened the primacy and wisdom of the male fishing community. Encountering nothing but resistance from the old men in town with money, Mehetabel travels to Boston to meet with younger fishing captains from her hometown preparing for sea who might be more interested in investing in new ideas. There she persuades Captain Aleck Nickerson to buy into the scheme, which he promises to do after he returns from his next trip to the Banquereau fishing grounds off Nova Scotia.

It is on the fishing grounds, however, where Nordhoff sets in motion the main conflict of the story. There, driven by low catches and declining numbers of fish, Aleck experiments with a new form of fishing—dory hand-lining—and sets out on his own to look for fish about a mile distant from his schooner and fellow fishermen. As the crew, now under the command of Aleck's brother Mulford, watch in amazement, Aleck hauls in fish after fish, and soon the rest of them do as well. Immediately, however, Nordhoff sends a metaphorical fog of change to swallow Aleck in his distant dory. After a frantic but fruitless search, Mulford gives his brother up for lost and continues the voyage. Here Nordhoff presents the moral of this tale, of how hard circumstances bring out the worst in a close community. As Mulford sails back to Cape Cod to tell Mehetabel and the rest of the community of Aleck's loss, he considers how his brother's death might benefit him in some way. "And yet it was pleasant to think that now he might win [Aleck's betrothed] Rachel for himself. . . . So long as Aleck lived Mulford had been content that Rachel should be his sister-in-law; it was not till now it occurred to him that she could be his own wife. . . . Why not?" The story moves ashore, where Aleck's loss is mourned, but not for very long; and soon Rachel, to her own eventual disgrace, agrees to marry Mulford, who as a fishing captain holds good pros-

pects for future material wealth. Predictably, Aleck unexpectedly returns a
year later and is shocked by the speed with which his world has adapted to
his presumed death. "'Was it so long to wait,' [Aleck] asked, conscious that
he would have waited twice a twelve-month for [Rachel to return]."

Through the ensuing internal discussions between what is right and what
is expedient, Nordhoff suggested that Cape Codders' efforts to turn their
wastelands into workspaces threatened relationships between neighbors,
kin, and fellow fishermen. In the face of economic and then ecological change,
friendship, family ties, even love, teetered toward becoming mere means to access credit, or achieve material comfort. In a vein hauntingly familiar to early
twenty-first-century eyes, Nordhoff challenged the reader to balance the moral
seediness of crass opportunism against emotionally numb, Pollyanna-like visions of making "good" of a bad situation.

Nordhoff occupied a good position to see the long-term tensions generated by the coastal prosperity witnessed by Thoreau a decade before. As a
journalist who had supported himself for some time in the banks mackerel
fishery, Nordhoff saw firsthand how new technology, changing natural resources, and commerce were arrayed against the very community values that
had allowed Cape Codders to thrive in their wasteland in the first place. As
the natural resources that Cape communities relied upon dwindled, so too
did the communities, and by the mid-1860s, when Nordhoff wrote, it was
becoming clear that the prosperity Cape Codders pulled from the sea might
not last.

Nordhoff, however, was not completely correct in indicting cranberry agriculture as the sole agent of social and economic change. The expansion and
celebration of Cape Cod's offshore fisheries between 1818 and 1865 resulted
in an equally marked expansion in Cape Cod's inshore bait fishery. Expanding mackerel fleets, the expansion of tub trawling for cod, halibut, haddock,
and other groundfish, and the opening of Georges Bank brought commercial
growth and developmental pressures onshore to Cape Cod's towns. As these
offshore industries expanded, they also changed the inshore fishery from one
focused on local production and local markets to one providing bait for
highly capitalized banks fisheries. Thus, it was the bait fisheries, rather than
Mehetabel Rogers's berries, that reshaped Cape Cod communities. As innovations on the banks created new demands for Cape Cod's inshore fish,
Cape Cod people developed new ways of taking, managing, and profiting from these local fish. The resulting commercial success led, in turn, to

new economic, social, and ecological challenges that would force profound change upon the Cape and bring about the area's largest grassroots movement since the American Revolution.

As banks fishermen demanded more bait, and later, as those fishermen grew more particular about which baits they carried, an entirely new bait fishery developed not only on Cape Cod but all along the New England coast. From Seaconnet Point, Rhode Island, to Eastport, Maine, shore installations began targeting bait species, such as herring and menhaden, not for local use, but for sale to the increasing number of banks vessels sailing out of Gloucester, New Bedford, Portland, and Boston. The Cape's newfound prosperity from banks fishing provided its residents with the investment capital needed to further cash in on the bait-fishing boom, and as a result, bait fishing created a niche industry where none had previously existed. Beginning around 1840, dedicated bait fishing and an ancillary fresh-fish export industry brought an inshore prosperity that had only previously existed from banks fishing. Consequently, by the end of the 1860s, prosperity, rail links, and the new bait business changed the way Cape people related to their inshore fisheries. In the eyes of fishermen with access to investment capital, southern New England beaches were far from the harborless wastes of shifting sands and windswept dunes that earlier visitors had despaired to see; on the contrary, they were ideal for a bait fishery that maximized catches and minimized labor.

The growing bait fishery fundamentally challenged Cape Cod's traditionally conservative inshore fisheries management regimes. The first places where more bait could be obtained were the town fisheries that had been at the root of community survival in the seventeenth and eighteenth centuries. And it was there that local bait fishermen pressured governments to end restrictions on river herring catches and exports—restrictions that had previously preserved those fish for long-term local benefit.

These pressures began soon after the American Revolution. In the 1790s, for example (and before the universal acceptance of the dollar in American accounting), Sandwich was selling between two hundred and four hundred barrels of river herring each year and making annually between 38 and 58 pounds sterling in town income by doing so.[2] Rochester also sold fish out of town to raise revenues. In 1789 the town meeting voted to sell to the highest bidder the exclusive right to take fish from town rivers. Like Sandwich, Rochester sought to balance profit with local support, in this case by attaching provisions to the sale of fishing privileges. Purchasers could take fish at only two places, only during three days in the week, and only with specified gear. Furthermore, the purchaser was required to sell fish to town residents at a fixed rate before curing and selling them to outsiders. Despite these encumbrances, the auction still attracted bidders who, in 1794, provided the town with over £22 in revenues, and for the rest of the century (and as the dollar was finally adopted), between $40 and $104 annually. In 1812 war drove the bid price to $443, and two years later it rose again, to almost $500. Even after the war, Rochester continued to enjoy significant income from the sale of town fishing rights, realizing over $300 per year in 1815 and 1816.[3] It is difficult to accurately and reliably compare historical currency values to one another or to compare changing values of a single currency over time. There are many ways to do it, and each has its limitations. Using two opposing methods to give those numbers some context, however, Rochester's $100 in 1800 represented the same equivalent share of gross domestic product as $2.9 million did in 2009. On the opposite end of the spectrum, an unskilled worker earning $500 in 1814 (as Rochester did) translates into an annual income of $88,000 in 2009 terms. In either case, fishing revenues represented a significant sum for the towns auctioning off their fishing rights.

With major fishing towns on all sides, Harwich similarly profited from increasing demand for fish from public fish runs. In 1814 the town voted to end restrictions barring outsiders from buying local fish, and fixed prices at 40 cents per barrel for residents and $1 for others. For the residents of Chatham and Orleans, Harwich charged as much as $1.50 a barrel. In 1818 the town raised prices for residents and nonresidents alike to $1.50 a barrel. The following year it changed fish prices again, this time to $1 for residents and $2 for nonresidents, as demand for inshore fish for bait mounted.

Despite these early, tentative forays into commercially developing town fish runs, through the nineteenth century Cape towns soon abandoned any pretense of preserving local runs for local tables. In Mashpee in 1801, for example, the town restructured its management of the Mashpee River to invest the (white) guardians of the Native American community with the privilege to sell the rights of the fishery. In 1836 both Wellfleet and Harwich began selling the rights to the town fish runs to private bidders who assumed the overhead costs of managing the fishery in exchange for the exclusive right to fishing profits.[4] Other town river fisheries were managed in similar fashions: Falmouth in 1847, Martha's Vineyard in 1855, and runs on the various tributaries of the Taunton River between 1792 and 1875 were all put up for auction and development.[5] Nor were the sums involved inconsequential. By the middle of the century, revenues from the leased weirs in Rochester, for example, came to represent a significant source of town income: in 1860 the $725.59 generated by fish runs represented 7.8 percent of the town's total annual budget. In 1861, with the Civil War raising prices, that figure jumped to 10.8 percent, and it rose again in 1862, to 11.3 percent.[6]

Fisheries proceeds were not simply pocketed. Initially they went to offset town expenses for maintaining the fishery, and then to lower poll taxes, meet educational costs, or sent toward poor relief. As fishery proceeds helped towns offset costs, however, those fisheries ceased to be seen as an integral part of an annual subsistence strategy. The value of these resources to townspeople changed from a tangible benefit in the form of fish on the doorstep to one more abstract. The fish became figures tallied in town account books, largely invisible to residents whose general prosperity meant they no longer needed local fish as food or fertilizer. Town fisheries went from sources of needed protein and nutrients to merely one more revenue stream to be optimized for profit maximization. Without the physical link between humans and local fish, most town residents stopped thinking of the health of the herring rivers. With that lapse, the foundations for mismanagement were laid.[7]

As demand for baitfish increased, landowners, too, looked for new ways to increase baitfish catches. With the best runs owned by towns, private investors began constructing artificial ones to avoid the limitations on gear, fishing days, and prices required by town regulations. Rich with barrier beaches, salt ponds, and small, easily manipulated streams, Cape Cod was the perfect place where small investments could yield big returns in the construction of artificial, privately operated fish runs. With fishing vessels already coming from Boston, Cape Ann, Long Island, or the middle Atlantic states for baitfish, the market was already in place for private landowners and investors to change the very shorelines to harvest more fish.

Before the 1830s the creation of artificial runs had occurred only sporadically. Hingham residents in the 1740s, for example, had sought to expand the alewife fishery through manipulating waterways, connecting streams to ponds, or by digging breaks in barrier beaches to allow fish to pass from the ocean into salt ponds. Falmouth's 1802 Herring War, too, revolved around the question of whether fish passed above Hinckley's dam to Coonamessett Pond through an artificial waterway dug in the 1740s. Between 1831 and 1863, however, the number of artificial runs grew significantly. During those three decades, the Massachusetts General Court issued twenty-seven acts of incorporation for companies seeking to enclose streams or ponds for promoting the alewife fishery. In 1831 the first such company included nine investors, who received permission from the state to develop and independently manage an alewife run in two small rivers that ran between Chatham and Harwich. Under the incorporation, the Skinnaquits fishing company could exclude anyone from taking fish from the streams and was entitled to operate the fishery as it wished. Five years later, two more fishing companies were founded in Harwich and Orleans that also enjoyed exclusive rights to the fish and the fishery within a set radius from the river mouth. One of these, the Andrews Fishing Company, also received permission to build at its own expense a passage between its private stream and the public millpond to allow the free passage of fish.[8]

As private runs became more popular—another two dozen would be incorporated between 1837 and 1863—companies received greater authority to fundamentally alter town landscapes and beachfronts. In 1840, for example, the owners of the Sanchachantacket Fishing Company in Edgartown received permission to "alter the present outlet of Sanchachantacket Pond, so called, for the purpose of flooding the meadows in the winter season, and for a herring fishery therein, and to regulate the same."[9] In 1842 the Long Pond Fishing Company in Yarmouth was empowered "to open a brook or outlet from Long Pond to Swan Pond, so called, and also improve Parker's River (into which said ponds empty), to the sea, so far as may be necessary for the purpose of an alewife fishery."[10] That same year the Coy's Brook Fishing Company received permission to undertake an even more extensive fisheries development plan that seemingly spanned the entire town:

> The Coy's Brook Fishing Company . . . are hereby empowered to open said brook, commencing at the point where it empties into the Herring River; thence up said brook to Coy's Pond (so called); thence through the bridge, swamp and land of Nathan Ellis and others [who were not company owners], to the valley swamp; thence across the highway to Brier's Pond; thence through a swamp to Eldridge's Pond; thence from said Eldridge's Pond, to terminate in the Long Pond,—for the purposes of carrying on the herring fishery therein and to regulate the same.[11]

Through such extensive channeling works, private fish runs not only re-shaped the way communities took inshore fish, but also reshaped the very seascapes in which both people and fish existed.

Far from an invasion of foreign capital despoiling local lands, however, the manipulation of the local landscape and beachscape for artificial herring runs was undertaken by local residents who knew the streams, brooks, ponds, and beaches best suited for fish breeding. Investors hailed almost exclusively from Cape Cod, as most articles of incorporation list company owners as residents either of the town in which the run was to be built or of a neighboring town. Many also shared last names, suggesting family ties uniting the firm. If the Marstons Mills Fishing Company, incorporated in 1867, is representative of earlier companies, these firms also drew upon other local residents looking to invest small sums. According to the company's 1868 capital stock allocation, for example, over thirty local residents bought one-dollar shares, with only three purchasing more than five shares. Just over half the investors bought only one or two shares. Clearly, the creation of private alewife runs was no invasion of outside capital; rather, this was a local effort to cash in on local resources in high demand.[12]

By the 1840s, however, the state was getting less generous in its allocation of rights to private fish-run owners. Companies incorporated in 1836 saw the area where they enjoyed exclusive rights at river mouths drop to one-eighth mile, and by the 1840s the state rarely included the clause at all. Companies' exclusive rights to a pond system's fish also waned through the 1840s. In 1848, for example, when the Pocha Pond Meadow and Fishing Company received the authority to undertake substantial restructuring of water flows around Edgartown, it secured the right to "close the outlet of said pond by building a causeway from the twenty acre lot, so called, to Cape Poge Beach in Edgartown." In exchange, however, the town received some important perks. First, the causeway had to be free for all uses, and unlike in earlier articles, the state protected town residents' rights to take fish other than herring from the pond complex.[13] Despite state-imposed restraints, however, private fish runs continued to change Cape landscapes and seascapes, as companies continued to dig ditches and reroute streams in order to profit in an expanding market. Once the more readily adapted ponds and streams were developed, investors embraced increasingly ambitious projects to make less-optimal waterways fit the business plan. In one of the last private fishing companies to be incorporated before the Civil War, for example, the company was allowed to "open a brook or ditch through their own land from Ashumet Pond to Bourne's Pond, so called, and from thence to the Vineyard Sound." Despite this license, however, the effort failed, because the pond itself was too low to ensure a consistent flow.[14]

Leased public runs and artificial fish runs reveal that Cape Codders were drifting away from earlier tenets of limited local use. It was along the beaches, however, and not along the streams, that the full force of new fishing patterns both inshore and offshore were to come to bear. The most dramatic and visible change in Cape Cod's inshore fishery came from the expansion of the pound net fishery along its shores (Fig 4.1). In no other place was evidence of Cape Cod's transformation from wasteland to workspace so visible. And from no other innovation were Cape Cod's fish and small fishermen to face as great a challenge. Beginning in the 1830s, some Cape fishermen with access to capital began setting up stationary pound nets along the Cape's shallow waters and beaches. Within a few decades, what had been empty stretches of ocean and beach during Thoreau's visits had filled with fishing crews busily transferring fish from nets to carts pulled into the shallows or into anchored vessels offshore.

Pounds nets' earlier manifestation, weirs, had long been used by Europeans and Native Americans as remarkably efficient labor-saving devices that allowed humans to catch fish without having to continuously tend gear. The two were so similar that the terms were often used interchangeably throughout the nineteenth century (for this discussion, the more technically accurate term "pound" will be used consistently). Both pounds and weirs were composed of a fencelike leader that ran from the shore to a corral-like pen set up in deeper waters. At this corral there may have been a number of antechambers funneling fish into a "heart" or "bowl" that fishermen could open or close. When fishermen emptied the nets, they closed the heart or bowl and transferred the fish from the net into either a boat designed to haul the catch inshore, or into barrels or crates taken out to the net at low tide by horse and carriage.

Weirs, the oldest form, were the least expensive to set up. Made of thin sticks, twigs, lath, or slats driven into the sand close enough together to prevent fish from passing through, weirs were easy to build but were easily destroyed by the weather. Pounds, which were more popular on Cape Cod's exposed beaches, operated on the same principle, except the barriers were made of netting and hung from anchored poles. Pounds cost much more, both for the nets and for the anchors and poles required to hold nets in place. They better withstood storms and were more easily cleared, however, and

FIG. 4.1 "Taking Fish from Pound Net, Cape Cod" [1891]. NOAA's Historic Fisheries
Collection, Image ID fish6892; Gulf of Maine Cod Project, NOAA National Marine Sanctuaries.
National Archives, Stefan Claesson, archival photographer

despite their expense, they soon became more popular throughout the nineteenth century.

Two principles allowed this stationary gear to function. The first was that
when forced by barriers to swim to either shallower or deeper water, fish will
swim to deeper waters. The second principle was the simple observation that
fish cannot swim backward, and as long as barriers were shaped so as to channel fish into a holding pen, few would escape. Using these basic tenets, fishermen designed these nets to corral fish swimming along the shore into holding
pens until the fisherman—whose day had been spent pursuing other work—
could get to the nets, clear them, and prepare them for the next day's fishing.

Spencer Fullerton Baird, whose role in fishing debates will be discussed in
the next chapter, described pound-net operations in his 1871 investigations:

> The most common form [of pound nets] on the south side of New England
> consist of a fence of netting, extending from the shore, and nearly perpendicu-
> lar to it, for a distance of 50 or 100 fathoms [300 to 600 feet] or more, as the
> circumstances require. The outer end of this straight fence or wall is carried

into a heart shaped fence of netting, the apex of which is connected with a circular "bowl" of net work, the bottom of which lies upon the ground, at a depth of 20 to 30 feet.[15]

Each pound net was made of a complex array of nets, lines, poles, and anchors, all set to best enable the trap to withstand waves and weather along exposed coastlines. Isaiah Spindle's trap in Woods Hole, for example, had a leader 795 feet long (265 yards) held in place with about forty poles, set at 20-foot intervals (Fig 4.2). Where the leader entered the heart, the pound net was 126 feet wide, tapering along 130-foot walls to an opening at the bowl of 6 feet. The bowl itself had a 90-foot diameter and included a net floor. About forty-five poles held the heart and bowl in place, each guyed to the bottom by a line to a single anchor. Taken in total, this pound net used eighty-five poles, at least that many anchors, and judging from the perimeter distance (which is likely slightly more than the actual net itself), 1,379 feet of netting ranging from 10 to 30 feet tall or taller. In total, Baird estimated each pound net to be worth between two thousand and three thousand dollars.[16]

If pound nets themselves were complex operations to situate and set up, working them was not, and as a result pound fishing replaced fishermen's more valuable skill with his less valuable muscle.[17] Pounds in shallow waters did not even require fishermen to step into a boat: horses and carriages could be driven out to the bowls at low tide to transfer fish directly into wagons. For pounds in deeper waters, work gangs used one or two boats to collect and transfer the day's catch. Theodore Lyman, Massachusetts commissioner of inland fish and game, described the process at length:

> The weir is hauled once a day, and always at slack water, because with a strong tide running east or west it is impossible to handle the bottom lines. The men pull out in two parties, of which one in a large scow passes around the outside of the bowl, casting off the bottom lines, while the other in a yawl-boat pushes inside the bowl, pulls up the sliding poles, and closes the entrances. The slackening of the bottom line allows the bowl-net to hang free, and the crew inside begin to haul up the bottom of this net in such a way as to work the fish toward one corner, letting the net as it comes to the surface pass under their boat, which is thus slowly drawn across the bowl toward the corner where the capture is to take place, and where the scow is already waiting outside.[18]

Hauling the net was not idle work: Lyman was struck by the energy and drama of fish and fishermen struggling, one for freedom and the other for

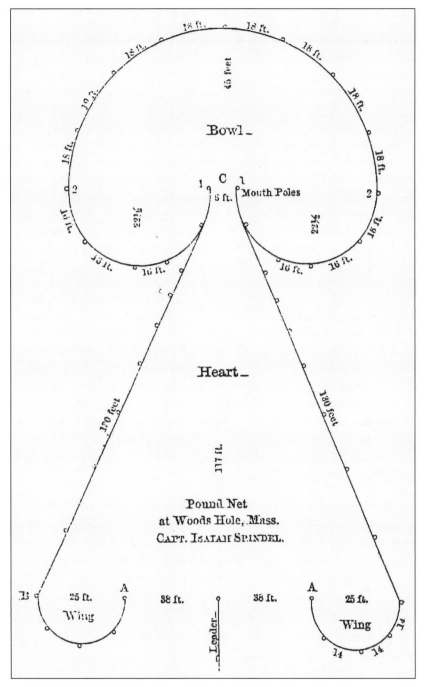

FIG. 4.2 Plan of Captain Isaiah Spindle's pound net, Woods Hole, Massachusetts, 1872. Spencer F. Baird, *Report on the Condition of the Sea Fisheries of the South Coast of New England in 1871 and 1872* (Washington, D.C., 1873), p. 262

profits, as vast numbers of fish of several different species were cleared for sale as food or bait.

> The scene now becomes an exciting one. The menhaden in thousands begin to show the upper lobes of their tails above the water; here and there darts a feverish mackerel like a blue and silver flash; great leathery skates, looking like pigs rolled out flat, raise their snouts in slow astonishment; here a shark suddenly works his way through the crowding mob; hundreds of goggled-eyed squid, smothered in the press, feebly ply their force pumps; and there the murderous bluefish, undismayed by imminent death, glares fiercely and snaps his savage jaws to the last. All these, with flat-fish, sea-robins, butterfish, and many more, are taken and rolled in a fluttering mass, iridescent with changing colors, and shower their silver scales high in the air. It moves even the weirmen, in their oilskin clothes, with a slight excitement as they cull out from the menhaden the choice and the offal fishes. There is Uncle Abishai smiting sharks with a spear, like so many Sauls, and he smiteth them not twice; and Captain Ed'ard endeavoring, with a swift scoop-net, to capture the dodging shad, because Mrs. Asa has boarders and needs a fish dinner; and Captain Charles, with the air of one who gets a toy for a good child, diligently striving after some of them [th]ere striped robins that the professor wanted. All this is strange and entertaining, even to a [state fisheries] commissioner, who, by the motion of a long swell and the evil piscatory odor, is somewhat afflicted with what the local satire terms "white ears." . . . And now the menhaden, bushels on bushels, are scooped all quivering into the great scow, for a little outside lies a mackereler who has just let go her anchor with a rattle, and a boat is pulling in with the skipper to buy bait.[19]

While apparatus such as this existed along the entire coast from New Brunswick to the Chesapeake, Cape Cod's location and local conditions were ideal for catching baitfish for passing fishermen. Cape Cod's physical shape concentrated schools of fish migrating north. At the same time, the shallow waters allowed fishermen to run their pounds farther out from shore, thereby increasing their ability to catch passing schools. On the western end of the Cape, where the Elizabeth Islands formed something of a fence to fish migrating from west to east, pound nets stretching into the passages through that fence—Woods Hole, Quicks Hole, and Robinsons Hole—targeted compacted schools of fish confined in these small passages. Key to the business before the growth of rail lines, however, was that fishermen from most northeastern fishing ports passed either north or south of Cape Cod en route to most of their fishing grounds. Vessels from Gloucester or Boston could make an easy stop in Provincetown for pound-caught bait on their way out to any of the northwest Atlantic banks. Vessels along New England's southern shore and from New York could stop at pounds and weirs that ranged from the eastern end of Long Island to Chatham to pick up fresh bait. As a result of its location and physical shape, Cape Cod became one of the most important pound-net fisheries in the United States in the second half of the nineteenth century.[20]

Once set up, pounds took large quantities of fish. While some days a catch could be very small, other days the volume of fish landed was monumental. Pound owner Jason Luce reported that in the eight weeks between April 4 and June 7, 1869, his single trap at Menemsha Bight caught 52,000 herring, 275 tautog, 79,000 dogfish, 125 striped bass, 380 barrels of scup, 300 shad, 15,900 mackerel, 2,500 barrels of sea robins, 1,590 barrels of menhaden, 300 sea bass, and 2 salmon. In comparison, Edgartown hook-and-line fisherman Josiah Pease caught only 26,542 bluefish in the six years between 1865 and 1871. Compared to Luce's net, Pease's more targeted and focused fishing could not compete in volume and efficiency.[21] Increased demand for bait, and the sheer volume of fish that could be landed in a pound, led to pound fishing's unprecedented proliferation and dramatic increase in size.

While banks vessels bought the baitfish, expanding railroad networks on the Cape hauled off the remaining fish to urban fresh-fish markets. After reaching Sandwich in 1848, rail connections opened in Yarmouthport on the north side of the Cape and Hyannis on the south in 1854. After the Civil War, rail lines continued to move eastward, with Orleans opening its station in 1865, Wellfleet in 1871, and Provincetown and Woods Hole by 1875. These railheads were essential for the expansion of the pound fishery. Without rapid rail connections, the massive volume of fish taken in Cape pounds, preserved first by ice and later in refrigerated cars, would never arrive in Boston, Gloucester, or New York in marketable condition.

As rail lines stretched eastward on the Cape, and as American fleets shifted over to more bait-intensive fishing gear in the 1850s, Cape Cod pound fishing expanded dramatically. No pound nets were capitalized enough before 1837 to warrant state articles of incorporation. In that year, however, three investors from Orleans incorporated the Fish Wear [sic] Company, based on Nanwicoit Point, Orleans. Between 1839 and 1852, three more companies also received incorporations. Three years later Cape Codders founded ten more pound fishing companies. In 1856 growing demand for corporate charters compelled the General Court to devolve the power to license and regulate stationary fishing installations to local municipalities, thereby removing itself as a hindrance to the process.[22] Other businesses grew to support the fishery, too. According to the 1855 state industrial census, whose agents began conflating weir and pounds into a single "weir" category, Brewster claimed four pound-net manufacturing operations capitalized at $600, annually employing six people, and producing $2,200 worth of nets.[23] By 1871, when Spencer Baird investigated complaints about pound fishing on the southern New England shore, one Rhode Island fishermen could claim that "there are three times as many pounds this year as last; it is [a] money making business, and all want to go into it."[24] Farther east, Baird counted forty-five pound nets lining Cape Cod's coasts. On the north side of the Cape alone, sixteen installations worked coastal waters: six pounds at the opening of Barnstable Harbor, including one with three hearts to accommodate larger volumes of fish; six more clustered on the southeast corner of Cape Cod Bay around Rock Harbor; another three lining the coast toward Wellfleet; and the sixteenth jutting up into Provincetown Harbor from Wood End. Twenty-nine more nets lined Cape Cod's southern coast. More spread-out than on the north side, a total of seventeen were located at Woods Hole, Naushon Island, Robinson's Hole, Falmouth Heights, Washburn Island, Lewis Bay, Bass River, and Old Stage Harbor. Monomoy Island itself hosted seventeen. Martha's Vineyard had twelve pounds along the north shore from Menemsha to Vineyard Haven (with two inside the harbor itself). Nor were pounds limited to Cape Cod proper: fishermen had built five more between Sippican and New Bedford Harbor.[25]

While financial records of the inshore fisheries are scarce—if not lost altogether—glimpses of the inshore fisheries' profitability, gained from the state's decennial censuses, explain why these operations expanded so quickly after 1856.[26] Between 1855, when the first Massachusetts industrial census was taken, and 1865, the inshore fisheries were delivering the highest returns on investment of all Cape Cod's fisheries (Table 4.1). In 1855, for example, the persisting inshore hook-and-line fishery and the nascent pound fishery together employed seventy-five inshore fishermen, who took 4,880 barrels of alewives, 450 barrels of bluefish (likely caught inshore), and 150 barrels of bluefish and bass (almost certainly caught inshore). It is not clear how much of these fish were taken by boats, pounds, or in private fish runs. Given that $9,758 of the total $13,058 in gross revenues came from alewives, most of

Table 4.1
Financial Overview of Select Barnstable County Fisheries, 1865

Fishery	Gross revenues	Capitalization	Hands employed	Return on investment (gross/cap.)	Share/fishermen (gross/hands employed)
Shore and menhaden	$18,500	$9,200	68	$2.01	$272.06
Weir fishery (Chatham only)	$3,150	$1,100	20	$2.86	$157.50
Cod and mackerel fleet	$2,143,802	$874,936	3,764	$2.45	$569.55

Source: Oliver Warner, *Statistical Information Relating to Certain Branches of Industry in Massachusetts for the Year Ending May 1, 1865* (Boston, 1866).

these earnings probably came from leased public fish runs. Using a crude—but available—comparison of gross annual revenue per hand employed, Cape Cod inshore fishermen's shares amounted to just over $140 per person. While this fell far short of the $213 of gross annual revenue each fisherman realized from the banks cod and mackerel fishery, given the low entry costs, inshore fishing offered hook-and-line fishermen decent wages, relatively speaking.[27]

A decade later, inshore fishing had grown sufficiently for Massachusetts census takers to create new special categories accommodating both the traditional inshore fishery and the new pound fisheries. The enumerated "Shore and Menhaden Fishery" represented the older inshore hook-and-line fishery. With sixty-eight fishermen working sixty boats, based largely in the town of Barnstable, this sector represented the inshore fishery that had operated along the New England shore for centuries. The shore fisheries consisted of a local fleet of small, owner-operated day-fishing boats using hooks and lines to take fish within a day's row or sail from the fishermen's homes and families. The menhaden fishery was likely made up of local farmers using beach seines to take the schools of menhaden for fertilizer. And, as of 1865, both fisheries were still significant. Using just over $9,000 in capital, small hook-and-line fishermen landed four thousand barrels of various fish that yielded $18,500 in gross revenue.

In contrast, the newly designated "Weir Fishery" represented new inshore fishing companies that used more efficient pound fishing technologies. It is important to state that the 1865 figures hardly represent a comprehensive overview of the industry: while the shore and menhaden figures were available for several Cape towns, only Chatham provided information from the pound fishery pertaining to capitalization levels, hands employed, and volume and value of catch. Aside from Chatham, Dennis was the only other Cape town to offer any information about pound fishing (and then only information on hands employed and total value of catch). Consequently, the 1865 figures underrepresent the magnitude of the nascent pound fishing industry.

But the figures, as limited as they are, do provide a glimpse of why people invested in stationary fishing gear. Comparing countywide figures of the shore and menhaden fishery, the cod and mackerel fleets, and Chatham's pound-fishing figures, it is clear that this new gear represented new opportunities to pull money from inshore waters. Chatham's inshore nets employed just twenty workers and landed $3,150 in mackerel. Requiring only $1,100 in capitalization, the pounds provided the highest return on investment (defined as gross revenues / capitalization) of any of the other major fisheries on the Cape: $2.86 for pounds as compared to $2.01 for shore and menhaden fishing, and $2.45 for cod and mackerel banks fishing.

The people losing in pound fishing's financial calculus were the men working the gear itself. These figures suggest that in the banks fisheries, where each fisherman was part owner of each voyage, each took a larger share of the whole venture: in this case almost $570 per fisherman. Shore fishermen, however, while not earning as much ($272) as their banks counterparts, fared far better than their weir-fishing neighbors, who earned only $157.50 per man. The difference in these figures derived from ownership. Inshore fishermen both owned and operated their vessels and as a result benefited as both investors and fishermen. Pound fishermen, while paid either on shares or a flat wage, depending on where the gear was set up, were employees working for an owner, whose investment secured for him a greater share of the profits.[28] In addition, pound net fishing in 1865 represented a more attractive investment than even the capital-intensive banks fishery. Without the overhead costs of larger vessels, their maintenance, repairs, and insurance, and without the need to share profits with a larger crew, pound net investors realized almost a one-third greater return on investments than their banks fleet counterparts. Quite simply, Barnstable County data shows that by 1865 pound fishing had grown because it represented to those with the capital a profitable, easily entered alternative to both banks and inshore fishing.

Taken altogether, then, Cape Cod's inshore fishery saw fundamental changes in the middle third of the nineteenth century. As offshore fishing expanded between 1818 and the Civil War, new demands for bait transformed how Cape Codders used their inshore fish stocks. With new rail links stretching along Cape Cod after 1848, more and more beaches were tied to major population and fishing centers desiring fish as food or as bait. In addition, Cape Codders dedicated more inland waterways to the artificial production of baitfish, and incorporated an increasing number of shore-fishing stations along the coast. Furthermore, as a means to yield greater returns on investments, Cape Codders discarded older regulatory regimes that limited both catch and markets for publicly owned alewife fisheries, as they embraced new technologies that took more fish through the labor of fewer fishermen.

Two circumstances permitted local fishermen to bring this increased pressure to Cape Cod's shores. First, ties to external markets now gave a value to resources whose use, when confined to limited markets, outweighed their conservation. Secondly, prosperity removed any reason why inshore fish—especially alewives—should not be fully commercialized. Rather than manage these resources for long-term public benefit, Cape Cod fishermen and investors turned very real fish into mere revenue streams to be optimized for short-term private gain. In short, Cape Cod residents between 1818 and 1860 had transformed their coastal wasteland into productive workspaces. In doing so, however, they also abandoned the controls that had sustained both communities and resources for more than a century.

Cape Cod's hook-and-line fishermen were not blind to the dramatic changes that were transforming their coastlines. For these small fishermen, the expansion of the pound fisheries created a fundamentally different world, where both economic and ecological changes redefined relationships between public resources, private capital, and fishermen's labor. First and foremost, with increasing numbers of private streams, larger pounds nets, and privately leased public herring runs, small fishermen were finding it more difficult to get access to the small fish on which they relied for bait, food, or fertilizer. Communities' willingness to lease public fisheries—if only for short terms—also meant that fewer and fewer small independent fishermen could find subsistence in waters and ponds along Cape Cod's shores.[29] Finally, by changing relationships between labor and capital, pounds also threatened to destroy the fishery both economically and ecologically. As hook-and-line fishermen watched pounds spring up all along Cape Cod's shores, they also noted what they believed was their effect on local fish populations, and what they knew was their effect on the local fishing economy.

After four decades of increasing fishing pressure, by the late 1860s small fishermen claimed they saw a steady and alarming decline in the abundance of inshore fish. Newport fisherman Nathaniel Smith said best what all other hook-and-line fishermen from Westerly, Rhode Island, to Provincetown, Massachusetts, feared: "I am seventy-three years old. I have fished for forty-six years. There were scarcely any fish when I left the business, three years ago. . . . Fish used to be very plenty, so that any one could get as many as he wanted; they were plenty until the trapping [pound fishing] was commenced. That was about 1828 or 1830."[30] Other lifelong fishermen disagreed with the timing of the region's declining inshore fish stocks. Captain Almoran Hallett testified that "the diminution began about ten years ago [1861], and there has been a falling off every year."[31] In either case, what was clear to these inshore workers was that fish stocks had declined at some point in living memory.

If fishermen could not agree when the decline began, they could agree that pound fishing was the cause. Most argued that pounds took too many fish. The comments of Henry Lumbert, a fisherman from Centerville, were typical: "No fish are as plenty as they were years ago. I suppose the traps and pounds, and their being caught up makes them scarce."[32] Some, like Hyannis fish dealer Joseph G. Loring, took more sophisticated approaches: "We think that the pounds keep the fish from the shores . . . whether the pounds break up the schools or what the trouble is, we do not know; but we know the fish are much more scarce than they used to be."[33] Based on their understanding of the regional movements of fish and of how fishing was changing in other neighboring areas, Cape inshore fishermen viewed this as a regional—not a local—problem. "I think they catch our scup about Soughkonet, in Rhode Island. They get them sooner [in the fish's migrations] at Soughkonet than at Vineyard Sound, and about a week earlier at Waquoit than here."[34] Pounds, traps, and weirs, whether on Cape Cod or farther west along the shore, were seen as collectively driving down stocks of inshore fish upon which Cape Cod fishermen relied.

Potter Brightman, a Westport hook-and-line fisherman, offered perhaps the most compelling argument as to why pounds reduced stocks of inshore fish. He recognized that pounds cut at the very foundation of fish populations. "In one night [pounds] caught 200 barrels of tautog; and not only that, they take them as spawning fish."[35] To him, pounds bypassed natural mechanisms that helped fish survive until after they had spawned. "Fish will not bite [a baited hook] when full of spawn. . . . Then you cannot get a fish to touch your hook. . . . They will not bite then, and you cannot do anything with them."[36] Two fishing captains from Edgartown, Josiah and Rufus Pease, also balked at the traps' ability to take spawning fish. "The pounds take all the breeding fish that come into the shores. I saw in New Bedford, the first of May, large scup, full of spawn, and rock-bass. They were taken in the pounds, and could not have been caught with lines; it was too early." His fellow captain agreed. Rufus Pease claimed, "They had so many tautog taken at Woods Hole at one time that the net sunk and the fish died, and they had to turn them on shore. They were chock full of spawn; large breeders in there, looking for a place to deposit their spawn."[37] In what can only be viewed as a remarkably prescient understanding of fish population dynamics, these fishermen recognized that because pounds caught fish before they spawned, stationary gear promised dire consequences for inshore fishermen.

Pounds made money—a lot of money. When asked if he would rent out his operation for five hundred dollars a month, one pound owner replied, "If you would say five thousand dollars a month, we might talk about it."[38] No inshore fisherman working his own hook and line and selling to a local market could ever see revenues on that scale. Furthermore, as pounds daily landed vastly greater volumes of fish, they glutted local markets and collapsed prices, squeezing inshore fishermen even more. For fishermen living on the margins, such changes caused great concerns—concerns they shared with Spencer Baird in 1871 when the naturalist investigated claims of stock declines. According to one man who had been fishing out of Edgartown since at least 1840, "The mischief of the pounds is, they keep the price down."[39] Potter Brightman, who fished at the head of Buzzards Bay, agreed: "The traps and pounds here catch [scup]; they catch more in one night than all the smack-man can catch in a season. . . . There are very few hook-fishermen now. Most of them have given it up because they cannot make a living." For Brightman, it may have already been too late. At some point between 1860 and 1870, his father, Elias, had lost their house, and the whole family had been forced to take rooms in the home of another mariner. With pounds taking so many fish and glutting local markets, Brightman's experience was likely repeated often in other fishing families.[40]

Even fish dealers felt compelled to testify on small fishermen's behalf. One Hyannis monger claimed that "the fishing business has gone down so [much] that it is not more than one-fourth of what it was four years ago."[41] Another stated, "There are not more than one-third as many persons employed in connection with the fisheries on the shore as there were five years ago. Those who have lost their business of fishing have gone away." And they recognized that they were, unwillingly, part of the problem: "We give two cents a pound this year. . . . We used to give three and four cents a pound."[42]

In fact, fish sellers saw clearly that their fates were tied to those of the fishermen and the fish. One dealer, Captain Hetsel Handy from Hyannis, made the connection between declining fish stocks, pound nets, and business prospects most succinctly. "Fishermen who have been in my employ two years say they used to fetch in five hundred pounds of fish in a day and get a cent a pound for them. Now they go out and try from 2 o'clock in the morning, and come in at night with one or two fish. . . . Twenty boats will not bring in more than two barrels." More than just declining stocks imperiled both fisherman and his buyer, however. The economic consequences of decimated stocks, glutted markets, and collapsed prices ushered in human calamities far beyond the calculus of profit and loss. "I have handed a man a quarter of a dollar, and even less, for his day's work in fishing; and they would say their arms felt as though they would drop off. . . . What are they going to do next winter? If they are well they may keep out of the poor-house."[43] For Cape Cod fishermen and the fish dealers, pounds served as a catalyst for ecological, economic, and individual human tragedies.

Handy also vocalized another widely held belief. The impending crisis represented an end not just of individual livings, but of an entire region's livelihood. Through careful management, and thanks to abundant seas, Cape Cod's people had finally managed, despite their poor lands, to hammer out an existence that was more than marginal. Now, to Captain Handy, that all appeared in peril. "We must either take our families and go away or else something must be done to enable us to live here. With a weir two or three men can catch more fish than all the other fishers on the coast." Handy also pointed out that, adding insult to injury, such predation was more than just destructive—it was also wasteful. "[Pounds and weirs] ship off a hundred tons a day to New York, and [so the fish] must be used up or spoil; whereas if they were caught with a hook and taken care of they would be good healthy food for men to eat."[44] In short, pound fishing threatened to undo in just a

few years with wasteful carelessness the life that Cape Cod communities had
taken generations to establish.

Squeezed between collapsing prices and collapsing stocks, small fishermen faced a relentless bind. Unlike the pound men, whose living came from
passive gear and state-of-the-art preservation and transportation links, independent fishermen recognized that their families and towns were tied to the
health of the fish themselves. Pound fishermen, who landed thousands of
times more fish and shipped them off to inexhaustible urban markets, simply
did not feel the local economic pressures and, as will be seen, did not believe
fish stocks could be permanently depleted. As hook-and-line fishermen perceived fish populations declining, however, they feared not only for their financial prospects, but for whole families and communities. One fishing captain from Hyannis stated, "The matter of fishing is one of great importance to
the people here; many get their living by it. In these places, Barnstable and
Osterville, there are a hundred boats employed in the business of fishing,
which would represent more than a hundred families." The consequences of
failed inshore fishing would hit families, communities, and the entire region.
"If the fishing is broken up, the people will have to go to sea [on long-term
merchant voyages] or to work on the land. Most of them are old men, and,
like myself, have no trade. I do not know what else I could do. The biggest
part of the men in the fishing business have no trade, and must fish or go to
sea [away from their families]." Furthermore, those ill effects would ripple
out across the community. "It would affect the sail and boat making businesses, too, if the fishing were to fail; they cannot get half price for their
boats."[45]

Another fisherman perhaps put it most succinctly: "If the work is given
up to the pound-men, I do not know what will become of the fishermen. It
seems as if they cannot exist together—the rich [man] or the poor man must
have it."[46]

By 1869, Cape Cod's coastal workspace was no longer a haven for iconic
fishermen to pull wealth from an ever-abundant ocean. New gear and new
economics had combined to make the futures of small fish and small fishermen dire indeed. As new gear and expanded bait fishing brought new prosperity, that prosperity compelled Cape Cod communities to walk away from
resource-conservation traditions that had served to limit fishing pressures for

the first two centuries of settlement. For those with capital, this new business environment allowed for tremendous economic gain. For those without, however, the consequences of pound fishing pushed many to the brink, as both economic and ecological trajectories converged to turn the vibrant Cape Cod communities witnessed by Thoreau into the grasping, opportunistic ones described by Nordhoff. In many ways, these pressures represented the logical outcome of the transformation of Cape Cod from a wasteland to a workspace. New markets, new money, and new visions of how a region should look and operate justified Americans' expanded exploitation of natural resources before the Civil War. On Cape Cod, however, separated and free to find its own way for generations, prosperity, cultural visions, and their legacies engendered disastrous consequences.

CHAPTER 5

Abstractions

*It should therefore be understood that the exhaustion of a local fishery is not like
dipping water out of a bucket, where the vacancy is immediately filled from the
surrounding body; but it is more like taking lard out of a keg, where there is a
space left that does not become occupied by anything else.*
 —Spencer Fullerton Baird, *Report of the Condition of the Sea Fisheries of the
South Coast of New England in 1871 and 1872*

*Like the many fishermen that I know, the witnesses were not well acquainted with the
habits of fish. They study them no further than they contribute to their pecuniary interest.
At most, they possess only a local knowledge of the fish with which they come in contact.*
 —Nathaniel E. Atwood to Massachusetts State Senate, April 19, 1871

By 1869, southern New England's inshore hook-and-line fishermen had
come to a breaking point. As pounds took more fish and collapsed prices,
those who continued to fish as their fathers and grandfathers had done saw
their lives and livelihoods as endangered as they believed were the fish they
chased. The question that lay at the heart of their frustration was how to
convince others that pounds destroyed stocks of inshore fish. To address this
issue, hook fishermen began a grassroots campaign in the winter of 1869 calling for legislative action. Beginning in Rhode Island, fishing-community
leaders circulated petitions calling for bans on weirs and pounds, and a
Rhode Island derivative called traps, all of which they believed both destroyed a common resource and, in doing so, violated common resource-
access rights. Soon the movement spread across the border into Massachusetts, and by the spring of 1870 both states were convening hearings on the
health, sustainability, and uses of southern New England's inshore fishery.

On the surface, these hearings focused on whether weirs and pounds were destroying inshore fish stocks. Whether they were doing so or not, however, a deeper, epistemological problem was also at issue: as sides formed, and as arguments developed, it became clear that beneath the economic and ecological arguments lay the question of who should have the authority to speak for the fish. As discussed earlier, that authority had long rested with those most familiar with local conditions—local fishermen—and as long as southern New England's inshore fishery remained healthy, that regime remained in place. By the late 1860s, however, even as most observers believed inshore fish stocks were declining, new gear divided local fishermen between those who could purchase weirs and pounds and those who could not, and as a result the previous unanimity that had existed was now sundered. Consequently, by 1869 the debates focused upon two deeper questions: first, why were stocks of fish declining, and second, how could that question be answered?

Far more was at stake than just fishing regulations. The conflict over weir and pound fishing involved conflicting visions of how humans should relate to the inshore fishery. Hook-and-line fishermen took fish one by one through a labor process that, ironically, created intimate bonds between the fisherman and the fish he killed for food and gain. For the weir and pound fishermen, however, the inshore fisheries were just one more place where man could pull wealth from the coastal workspace. Their industry took fish by the hundreds, if not thousands, and rarely did any individual fish come into clear focus. In order to handle, manage, and comprehend this magnitude of fish, pound and weir operators, and their later allies, had to view fish as numbers of an aggregate catch. These numbers were then integrated into a larger banks fishery, which used these fish as inputs into a larger industrial enterprise bringing cod, mackerel, and other market fish from the banks to local and distant markets. As such, these operators related to fish not on the intimate one-by-one basis of the hook-and-line fishermen, but rather in abstract terms more concerned with volumes of fish caught, shipped, and sold. In other words, fish were not entities to pound and weir owners; they were numbers within a larger industrial calculus aimed at maximizing production and profit.

As events would show, the controversy over fishing gear, and who should speak for the fish, introduced another group of people who also viewed the inshore fisheries from a more distant, abstract, position. As hearings stalled and protests mounted, a new group of men—fisheries scientists—entered the fray on both sides of the argument. Just as divided as the fishermen were as to whether humans could affect stock sizes, academically trained scientists viewed fisheries problems in ways similar to those of the weir men and the banks fishermen. In entering into these debates, scientists—intentionally or not—rendered both fish and hook-and-line fishermen into mere numbers—abstractions—which could then be more easily manipulated, managed, and even erased. And while the involvement of scientists did little to effectively curb weir and pound fishing and preserve stock sizes, such involvement fundamentally restructured the way people managed local resources.

The attack on pounds and weirs began in Rhode Island under the leadership of respected fishing veterans. One petition, championed by forty-six-year fisherman Nathan Smith, enlisted 170 supporters. Another longtime fisherman, Sam Brown, recruited 100 signers more for another.[1] The campaign's legal implications drew others to the anti-weir cause as well. Since its renewal in 1842, the Rhode Island state constitution guaranteed the rights of free fishing to all state citizens—a right that dated back to Rhode Island's original royal charter, granted by Charles II of England. As hook-and-line fishermen and their supporters read it, weirs, pounds, and traps violated individuals' constitutional rights to free fishing by taking far more fish than an individual could with hook and line, and therefore leaving far fewer for others to catch. If the ban was approved, then new definitions of common resource use would need to be established that protected individual access to fisheries resources. There were political repercussions, too. The petitioners tied their efforts to the state's gubernatorial election, and in 1870, when the Republican candidate for lieutenant governor was surprisingly defeated in a typically Republican state, the message was clear: bans on pounds, traps, and weirs garnered the support of many people willing to do what was necessary to enact them.[2]

With strong popular support and the leverage of the election cycle, hook fishermen had little doubt that their case would prevail. To be sure, however, they kept another ace in the hole. Hook fishermen could reasonably anticipate that when their petitions were presented to the legislature, the body would investigate their claims in the same way southern New England legislatures had investigated all similar cases previously: a committee would be convened, chaired by a legislator with political ties to the issue, and would then collect testimony—in this case from fishermen—about the effects of stationary gear. With many hook fishermen in agreement about the effects of stationary nets on inshore stocks, much of the evidence the committee would hear would support the ban on traps, pounds, and weirs. In that case, the investigating committee would be hard-pressed not to recommend that the petition be granted.

The Rhode Island hook-and-line fishermen got most of the scenario right. Enjoying significant popular support, the legislature assembled an investigating committee in the winter of 1870. It was chaired by Newport representative Francis Brinley, who held significant ties to both hook fishermen and weir fishermen. And, as hook fishermen anticipated, Brinley turned to local residents to assess the health of the local marine environment through a series of public hearings that ran through the spring in Providence, Tiverton, Seconnet, Newport, and Narragansett Pier.

At this point, however, events failed to follow the course that hook-and-line fishermen had plotted. Local hearings brought out so many heatedly opinionated and contradictory witnesses that Brinley himself conceded there was no chance he could finish the investigations as planned. "The process of oral examination was so exceedingly slow and tedious that the committee were soon convinced of the impracticability of continuing it."[3] This should have surprised no one, for after two decades of hardening markets and declining fish, all leading to increased competition over the fish that remained, whatever unified voice that may have once existed within the fishing community vanished as individuals presented competing claims. In an effort to pursue its investigations more efficiently, the committee sent out a questionnaire with eighty-two questions inquiring into the health and function of the inshore fishery. That changed the whole game. The collection of information outside public view allowed weir and pound fishermen's testimonies to stand equally alongside those of their hook-fishing opponents. Without a public forum, where a general consensus could be hammered out through discussion and debate, and where dissent could be drowned out, it was far more difficult for hook-and-line fishermen to impose a consensus. Brinley's questionnaire, in short, marginalized the power and the persuasive tactics that hook fishermen could use in a public forum, giving weir fishermen a better chance at defeating the bans.

Even with questionnaires, however, Brinley still sat on a pile of conflicted, confused, and contradictory pictures of the health of the southern New England inshore fishery. To clarify the rancor, the committee tried to find the best examples to represent each side of the argument. For the case against traps, the committee selected the responses of C. H. Bassett, "a very intelligent man" and a banker with ties to workers and fishermen in Barrington, Rhode Island, all of whom relied upon the inshore fisheries for employment or subsistence. Bassett reported that "they all tell one story. Before traps were allowed, there were plenty of fish; could catch enough [for a meal] in half an hour . . . in former years the Providence market was almost wholly supplied with fish from [Narragansett] bay. The bay and the river was a vast reservoir from which we took out fresh fish from day to day, as we wished." Only traps could have caused the decline, Bassett claimed, for he had not observed any change in the availability of food for target species, nor had pollution levels appeared to change over the years. Regardless of the cause, though, the costs of declining fish stocks were hitting working people hard. "One very intelligent man thought it made one hundred dollars difference in the cost of living to those persons living on the shore and in the small towns on the bay." From Bassett's perspective, for the one thousand or so families he believed so affected, that figure amounted to a tax of about one hundred thousand dollars. Nor were just fish consumers suffering. Bassett also recounted how those who earned livings supporting the inshore fisheries also lost as new gear changed old fishing ways. "Boat building was formerly carried on here [in Barrington] by six or seven different concerns. I know of but two now, who build a few boats."[4] Bassett's testimony, in short, presented an image of pounds, weirs, and traps imposing a heavy tax on coastal residents that threatened the region's entire economy.

The investigating committee looked to Benjamin Tallman of Portsmouth, Rhode Island, to defend weirs and traps. "Well known as a fisherman of great experience, and who may be considered as the inventor of trap fishing," Tallman provided a detailed list of the species his traps took and offered recent price fluctuations as a rough indicator of those species' relative abundance. Tallman acknowledged that he, too, had observed changes in the inshore fisheries. Sea-bass and scup had both declined, sending market prices upward. Despite that, however, Tallman contended that traps took the fish that would otherwise not be available to Rhode Islanders because of the industrial cities nearby. "Mr. Tallman is of the opinion that if these methods for taking fish were disused, the market would not be better or fish more plenty, because the fish the trappers take would not have stopped in the bay; all the impurities of the waters at Fall River, Providence, &c., deleteriously affect the fish."[5] Standing on the argument that shore gear was taking only those fish that would otherwise escape Rhode Island's nets and hooks, weir, pound, and trap fishermen deployed a defense similar to Hinckley's from the turn of the century, one that challenged their opponents to prove fish behaviors.

Based on these two representative testimonies, Brinley's committee recommended in June 1870 imposing a ban on traps along Rhode Island shores. While the ban passed in one house, it was ultimately tabled in the other and never enacted. What is telling is not so much Brinley's final recommendation and its fate, however, but how the committee arrived at its decision. As other southern New Englanders had for centuries before, this committee looked to local people to assess the health of the local marine environment. What emerged, however, was not the clear consensus that the petitioners had hope for. Aided by Brinley's abandonment of public hearings, trap fishermen were better able to present—without fear of public recrimination—a different image of the health and function of the inshore environment. And to the weir fishermen's credit, and despite the economic stakes in play, Tallman and his trapping colleagues reported their observations that fish had indeed declined. As noble as it might have been, however, that integrity did not help sway Brinley to their side. Nevertheless, through Rhode Island's hearings it became clear that inshore hook-and-line fishermen no longer had a monopoly on interpreting the health of the inshore fishery.

When the anti-weir campaign crossed over into Massachusetts in 1870, it turned bitter. Through the winter of 1869–70, hook-and-line fishermen found as much support among Massachusetts fishermen as the cause had in Rhode Island. Coming mostly from New Bedford, a total of twenty-six petitions calling for bans on weirs and pound nets garnered the support of three thousand hook-and-line fishermen from Westport to Provincetown. In addition, and like Rhode Island's case, the hook fishermen's cause attracted wide popular support. Hyannis fish dealer Hetsel Handy claimed, for example, that "if the question of having pounds or not was put to vote in this county, seven-eighths of the people would vote against them."[6] Others were willing to use extralegal means to advance the anti-weir agenda. In Westport, for example, the head man of the town's only weir was "accidentally" shot by unknown parties, effectively shutting down that weir and discouraging the construction of any more.[7] Other southern New England residents heard "men solemnly swear they would destroy the pounds and everything connected with them that they could lay their hands on before they would submit to have the maintenance of their families thus taken away."[8]

Not only did the movement enjoy broad popular appeal—petitioners also secured the support of the prominent progressive politician Thomas Dawes Eliot, who had built his career around defending the prospects of working-men in the post–Civil War republic. A former member of the Free Soil Party, a congressman through the Civil War, and former chairman of the House Committee on the Freedmen's Bureau, Eliot was likely drawn to the cause of the fishermen by his son-in-law, artist Robert Swain Gifford, whose father was a fisherman and whose artwork celebrated the vibrancy of coastal fishing communities. With such an august and well-respected champion, who in one of his last political efforts before passing away presented the New Bedford fishermen's petition to the Massachusetts General Court in January 1870, Massachusetts petitioners had good reason to be optimistic.[9]

Pound fishermen and their supporters did not sit idly by. While hook-and-line fishermen canvassed fishing towns, pound owners enlisted the aid of those industries reliant upon their catches. By the beginning of the hearings they had amassed sixty-two documents with a total of almost eight thousand signatures that they presented to oppose bans on stationary fishing gear. Among the signatories were representatives from the banks fleets, which needed cheap bait, and the Cape Cod Railway, much of whose revenue came from hauling fresh fish from the Cape to Boston and New York. Other industries also opposed the ban on pounds. The highly capitalized Pacific Guano Company in Woods Hole opposed the ban, not surprisingly, as the company had shifted over to weir-caught menhaden as a substitute for dwindling supplies of bird guano on the Pacific's Howland Island. So, too, did farmers from across the state, who purchased the company's cheap, fish-based fertilizers. In sum, Cape Cod weir fishermen enjoyed sufficient support to pay the more than three thousand dollars in legal fees that the entire proceedings would cost.[10]

Like the Rhode Island legislature, Massachusetts assembled a committee, again chaired by a lawmaker with many ties to the issue and the region most concerned with it. In this case, the nod went to the former fisherman and well-connected Provincetown state senator Nathaniel E. Atwood. Atwood was the fisherman Humphrey Storer had gathered information from in the 1850s, and through that connection he was recommended by Louis Agassiz to lecture on fishes at local learned societies. In addition to these ties, Atwood found further support for his chairmanship from Massachusetts commissioner of inland fish and game Theodore Lyman. Atwood certainly knew the industry well—perhaps too well. Many of his Provincetown constituents had direct interests in pound fishing, either for the banks bait industry or for the fresh-fish market. Furthermore, many other voters in Provincetown were banks fishermen themselves, who relied upon cheap pound-caught bait. In 1870 Provincetown still hosted a banks cod-fishing fleet of over one hundred vessels whose overhead costs, including that of bait, were evenly shared by each fishermen working the vessel. Consequently, more expensive bait would cut into the revenues of the fishermen-voters, who also landed about half a million dollars in gross revenues each year.[11] Finally, Atwood's own family— both immediate and distant—had significant interests in pound fishing. The Atwood Company of Provincetown, for example, owned railcars, wharves, chandleries, and refrigeration facilities, all geared toward exporting fish to Boston and New York markets, or to selling it to banks-bound vessels buying bait.[12] As Atwood clearly recognized, without cheap bait, Provincetown's cod, haddock, and halibut trawl-line fleets would move elsewhere. It was in his political, personal, and economic interests to play an active, even leading, role in the Senate investigations into hook-and-line fishermen's petitions.

Beginning in February 1870 the committee convened a series of eighteen public hearings to collect testimony from witnesses on both sides. Soon it became evident, however, that Atwood would run into the same problems that Brinley had in Rhode Island. As Lyman characterized the proceedings two years later, "There was, indeed, little to sway a looker-on towards either party. The witnesses generally had limited information, coupled with pretty strong prejudices." Furthermore, Lyman believed that had it not been for more professional men in the hearings, the entire proceedings would have been a complete waste of time: "What real information was to be got was violently pulled and twisted by the half-dozen lawyers engaged by the combatants."[13] As hearings dragged through the winter and into the spring, no clear picture emerged as to whether weirs and pounds were destroying stocks of inshore fish. And by April, the committee had heard enough to present its conclusions. It was clear that fishermen's testimonies—from either side of the issue—had failed to provide any clear consensus; and while it seemed that scup, striped bass, sea bass, and tautog had declined in Buzzards Bay, the committee rejected the petitioners' calls for bans on pounds and weirs, claiming that no positive link could be determined between inshore nets and the observed changes in fish stocks.[14]

Once the finding was announced, Bristol County representative John A.

Hawes, whose constituents largely supported bans, refused to vote until Atwood explained his recommendations. And here Atwood took a bold step. Rather than defer to local fishermen's experiences and observations and then select the clearest statement of each side's position, Atwood rejected the traditional a priori assumption that local fishermen were accurate observers of nature. Instead he conceded that, indeed, a general consensus had emerged through the hearings that some species of fish had declined along the coasts. Yet the question why they had declined remained unanswered, and in attempting to answer it, Atwood categorically rejected all fishermen's claims as unreliable. To the contrary, he urged the committee to listen to the testimony of a new group of experts, scientists, who brought a different kind of expertise to the issue:

> Sir, if any other matter upon which there were more than 11,000 names on the petitions and remonstrances should come before the legislature . . . [the committee] would expect that experts and men acquainted with all the practical workings would come before them . . . that possessed a knowledge of the geographical distribution, migrations, habits, food, time of depositing spawn, growth, and development of their young, as far as it could be known, and, besides, all the changes that have taken place during a long series of years.

The implication was that because the hook-and-line fishermen lacked ichthyologic and scientific expertise, the committee should reject their testimony as uselessly confused and partisan.[15]

Something had to justify Atwood's dismissal of such popularly supported petitions, however. And here Atwood drew upon his own experience and reputation as both a fisherman and respected naturalist to legitimate his version of the situation: "Mr. President, allow me to lay aside the evidence before the committee, while I briefly allude to the changes I have noticed during a long life of practical experience with the fisheries." Claiming that he could "go back [to] no earlier date than 1816, when I entered the fishing boat and followed fishing as a business for a period of *fifty-one* years," Atwood then proceeded to replace the petitioners' personal testimonies with his own, far more limited observations. After describing markets, prices, and personal reflections on the scup, mackerel, Spanish mackerel, shad, and squeteague fisheries, Atwood explained declining fish stocks through a reductive, anti-inquisitive, simplistic understanding. "Where are they now? All that can be said in answer, I can say in three words—they are gone." With one simple statement, Atwood replaced eighteen hearings' worth of testimony—presented by witnesses with decades of their own "practical experience" in the fisheries—with a single explanation that was more easily understood and more politically acceptable. Here, the practical fishermen-naturalist turned the issue back into a mystery beyond the powers of the legislature to address, obviating any need for legislation and leaving the coasts as workspace free to be exploited as industrial fishers deemed appropriate.[16]

To support his position, Atwood cited the findings of the 1863 British commission that investigated claims of declining catches in the sea herring fisheries. Led by renowned naturalist and Darwin champion Thomas Henry Huxley, the British commission had interviewed thousands of fishermen along Britain's coastlines. Huxley's final 1866 findings provided Atwood with his argument's most important support: "[The British commission] came to the unanimous conclusion that there was no danger of exhausting the fisheries, either in the open sea or in any of the arms or estuaries along the coast, with all that men can do."[17] Huxley's conclusions were simply too convenient for Atwood not to use them to further his claim that weirs and pounds could not possibly drive down fish stocks.

Atwood still needed to provide some explanation for the hearings' one agreed-upon fact—that fish stocks had declined along the southern New England shore—and the committee would not be satisfied with just a theoretical reason to deny the request of one of the largest grassroots movements in southern New England since the American Revolution. To explain declines, Atwood argued that the environment itself was causing fish stocks to fail. In particular, bluefish, he claimed, represented the root of southern New England's environmental and social collapse: "The bluefish affected our fishery so much that the people were obliged to leave [Provincetown]. Family after family moved away, until every one left, leaving that locality . . . a desolate, barren, sandy waste. . . . These [bluefish] not only depopulated our bay of nearly all other species, but they depopulated my village and my home."[18]

Atwood then argued that any ban on traps and weirs would harm more than just those fishermen currently employing would-be banned gear, and in making this case he revealed the larger economic interests at stake in the proceedings. "The large fleet of vessels belonging to Gloucester are a part of the season dependent upon these fisheries for bait to be used in their bank-fisheries." Cod fishermen, halibut fishermen, and mackerel-catchers would all suffer for want of inexpensive bait. Furthermore, larger society would also

MONEY TALKS"...

be hurt. "There is a large amount of capital invested in our fisheries, giving employment to a great number of men, who follow a life of hardship and exposure. They are a useful class of men, as they are producers. By their labors they bring to our tables a large amount of wholesome and nutritious food, which is a blessing to our people."[19] In the face of Atwood's testimony, one that took listeners from fishermen's knowledge, to fish behavior, and finally to the economic importance of baitfish, few remained willing to press the issue further. By the end of the session, Bristol County's Hawes and his colleagues were forced to accept Atwood's findings and to continue to allow weirs and pounds to fish the southern New England shore.

Atwood's proceedings accomplished one other, fundamental feat. Through these hearings, Atwood not only defeated hook-and-line fishermen's efforts to preserve the inshore fisheries. He also removed hook-and-line fishermen and their uniquely intimate relationship to the marine environment from the management of inshore resources. Unlike Rhode Island's committee, which still relied upon local testimony for its conclusions, Atwood swept away the observations of countless witnesses, and with them, two centuries of local expertise controlling the use and management of the local environment. In their place he put weir and trap fishermen, and the fisheries scientists whom they referred to in defense of their position, all of whom approached the marine environment from a more distant and abstract position.

It was this more distant perspective of the marine environment that united pound owners and the scientists who supported them. Both viewed the environment in terms of massive quantities of fish that could only be accounted for—economically and intellectually—by rendering them into numbers. Once represented by numbers, fish became abstractions, without any links to a physical entity living in the coastal waters, or as even part of that environment. Such abstraction allowed men like Atwood, and later Theodore Lyman, to believe that the whole marine environment could be known mathematically and, as such, manipulated mathematically from a desk covered in pages of figures, counts, and tallies. Such representations turned fishing into a mathematical problem, and turned fish into massively large numbers that man could not conceivably affect on a large scale. Consequently, Atwood's hearings fundamentally changed not only *who* could speak for the fish, but *how* they would speak for them, and how fish would be envisioned in the future. Small fishermen, who knew local fish stocks and local habitats, were pushed aside and replaced by industrial interests, backed by scientists, both of which groups saw fish only as numbers within a vast, forever-abundant nature.

Finally, by discrediting fishermen as witnesses, Atwood also undermined one of the state's few means by which to assess, and then manage, its marine resources. No longer would fishermen be viewed as those most closely tied to the long-term health of the inshore fishery and therefore the most reliable sources of information. Instead—and as a result of Atwood's efforts to protect his own interests—fishermen's financial interests were now considered to taint their experience and observations, and certainly they could no longer speak for the fish. Replacing this old center of information about the marine environment would be a new one derived from formal education and the application of apparently universal laws of nature.

What sense could this possibly have made to the fishermen who were dismissed that day? What could a British naturalist working along the shores of the North Sea know about the Nantucket and Vineyard sounds? How, indeed, could anyone without any local experience be qualified to judge such matters? Those were good questions, and as of the spring of 1870, it was not clear how well formal academic science could fill the roles that fishermen had played. These questions would be answered in the subsequent two years, however. And those answers, in turn, carried profound implications for the management of inshore fisheries for the rest of the century.

Discredited or not, Cape Cod's inshore fishermen refused to accept the committee's findings. One month after Atwood's conclusions were presented, hook-and-line fishermen managed to push through a ban on weirs, traps, purse seines, and gill nets in the headwaters of Buzzards Bay.[20] While this represented an important, emboldening victory for small fishermen, for pound fishermen it represented but a small concession. With so many traps lying en route to Georges Bank or the Grand Banks, few banks schooners would bother to sail the extra twenty miles up into the headwaters of Buzzards Bay for bait and then beat back out against the prevailing southwest winds to resume their trip. In what was likely a tactical concession, pound owners decided not to obstruct the Buzzards Bay ban.

But that small victory put new life into the anti-pound movement, and once again, in 1871, more petitions appeared before the Massachusetts General Court. This time, rather than push for a statewide ban, hook fishermen presented what could only be seen as a test case designed to establish some legal precedent for future prohibitions on inshore stationary gear. In the small fishing town of Cotuit, on the south side of Cape Cod, petitioners claimed that a single weir—stretched out across the entire mouth of Waquoit Bay—was destroying the local breeding stock of alewives. Clearly, if there was a case that could be made for destructive effects of pounds and weirs on public fisheries, this was it, and proponents pushed this case to the statehouse in a new attempt to establish some precedent for broader regulation.

When the hearings convened, it was the state inland fish and game commissioner, Theodore Lyman, who this time found himself listening to fishermen arguing over the effects of gear on the fishery. As he later recalled, "The hearing [on the Cotuit petition] proved of the usual kind. None of the petitioners knew much about the weir, but they were sure it was bad, because they got fewer alewives and bass than they used to do, and no scup at all." Not even the defense was well informed. "On the other part, the remonstrants stated that their weir was quite a blessing in disguise, and that it captured only such alewives as did not breed in that neighborhood."[21] Lyman, like Atwood before him, recognized that larger economic stakes were at issue than the survival of a small town's public herring run. He put it quite simply: "The vital matter of *bait* lies at the bottom of the weir question."[22] To highlight the point, Lyman provided an overview of the Provincetown fisheries that would be affected by any ban on pound fishing. These included a "local fishery pursued near the shore to supply the daily market," "the Grand Bank and the Gulf of Saint Lawrence Fishery," and "the George's Bank fishery. The last two are of the greatest importance." To make that point abundantly clear, and to justify why he favored the banks fisheries so heavily over the inshore hook-and-line fishery, he included in his final report statistics from the Provincetown banks fishery, including the amount of clam bait carried, salt used, men employed, cod and halibut caught, men lost, and, curiously, vessels cast away for 1868.[23]

If Atwood saw bait as an immediate economic issue in 1869, Lyman saw it in a larger ideological framework that had defined his tenure as fish and game commissioner. Since the 1850s, Lyman had applied his naturalist education to convert Massachusetts' inshore and inland fisheries into centers for economic growth. As early as 1857, for example, in commenting on stocking trout streams, Lyman had criticized local residents' failure to recognize the commercial potential of inland fisheries: "There are very few instances, where the owners of the lands over which the streams flow, take any pains to preserve or to multiply their stock of fish, or even to claim them as their property." Instead, disorganized and inefficient traditions controlled inland fisheries. "An implied license is given to all persons to fish at their pleasure. Hence the stock of fish is greatly diminished and very few fishes grow to their full size." In this, owners of riparian rights had failed to develop their resources, and a great potential lay wasted. "They are not regarded by their owners as valuable property, and fishing is pursued as a mere pastime."[24]

By 1868, Lyman had come to see the privatization of natural resources as undeniable, as "the march of civilization." But as with all history, according to Lyman, values and conventions needed to change over time, something that had not happened in the case of Massachusetts' inshore fisheries. "But in our march of civilization we have very thoughtlessly trampled under foot a most valuable property, because a vague idea that [it] was game, and, by immemorial right, belonged to anybody and to everybody." Initially, wild game played an important role in supporting a new nation. "In a new country, the first settlers may properly have, not only liberty, but in some things license; license to till land anywhere, to cut wood anywhere, to shoot and trap game anywhere, to catch fish anywhere and in any way." Such free access, however, had only a limited lifespan, according to Lyman. "As population increases, land and wood become PROPERTY, until, as in Tuscany, the one is cultivated by the square rod, and the other as in Paris, is sold by the pound."[25] Thus, Lyman reasoned, as the nation had changed, its laws and conventions regarding natural resource rights needed to as well.

To Lyman, Massachusetts had been swimming against the currents of history. For him, any attempt to preserve open access to resources or to curb the power of private property to transform nature represented artificial, anachronistic, and regressive attempts to restrain the inevitable privatization of natural resources. "At once the members begin to ask whether this [private] control [of common resources] would not abrogate . . . some ancient right of the inhabitants of Harwich Centre to dig one peck of quahogs per man on that particular ground." Not only were these preservation efforts anachronistic: communities attempting to curb history were acting against their acknowledged self-interest. "These same committee-men would not treat a petition for a railroad or a cotton mill in this way, and simply because they *believe* in the success of a railroad or of a mill, but they do not believe in and do not know about the success of fish or oysters." Thus, tradition fostered a false faith in open access that deprived the commonwealth of a valuable industry. "Let our people once clearly understand that these fish and these oysters are real *property*, to be increased and to be raised in value like other property, and there will be no more difficulty about the rights of owners."[26]

Given Lyman's crusade to privatize inland fisheries resources, it came as no surprise when, tasked with responding to Cotuit's petition to ban the Waquoit Bay weir, he saw the hearings as an opportunity manage inshore fisheries on rational grounds that optimized the economic development of an underdeveloped, even hobbled, industry.

To help accomplish his goals, Lyman brought the developing field of fisheries science into the hearings once again. Perhaps responding to criticisms of Atwood's reliance upon Huxley, Lyman decided to undertake his own experiments. He acknowledged that the observations collected through hearings, Rhode Island's reports, and through efforts of Spencer Baird and the U.S. Fish Commission (who had begun investigating the controversy in 1871) were valuable. "But let it be said, once and for all, that this investigation must go on like any other in science. The day is (or ought to be) long past when people will listen to a priori argumentation and attend to the nice weighing of probabilities and guesses." Unlike previous investigations, where fishermen's testimonies best represented the state of the fisheries, the new regime would look to professionally trained naturalists who would settle the issues through "close and protracted observation, and by collecting and comparing historical matter and oral testimony."[27]

Lyman was well equipped to lead such a charge. He had studied directly under Louis Agassiz at Harvard and eventually became one of the original trustees and the treasurer for Agassiz's Museum of Comparative Zoology.[28] With such training and education behind him, Lyman saw at once that the contest over the Waquoit Bay weir required that the ground rules for fisheries management be changed. "The only way to avoid [the costs of lengthy hearings] was to substitute the exact observation of unprejudiced persons for the inconsequent souvenirs of interested witnesses."[29] If Atwood's 1870 hearings undermined inshore fishermen's authority to speak for the fish, the 1871 conflict gave Lyman the chance to put formal, academic natural science in the fishermen's place.

To investigate whether the Waquoit Bay weir was indeed destroying Cotuit's fish run, Lyman leased the weir outright in the spring of 1871 and positioned a "man" to record the catch, weather, and air and water temperatures. These data, Lyman hoped, would help undermine petitioners' arguments and hearsay observations. He soon realized, however, that these numbers could not answer whether the fish caught in the Waquoit weir were those spawning in the rivers or those migrating along the coast. Such questions required additional contextual information, such as when each fish species arrived on the coast, how weirs operated, how fish behaved when encountering a weir, and other conditions that affected the health of the local fishery.

The problem was that, to get this information, Lyman had to turn to the same fishermen he had hoped to remove from the management process. Soon the "inconsequent souvenirs of interested witnesses" came to play increasingly important roles in shaping the opinions of the "unprejudiced persons" investigating claims of environmental disruption. Based on weir fishermen's reports, Lyman concluded that, for a sixty-day season, the 333,855 fish landed were "too large to pass a 2½ inch mesh" at the end of a 1,375-foot-long leader, and therefore remained caught in the weir's bowl. The resulting average of 5,500 fish caught per day did not, however, "represent all the marine travelers" passing by the weir. For all the fish the weir caught, many more escaped: "Many fishes doubtless 'strike back' and refuse to 'lead,' that is to say, instead of following close along the leader and passing into the bowl [of the weir], they retreat from the net, and with a sweep, double the whole weir."[30] Furthermore, and again based on weir fishermen's testimonies, those fish caught in the Waquoit weir could not be those swimming upstream to spawn. "Weir men say of fish that [fish] 'lead' best when passing rapidly towards some distant point; and worst when they are moving slowly or uncertainly." In that case, then, the alewives caught in the weir could not be those seeking to spawn in Waquoit Bay. Rather, fishermen contended that "the alewives taken are chiefly those which are bound for points farther to the northward and eastward; whereas, the schools which enter the streams near a weir [to spawn] proceed with deliberation, and are not led into the trap."[31]

With this questionable premise established, Lyman analyzed his data to conclude that the fish captured in the Waquoit weir, because they were caught in the weir, could not be the same fish that were migrating upstream to spawn. He also compared his own 1871 catch records with those from previous years and from different runs along the southern Cape Cod shore. He concluded that if 1871 was a typical year—an issue he acknowledged needed to be determined—the reasons for any decline in stock size "lie chiefly in the sea," for the spawning alewives were not taken in weirs, and therefore populations were dropping for other reasons.[32]

Lyman went on to argue that two different agents were driving down stocks of fish in Waquoit Bay. The first was a mysterious green ooze that both weir men and hook-and-line fishermen believed killed local fish. The second agent was the sea itself, which to Lyman represented a "teeming workshop, crowded with fabrics torn in pieces ere they are half finished, to be converted into other fabrics which, in turn, are as rapidly destroyed." In this milieu, it was a miracle that any life could survive for long: "The myriad forms of life scarcely take on their embryonic state before they are crushed, and pass, with a power that never dies and never sleeps, into new organisms, which are themselves struck down in the unceasing slaughter. It is a spectacle before which the mind quails!"[33] Given this vision, Lyman's chosen culprit, again bluefish, appeared as the most plausible agent of alewives' destruction. "On the whole, it will be perhaps pretty near the truth to say that, although the bluefish blindly destroys almost everything that comes in his way, his main food is the soft fishes and mollusks, such as menhaden, mackerel, alewives and squid."[34] In the end, Lyman confidently concluded it was the marine environment itself, and not man's use of it, that destroyed Waquoit alewives.

For a man so dedicated to scientific inquiry, Lyman's rhetorical flourishes appear out of place. Even so, Lyman successfully undermined anti-weir petitions and petitioners as effectively as Atwood had the previous year. Drawing conclusions from a single weir, and, acknowledged or not, drawing upon select testimonies he questioned from the beginning, Lyman once again defended the banks fishery's access to bait against a popular movement he saw as hindering statewide progress and economic development. In short, Lyman's conclusions satisfied only those seeking a reason to dismiss the petitions. Drawing on questionable science, questionable data, and offering questionable conclusions, Lyman's work, like Atwood's before, proved sufficient for hook-and-line fishermen's petitions to be dismissed for the time being. Like the previous year, however, hook-and-line fishermen were anything but quelled.

By the time Lyman commenced his studies of the Waquoit Bay weir, the controversy along the southern New England shore had attracted attention in Washington, D.C. Assistant secretary to the Smithsonian Institution Spencer Fullerton Baird had been working in Woods Hole, Massachusetts, in the summer of 1870 when local fishermen began to respond to Atwood's and Brinley's findings. After Lyman failed to effectively settle the matter, Baird began exploring how he, as a naturalist, could more effectively deploy scientific inquiries to put an end to the political controversy.

For Baird the conflict provided an ideal opportunity to demonstrate the benefits that federally funded science offered to help settle disputes with political and economic consequences. Few in Congress were interested, however, in spending federal funds to support work with little immediate practicability. The controversial Wilkes expedition in 1838—which as of 1870 had still failed to yield much more than crates of unlabeled specimens and a history of political rancor—had done little to encourage governmental support for the large-scale natural history work that Baird, Agassiz, and other naturalists believed would greatly benefit American science and industry. After two years of political and social conflict, unaffected by state efforts to solve either the human or the ecological problems, the southern New England fisheries controversy represented to Baird an ideal opportunity to show to Congress that federal funding of natural science research promised important scientific, political, and economic rewards. After a deliberate campaign over the winter of 1870–71 that involved delicate negotiations with congressional leaders, Baird secured permission from the federal government to conduct investigations into the southern New England fisheries conflict in Congress's name.[35]

Congress tasked Baird to investigate four fundamental questions: "first, to determine the facts as to the alleged decrease of the food fishes; secondly, if such a decrease be capable of substantiation to ascertain the causes of the same; and, thirdly, to suggest methods for the restoration of the supply." The fourth question was originally only an ancillary one: "A fourth object incidental to the rest was to work out the problems connected with the physical character of the seas adjacent to the fishing localities, and the natural history of the inhabitants of the water, whether vertebrate or invertebrate, and the associated vegetable life; as also to make copious and exhaustive collections of specimens, for the purpose of enriching the national museum at Washington."[36]

Arriving in Woods Hole in June 1871, Baird went to work investigating allegations along a wide front. With federal blessing, Baird called upon the help of academic colleagues from Yale, Brown, the Boston Society of Natural History, Tabor College (Iowa), and the Botanic Garden at Cambridge to undertake an investigation of not just the commercial species, but of what his team hoped would be the entire coastal environment. While his colleagues collected marine plants and animals, dredged bottom sediments, and analyzed plankton and algae, Baird, like Brinley, Atwood, and Lyman before him, traveled along the coast collecting testimonies. To ensure accuracy, Baird brought along a professional "phonographer" named Henry E. Rockwell, who used new voice-recording technology to document as accurately as possible people's testimonies. In the course of the summer, Baird held meetings with those interested in the inquiry, including "nearly all the leading fishermen, both line-men and trappers," as well as fish dealers who sent fish to New York and Boston markets. In addition, Baird elicited testimonies from "gentlemen of literary ability and research," such as weir-supporter and owner J. M. K. Southwick from Newport, and hook-fisherman supporter and New Bedford fish dealer George H. Palmer.[37]

First and foremost, Baird listened as scared people desperately sought to change the course of events destroying their livelihoods. One Hyannis petition, for example, presented the conflict as much a moral as an economic issue, which in both cases bore ominous consequences. This group called the legislature to task, begging "your honorable body to become interested in making laws to regulate the fishing business." If bans on weirs were impossible, then "at least regulate the fisheries, so as to secure to the fishermen a compensation for the toil and danger accompanying their business." For these fishermen, this was a battle between the virtuous workingman and the evils of excessive wealth. "We contend that the rich man's dollar, while he is asleep, should not be allowed to catch all the fish, while our lines, which are well baited and tended, find no fish to bite at them. We contend we can put as many and better fish into the markets where fish are sold than are sold in those markets [supplied by pounds, weirs, and traps]." The proof of this lay in the wasteful destruction witnessed in weirs during each spring spawning run:

> If any of you doubt it, let him visit the places [fished by pounds, weirs, and traps] where fish are induced to go and deposit their eggs. You will find fish taken in such quantities that, after taking care of all they can, the balance are thrown onto farmers' wagons that stand waiting to take them away to dress the land; catching as many fish at one time as it would take to supply all the markets for months; destroying hundreds of what would become fish where one fish is taken.

Ultimately, the Hyannis group argued that humble fishermen, as better stewards of resources, produced better fish, less waste, and provided more benefits to the larger community. This was as it should be. But pounds, weirs, and traps were changing that pattern in ways that violated moral as well as economic principles. "Shall the rich man's dollar be allowed to drive us from our home and all that is sacred to us in memory? Must we look on, and see the rich man's dollar rob our children of bread and clothing?" Should the state persist in ignoring appeals, the petitioners implied, small fishermen could not be held accountable for the destructive consequences of unrestrained capital development.[38]

As Baird took testimony along the coast, he saw firsthand how an academic question of natural history carried economic, political, social, and cultural significance for those tied to the fishery. The fates of whole communities rested in the health of the inshore waters, and as those people faced hardship and dislocation, they were willing to do what was necessary, for better or worse, to improve their lots. If Baird had previously viewed the southern New England fisheries controversy as an opportunity to secure federal support for marine science, his travels along the coast during the summer of 1871 showed him that the controversy concerned people's well-being, too.

In the end, Baird found the testimonies impassioned, emotional, and, as had Atwood and Lyman before, often contradictory. "Many of these persons eagerly embraced the opportunity to tell their story of alleged wrongs, to urge various means for their redress, or else to claim the possession of certain inherent rights which it were rank injustice to deprive them of." Baird developed very different conclusions from Lyman and Atwood, however. By the time he had finished his interviews and research, Baird found that both the scientific surveys and the experiences of all fishermen along the shore formed a consensus on at least one point. "I have no hesitation in stating that the fact of an alarming decrease of the shore-fisheries has been thoroughly established by my own investigations [and] by evidence of those whose testimony was taken upon this subject." Baird made this conclusion on two temporal scales. First, referring back to early European descriptions of the abundance of the southern New England fisheries, Baird could see that there were certainly far fewer fish than what the first Europeans described. More recently, Baird also found, things were getting even worse. "The evidence of the fishermen . . . and of others familiar with the subject . . . goes to prove that the decrease has continued in an alarmingly rapid ratio during the last fifteen or twenty years, or even less."[39]

Baird was, in fact, working with very different assumptions from those of Atwood and Lyman before him. Where the latter two had looked exclusively to Huxley's conclusions in 1866, Baird also considered the criticisms that Huxley's work had received, as well as the contradictory findings by other fisheries scientists who believed that human action could indeed affect fish stocks in the open oceans. In 1854, for example, John Cleghorn (who coined the term "over fishing") concluded at the British Association for the Advancement of Science that British smacks were indeed fishing down herring stocks.[40] Furthermore, during the 1870s, another British scientist, Ray Lankester, was developing his opposition to Huxley's notion of the inexhaustibility of marine stocks, which he would present in 1883 at the Great International Fisheries Exhibition in London. Thus, while Atwood and Lyman relied solely upon Huxley, Baird drew upon a number of other theories concerning humans' ability to affect natural systems.

Academic disputes aside, Baird recognized that the real issue was larger than stock sizes alone and included the social and economic consequences surrounding the health of the fishery. "If the scarcity of the fish be due to their going off into deep waters of the ocean, it is, of course, of very little moment to the fisherman that they are as abundant in the sea as ever, if they do not come upon such grounds as will permit their being taken by his lines or nets." And Baird was no follower of Huxley in this regard; for the Smithsonian's assistant secretary, man had, and had manifested, a distinct ability to affect the abundance of the ocean. As a result, it simply would not do to ignore changes in fish populations—and hence ignore calls for gear regulations—because of a theoretical abundance in another area. Rather, investigations into the fishery must also include the tremendous human costs of fisheries decline, for fishermen and their communities were suffering along with the fish. Prophetically, Baird warned that

> at the present time [shore fishing] is cut-off to a great degree from [fishermen] in many places on the Massachusetts coast, where, as on Nantucket, Martha's Vineyard, and elsewhere, the deprivation from the loss of profits by fishing is being most seriously felt. The result, of course, of the inability to make a living in this manner is to drive the fishermen to other occupations, and especially to induce them to leave the State for other fields of industry. In consequence the population is reduced, and the community feels this drain of some of its best material in many ways. Furthermore, property depreciates in value, farms and houses are abandoned, the average taxation is increased, and many other evils, readily suggesting themselves, are developed.

Where Lyman and Atwood dismissed fishermen's observations, and hence the fishermen themselves, from the management process, Baird recognized that fishermen, in their own way, were also part of this world and that their social and economic concerns, like their observations, could not be simply dismissed.

As much as Baird may have wanted to help the small fishermen, however, the political pressures surrounding his investigations would come to make that impossible. As a scientist blessed with congressional support, Baird needed to prove that publicly sanctioned science could provide answers where traditional methods had failed. Thus, Baird could not ignore or dismiss Atwood's and Lyman's earlier investigations.[41] To do so would throw into doubt how useful formal scientific inquiries indeed could be. At the same time, any recommendations he presented would need to be approved by the states, and to get that approval, Baird would have to win the support of state fisheries managers. In Massachusetts' case, Lyman and Atwood had intimate ties to the banks fisheries agents eager to see weir fishing expand. Consequently, when Baird issued his findings in a report published in 1873, he needed to walk a fine line between disagreeing with colleagues, preserving the region's fisheries, and justifying federal scientific support.

To walk that line, he very carefully explained why he presented findings different from those of the Massachusetts contingent. Unlike previous fisheries scientists, Baird recognized that fish abundances could fluctuate regionally. Stock declines were not "felt uniformly over the entire coast, but in certain regions the complaint in regard to it is universal." Where Atwood and Lyman argued that perceived declines were caused by fish moving to different areas—a belief supported by Huxley in 1866—Baird drew upon human evidence to supply information unobtainable from the fish themselves: "It is difficult to point out any locality where, near the shores in the New England States, at least, under the most favorable view of the case, the fish are quite as plentiful as they were some years ago." To further prove his point, Baird presented a more sophisticated understanding of fishery performance. He conceded that Atwood and Lyman were correct in their earlier claims that previously stable catch rates suggested unaffected fish populations. Baird also argued, however, that more efficient traps and pounds could be masking declining productivity. "The scarcity referred to is better shown by the great difficulty experienced by line-fishermen on grounds where they were formerly able to catch all they needed for their own use and sale."[42]

Why regional stocks declined also represented a very delicate issue. Again, Baird was torn between offering explanations that were scientifically grounded and those that were politically acceptable. And here, Baird gave something back to Lyman, Atwood, and their weir-fishing constituents by supporting their findings that bluefish were causing much of the decline. "No one who has spent a season on this coast . . . can fail to have been struck with [blue-fish's] enormous voracity, and the amount of destructiveness which it causes among other kinds of fish." However, for a man whom contemporaries saw as reserved, empirically driven, and restrained, he embraced uncharacteristically dramatic language supporting the bluefish thesis, suggesting perhaps that he was not convinced of its merits:[43]

> The fish seems to live only to destroy, and is constantly employed in pursuing and chopping up whatever it can master. As some one has said, it is an animated chopping machine. Sometimes among a school of herring or menhaden thousands of bluefish will be seen, biting off the tail of one and then another, destroying ten times as many fish as they really need for food, and leaving in their track the surface of the water colored with the blood and fragments of the mangled fish. . . . No other seacoast than that of the Atlantic border of the United States can show . . . so destructive a scourge as the bluefish.[44]

Subsequent discussions that he held with Lyman in October 1871 also suggest that Baird was uneasy with this thesis. During a meeting that also included the Rhode Island fish commissioner and a Rhode Island congressman, Baird awkwardly compared the roles of humans and bluefish in the marine environment, granting them equal roles as predators. "There is a certain balance of fish, there being plenty to feed all these fish scavengers [in Vineyard Sound], and to feed mankind also. Now, if you bring in the bluefish, they disturb this balance; they take scup, sea-bass &c., that should be permitted to spawn. . . . Then having disturbed the balance to that extent, we come in with our traps and reduce the number of spawning fish and of spawn still further; and where the bluefish destroy many, we destroy even more."[45]

Baird's isolation of bluefish from all other species of fish seems odd. Yet given the political implications of blaming humans, such statements make sense. Baird may have made a calculated decision to balance science, politics, and economics. Weir fishing, with all its supporters, would not likely be banned, but restraining it was essential in order to defuse the political controversy that had inflamed the region for two years. If blaming the bluefish would ensure that Massachusetts and Rhode Island agents would support Baird's proposed policies, then so be it.[46]

Consequently, Baird's recommendations represented a compromise between what his research told him the ecosystem needed, what the fishermen
alongshore said they needed, and what would be found acceptable among
weir fishermen and state agents. First, while banning weirs may have seemed
the simplest approach, the economics and politics of the situation would not
allow it. "I am not prepared to advocate the abolition of traps and pounds, as
without them it would be extremely difficult to furnish the fish in sufficient
quantities to meet the present and increasing demand of the country." That
demand came not only from increasing numbers of urban workers who relied
upon cheap fish for their daily meals, but also from the banks fleets, which
would suffer without access to weir-caught bait. Nor was Baird prepared to
ban weir fishing during the spawning season, despite the potential of fixed
gear to take spawning fish. Baird's position was not in line with Lyman's,
however, which argued that traps did not take spawning fish. Instead, Baird
cited the simple economics: "It is consequence of the profits made during
that time that the fishermen are enabled to meet their expenses, and very few
would put down and maintain their traps for the summer-fishing [for food
fish] alone." Ultimately, Baird recommended closing traps and pounds from
Fridays at six in the evening to Mondays at six in the morning during the six
weeks of the spawning period. This, Baird believed, would not only preserve
stocks of fish, but also preserve prices fishermen realized at dealers.

After his 1871 and 1872 investigations, Baird and his colleagues published
their findings in 1873 in what would become the first of a series of annual reports of the U.S. fish commissioner. The final report ran over nine hundred
pages and included diagrams, plates, maps, and transcriptions of testimonies
and communications. Of those nine hundred pages, over six hundred were
dedicated to the scientific research conducted by the various naturalists who
came to Woods Hole during the two-year study. The remaining third focused
on the observations, pleadings, legal opinions, testimonials, and historical
sources relating to the southern New England fisheries. For its time, the report
was a masterly, thorough document, reflecting Baird's empirical conservatism
for both natural and human sources of information. Ultimately, however, Baird
came to the same conclusion that small fishermen had argued for years: "The
reduction in the cod and other fisheries, so as to become practically a failure, is
due to the decrease off our coast in the quantity, primarily, of alewives."[47]

Facing powerful interests in the banks fishery and from fisheries managers
like Atwood and Lyman, Baird proposed only modest regulatory changes—

and certainly not a ban on stationary fishing like the one that died in session in Rhode Island in 1869. In the draft legislation he presented to fisheries managers in Massachusetts and Rhode Island, Baird called for only three minor limits on the inshore bait industry: stationary operations should be licensed; licensees should be required to submit annually catch records for the previous season; and between April 20 and June 15 of every year, stationary gear should not be allowed to take fish between Friday evening and Monday morning. For the trap fishermen, these proposed regulations posed more headaches than hardships. Traditionally, traps tended to be left open on Sundays when no fishermen came to clear them.[48] Furthermore, trap fishermen who testified to Baird in 1871 largely accepted the idea of limiting takes during the spawning season. Mandatory annual catch records represented the most inconvenient element of the new regulatory system, and even these could be rounded, guessed at, or reconstructed from sales records of some sort—or, as would more often be the case, ignored.[49] Ultimately, Baird's recommendations gave something to everyone: small fishermen could claim a victory in forcing through some limits to trapping. Weir men, on the other hand, could operate more or less as they had before.

Looking back, Theodore Lyman saw the 1871 investigations as the culminating event in a decades-long struggle to centralize and streamline fisheries management. With new regulations that were adopted by Massachusetts after Baird's report, the waste and inefficiencies brought into the process by local tradition and local involvement were replaced by systematic, efficient, and forward-thinking management. As Lyman stated in the 1878 report of the Massachusetts Commissioners of Inland Fisheries, "At every session of the Legislature thousands of dollars' worth of time is consumed in committee-hearings and public discussions of ill-considered local laws for the limitation of fishing." Triumphantly, Lyman declared that science, and in particular his own research at Waquoit (he made no mention of Baird's work), provided the best foundation for fisheries management. "This experiment, which cost a few hundred dollars, gave more solid information than has come from all the legislative hearings during the past ten years; it did more than any hearing ever did, in this, that it *settled* one or two points."[50] Now, with local opinions marginalized, managers could simply collect the data "that give a certain basis for just laws which shall aid and encourage the fishermen instead of fettering and annoying him." Brushing aside the local traditions that sought to maintain the long-term health of local resources, Lyman instead institutionalized the commercial expediency that had emerged as coastal communities cashed in on inshore fisheries, a model that would form the foundation for fisheries management until at least the 1990s: "The problem [for fisheries management is] *How many fish may be taken and leave enough for seed?* The solution of this problem is deemed the most important that can be undertaken by the Commissioners."[51]

By 1872, Baird had defused hook fishermen's protests over weir fishing without closing the weir fishery and denying banks fleets and fertilizer factories their much-needed industrial inputs. Baird did little to preserve stocks of fish, but his success in quelling the dispute, in addition to securing federal funding for large-scale scientific research, also firmly replaced fishermen with fisheries scientists in fisheries management. For, indeed, while the dispute did not end after 1872, hook fishermen never again mounted as organized or effective a resistance to weir fishing—or any other highly capitalized fishing—for the rest of the nineteenth century. Arguments over weir and pound fishing would resurface beginning in the 1880s. Subsequent protests, however, took on very different characteristics from those mounted by inshore hook-and-line fishermen fighting to keep their fish, livelihoods, and communities alive.

Baird's report also served to complete a process begun by Atwood, the result of which would alienate communities from their local resources in ways that would prove disastrous. With the final removal of local fishermen from the management process, and their replacement by industrial interests, along with the scientists that supported those interests, Cape Cod's fish and small fishermen had become abstractions. That is, they were relegated to mere inputs in a larger industry, inputs whose individual natures had no place in influencing the decisions that affected them. As for the fish, the establishment of industry- and science-based management after 1871 meant that they would become mere numbers in a larger balance sheet of marine environmental production. The small fishermen would face a similar fate, as their knowledge and skills were undermined by expanding weirs and by pound owners who cared little for what fishermen knew of the local coastline, only for the labor they provided. Here, too, individuals were rendered abstractions, in what proved to be an ominous series of changes.

CHAPTER 6

Removals

*In view of the precarious nature of fishing as a means for the support of families,
I ask that the investigation of the Bureau of Labor be conducted with the desire to
ascertain how far the functions of the State can be exercised in the aid of the people
in the reclamation and adaptation of land for the ends herein set forth.*
—Edward H. Rogers, to the Massachusetts Bureau of Statistics of Labor, 1896

*Best of all, at the seaside resorts of Massachusetts one is among a nautical people—
old "salts" or amateur sailors from childhood—who know how to set a sail, handle
the oars, or steer a craft from a skiff to a skipper, with that ease and certainty that
can only come from the most thorough knowledge and a long experience.*
—Oramel Senter, "Civic and Scenic New England," *Potter's American Monthly*
(August 1877)

The investigations from 1870 to 1872 revealed that some fisheries scientists,
unlike local hook-and-line fishermen, envisioned Cape Cod's coastlines not as
the familiar and long-harvested resource whose management kept Cape Cod
communities alive, but rather as an extension of a boundless, ever-abundant
ocean capable of sustaining unlimited human exploitation. Following these
scientists' findings, others, too, came to the Cape seeking marine abundance.
By replacing local knowledge with academic training, and in turn successfully arguing that weirs could have no effect upon the ocean's bounty, Theodore Lyman and Nathaniel Atwood, and unwittingly Spencer Fullerton
Baird himself, removed the last barrier to the full-scale exploitation of Cape
Cod's inshore marine resources. Without the small fishermen to speak for
the long-term health of inshore fish stocks, and with the enactment of Baird's
recommendations providing the appearance of restrained fishing, there was

simply no reason for Cape residents to limit the number of their weirs supplying fish and bait to expanding markets. Consequently, Cape Cod's shore fisheries expanded dramatically and in doing so fundamentally changed the coastal environment for fish and fishermen alike.

In the aftermath of this removal of fish, and ultimately people, from Cape Cod shores, the region was transformed, once again, in ways almost as dramatic as its transformation from a wasteland to a workspace. As Cape fish stocks declined, and as fishing families fled, a new group of people came to Cape Cod to make it their own. After 1880, writers, authors, and painters, catering to a growing population of middle-class urban residents seeking escape from industrial cities, began to call attention to Cape Cod as a place where weary industrial man could reconnect with a pristine and powerful nature. Yet to accomplish this feat, those producing new visions of the Cape faced the ironic necessity of recasting Cape Cod's fishing past, its industrial fishing present, and the social consequences of ecological decline in ways that would appeal to tourists and vacationers looking to escape from their own problems in urban communities. How writers, artists, and tourist promoters met this challenge by the 1890s added one more chapter to this story of removals, but one with ominous and long-lasting consequences.

Baird's 1872 report and his awkward meeting with state fish and game commissioners allowed pound fishing to expand along the southern New England coast. With weekend pound closings providing the semblance of regulation, and with claims of inexhaustible marine bounty established by Lyman and Atwood, Cape pound owners multiplied the number of operating installations. From the thirty-three tallied by Baird in 1871 along the Cape Cod and Martha's Vineyard coasts, by 1878 there were fifty-two. Fourteen of these sat along the fourteen-mile shore from Brewster to Lieutenant Island, just south of Wellfleet. Another eleven were clustered in the shallow waters between Harwich and the southern point of Monomoy Island. In addition to the fifty-two on Cape Cod, fourteen more lined the mainland shore of Buzzards Bay, with six on the three-mile western shore of Sconticut Neck.[1]

By 1885, Cape Cod supported eighty-two pounds and weirs, representing just under $133,000 in invested capital. In that year, fifty-two installations operated in Chatham, Provincetown, Truro, and Eastham alone. The forty-eight weirs that lined the roughly thirty miles of coast from Brewster to

Provincetown averaged about one installation (with its eight-hundred-yard leader) every mile and a half.[2]

In 1895 the total count of Cape weirs rose to over ninety. Had Thoreau sought solitude in the mid-1890s on the same shores he walked forty years earlier, he would have run across, on average, one weir every half mile.[3]

In fact, after 1872 weir fishing represented one of the few bright spots in Cape Cod's fishing economy. The last third of the nineteenth century witnessed challenges across all of Cape Cod's fishing industries. Just as the banks fisheries had fueled the economic growth of Cape communities before the Civil War, those fisheries' subsequent decline pulled down the same communities. For the whole Cape, investment in the fisheries dropped from $1.9 million to $690,000 just between 1885 and 1895. The value of fishing products also declined, from $1.2 million to $748,000, during the same period.[4] Where once almost every town hosted both banks and inshore fisheries, changes in the shore-side organization of the banks fishery drove Cape Cod's deepwater fleet away from its towns. These changes on shore reflected the developments that had allowed Cape towns to compete in the fisheries in the first place—rail connections, access to markets, cheaper outfitting and refitting supplies. But now it was Boston and Gloucester that expanded on these initial advantages to become New England's fishing centers. And while vessels remained owned by Cape Cod investors, vessel business was increasingly pulled to those ports, where auction houses, better ice and refrigeration facilities, and a concentration of buyers and business contacts all helped lure banks schooners away from small fishing towns and consolidate the fleet.[5]

Changing conditions on the banks themselves also contributed to the departure of Cape-owned schooners for larger ports on the mainland. Recent studies have shown that, even on the offshore banks, late nineteenth-century fishermen faced declining stocks of cod, halibut, and other prized commercial fish.[6] In the face of such ecological and market challenges, fishermen and vessel owners built larger schooners, adding speed and capacity in order to better find and catch increasingly fewer and smaller fish. And as banks schooners grew in size, they simply became too big to enter Cape Cod's small, shallow harbors. The few larger harbors on the Cape, such as Chatham and Provincetown, did retain some of their fleets and even managed to attract those from neighboring ports. But even in Chatham, increased silt deposition and shifting sands choked the mouth of the harbor, further accelerating the consolidation of banks fishing in Gloucester and Boston.[7] Consequently, by the 1890s, with the exception of Provincetown, most of Cape Cod's large banks schooners had shifted to mainland ports, taking fishermen, outfitters, and most of fishing's ancillary industries with them.

In contrast, inshore pound fishermen thrived once the debates over the effect of their gear had been put to rest. Now permitted to operate without fear of recrimination and under less-than-effective limits, pound owners landed increasing numbers of alewives, menhaden, mackerel, scup, and other inshore species. Because alewives were almost always caught inshore, landings for these fish paint a clear picture of the dramatic increase in inshore fishing pressure.[8] In 1875 Massachusetts decennial census investigators reported that Barnstable County inshore fishermen landed 460,000 individual alewives and 553 barrels of herring. Conservatively estimating that each barrel held 300 fish, the 1875 catch totaled about 625,900 fish.[9] Ten years later, fishermen landed 4.6 million individual alewives and herring. In 1895 Barnstable County produced over 11,642 barrels of salt and fresh alewives, along with 35,418 barrels of salt and fresh herring. These catches totaled, conservatively, roughly 14.1 million individual fish. In just two decades, the reported catch of alewives and herring increased over 2,200 percent.

The significance of this growth was made clear by bait fishing's changing prominence within the larger fishing industry itself. When the U.S. Fish Commission took a census of all American fishing industries in 1889, Cape Cod's bait and inshore fishery had grown to sufficient stature that census takers considered bait fishing a separate and distinct fishery. The new U.S. fish commissioner, Marshall MacDonald, further reported that "Barnstable County occupies a very prominent position in the shore fisheries, for, of the 3,748 shore fishermen in the State, no less than 1,840 are credited to that county."[10] And those fishermen were busy. In 1889 the shore fishery as a whole landed a total of 7.3 million pounds of alewives and herring for use as food or fertilizer. Of those, pounds took just over 5 million pounds (almost 70 percent), with the rest taken by dip nets, gill nets, and seines. In addition, the now administratively distinct bait fishery took another 5.4 million pounds of herring and alewives in its total catch of 6.1 million pounds. Pound landings accounted for 90 percent of this total. Assuming each fish to weigh about three-quarters of a pound, the combined 12.8 million pounds of alewives and herring represented about 17 million individual fish taken in weirs alone.[11]

With such monumental catches continuing into the foreseeable future, on the surface at least, Cape Cod pound fishing appeared to be one of the few strong sectors in an otherwise declining industry.

Closer study of pound net landings, however, suggests a very different story. While overall landings continued to rise over the last third of the nineteenth century, catch records submitted to the Massachusetts Commissioners of Inland Fisheries between 1879 and 1886, and data collected by the U.S. Fish Commission between 1885 and 1905, reveal that these apparent increases masked declining efficiencies in pound nets' ability to land the bait and food species that hook fishermen were most concerned about in 1872.[12] Because not every installation owner submitted catch records, and numbers of records submitted varied from year to year, comparisons of total landings are difficult to determine. To make some comparisons, however, marine ecologists use a calculation called "catch per unit of effort," or CPUE, to measure relative catch as an indicator of abundance over space and time. CPUE figures derived from records submitted between 1879 and 1886 indicate that Cape Cod pounds caught fewer fish per unit of effort as the period progressed, indicating fewer fish in the local population. For the bait fish alewives and menhaden, the downward trend was momentarily interrupted by a strong run of the latter fish in 1883 (Fig. 6.1). Aside from that, however, the average annual number of baitfish caught by each shore operation fell during this period from between twenty thousand and forty thousand between 1879 and 1882 to just over ten thousand from 1884 to 1886.

Again, the 1883 menhaden event distorts these figures. In 1881, 1882, and between 1884 and 1886, pounds recorded widely varied landings that offered, on the one hand, low catch rates ranging from 276 fish per weir annually to 5,831. On the other hand, in 1879, 1880, and 1883, landings rose by orders of magnitude as weir men on average hauled in just under 300,000 fish per run in 1879, 1.2 million in 1880, and 2.9 million in 1883.

Separating menhaden landings from alewife landings, however, provides a clearer image of more regular changes in the fisheries, one that reveals a more consistent decline in Cape Cod alewife landings (Fig. 6.2). On the surface, alewife catch rates appeared relatively stable, for annual catch-per-weir figures held between roughly 8,000 fish per weir to around 19,000 for the whole period.

Behind these countywide figures, however, lies a very different story. A vast majority of the reported alewife catch on Cape Cod was taken by Har-

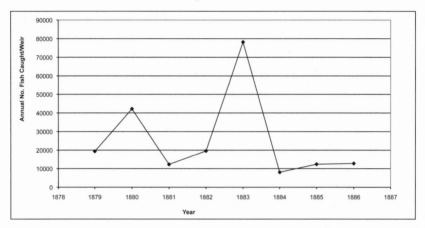

FIG. 6.1 Annual average baitfish catch per weir, Barnstable County, 1879–86. Massachusetts Commissioners of Inland Fisheries, *Annual Report of the Commissioners of Inland Fisheries* (Boston, 1880–87)

wich and Chatham pounds, whose positions on Cape Cod's southeast corner better allowed them to take congregated schools of fish headed out Pollock Rip Channel. These installations typically landed about half, and sometime as much as 90 percent, of all the alewives reported as landed for the whole Cape (Table 6.1).

While the rest of Barnstable County's pounds landed between 10,000 and

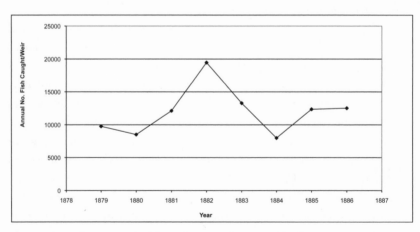

FIG. 6.2 Annual average alewife catch per weir, Barnstable County, 1879–86. Massachusetts Commissioners of Inland Fisheries, *Annual Report of the Commissioners of Inland Fisheries* (Boston, 1880–87)

Table 6.1

Alewife Catch, Barnstable County, 1879–86, with Chatham and Harwich Catch Proportions

	All Barnstable County		Chatham		Harwich		All Other Barnstable County	
Year	No. fish	Annual percent	No. fish	Annual percent	No. fish	Annual percent	No. fish	Annual percent
1879	302,524	100	172,405	57	56,220	19	73,899	24
1880	306,635	100	59,566	19	179,637	59	67,432	22
1881	436,213	100	282,922	65	48,363	11	104,928	24
1882	837,087	100	511,844	61	77,585	9	247,658	30
1883	597,903	100	307,749	51	45,789	8	244,365	41
1884	375,845	100	320,836	85	20,054	5	34,955	9
1885	345,981	100	101,422	29	24,206	7	220,353	64
1886	288,020	100	149,677	52	4,764	2	133,579	46

Source: Massachusetts Commissioners of Inland Fisheries, *Annual Report of the Commissioners of Inland Fisheries* (Boston, 1880–87).

20,000 fish per pound over the entire period, Harwich and Chatham experienced a marked drop in their alewife catch rates after 1880, just when the weir fishery seemed in the middle of its rapid expansion (Fig 6.3). Harwich operations, for example, annually took just over 44,000 alewives per pound in 1880; after that, annual catch rates fell appreciably, bottoming out at about 4,700 fish per pound by 1886. Chatham nets saw the same decline: after a high of over 100,000 alewives taken annually per pound in 1882, catch rates fell consistently, to under 20,000 in 1885 before rebounding somewhat to around 30,000 by 1886.

Declining catch rates suggest that fewer menhaden and alewives were coming inshore. Whether that represented a decline in the total population or just that the fish were elsewhere remains unknown. What was not unknown, however, was that as fewer alewives and menhaden came inshore, fewer larger food-fish species came inshore as well. If declining Barnstable County pound landings suggested declining stocks of baitfish running inshore, the recorded catches of food-fish species followed a much clearer downward trend. Annual landings per pound net of bluefish, tautog, squeteague, scup, and striped bass all fell appreciably for the period in question, from a high of around 25,000 fish per weir in 1881 to a low of just over 5,000 fish per weir in 1885 and back up to just over 10,000 fish per weir in 1886 (Fig 6.4).

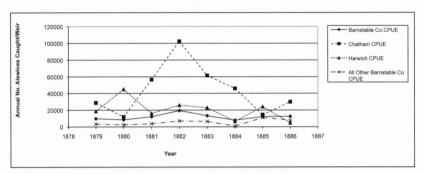

FIG. 6.3 Annual alewife catch per unit of effort (CPUE, in number of fish caught per weir), all Barnstable County, Chatham, and Harwich, 1879–86. Massachusetts Commissioners of Inland Fisheries, *Annual Report of the Commissioners of Inland Fisheries* (Boston, 1880–87)

Broken down by species, the story is even more dramatic. Scup catch rates fell from a high of almost 20,000 fish per weir per year to about 10,000; bluefish from 9,000 to almost nothing; and the remaining food fish appeared so infrequently that no major landings were registered (Fig 6.5).

Expanded weir operations allowed humans, perhaps for the first time, to effectively compete against other marine animals for small fish found inshore. Pound men on Cape Cod targeted the same highly abundant, highly migratory, and small-size fish, such as alewives and menhaden, that larger, "food

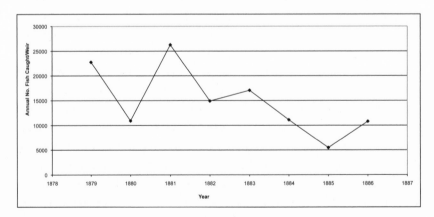

FIG. 6.4 Annual average "food fish" catch per weir, Barnstable County, 1879–86. Massachusetts Commissioners of Inland Fisheries, *Annual Report of the Commissioners of Inland Fisheries* (Boston, 1880–87)

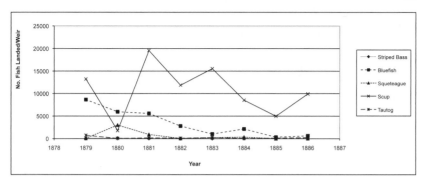

FIG. 6.5 Annual "food fish" caught per weir, by species, Barnstable County, 1879–86. Massachusetts Commissioners of Inland Fisheries, *Annual Report of the Commissioners of Inland Fisheries* (Boston, 1880–87)

fish" species most commonly ate as prey. For marine ecologists, alewives and menhaden represent two species of "forage fish" that serve as food for larger predators in the marine environment. As such, these fish, whether termed "bait" or "forage," play an important ecological role. By feeding upon detritus, plankton, and small shrimps and crabs, these fish transfer energy from the base of the food web to species further up. In other words, these fish, by serving as a conduit through which the sun's energy gets passed from single-celled animals to top-level predators, were a significant reason why Cape Cod enjoyed such abundant fisheries in the first place.

To better identify how changing fishing patterns affected the inshore ecosystem—and how that ecosystem in turn affected the fishermen—we have to borrow some more analytical concepts from marine ecology. Marine ecologists assign each species in a food web a numerical value—called a trophic level—that ranks it on an energy-transfer scale ranging from the smallest marine organism—phytoplankton—to top-level marine predators, such as whales, dolphins, tunas, and humans. These values are relative, to be clear, but despite this, comparing values between species within an ecosystem does allow ecologists to better understand how fish species relate to a wider web of predators and prey. While this sounds simple and clear, it is anything but. Nonetheless, such studies have allowed marine ecologists to develop better conceptual understandings of how fishing for one species affects the prospects of all the others. Trophic-level calculations place menhaden and alewives lower in the food web than those fish hook-and-line fishermen took as food (Table 6.2). For example, alewives and blue-black herring, which sit on the trophic scale between 3.5 and 3.6, feed upon species at levels 2.2 and higher and carry that energy offshore to be taken up by larger predators.[13] Menhaden occupy an even lower position. Like alewives, these fish feed on detritus and plankton and therefore play an even more critical role in transferring energy from deeper down the food web up to higher levels.

"Food fish" species tend to sit higher up the trophic web. Mackerel, squeteague (weakfish), scup, striped bass, and bluefish all occupy positions above 3.7 and feed on trophic levels 2.8 and higher.[14] Therefore, the "food fish" Cape Cod people relied upon the same smaller fish for sustenance that weir fishermen were taking out of the inshore ecosystem in such vast quantities for bait. And as more pounds took more bait, pound net catches detailed above suggest that food-fish species went elsewhere—away from all Cape Cod's inshore fishermen—to feed.

Other data further suggest that localized changes in the inshore ecosystem continued through the nineteenth century and into the twentieth. Pound net landing data collected by U.S. Fish Commission naturalist Vinal Edwards between 1885 and 1895 and between 1905 and 1915 indicate that Woods Hole–area operations experienced declines in catch efficiency similar to those on the Cape a decade previous (Table 6.3).[15] Beginning in 1885, Edwards traveled to nets in and around Woods Hole to record daily catches. For the first year Edwards reported catches as the fishermen described them, using common fish names and reporting quantities in units used by the commercial fishery—so many buckets of alewives, so many barrels of scup, etc. That ceased after 1885, when it appears that Fish Commission agents in Washington needed numbers of fish, not estimated volumes, and they needed more accurate names for species than the common names Edwards supplied. Thus, in 1886 Edwards reported not only the numbers of individual fish (with whole-number estimates for very large catches from two hundred to over one hundred thousand fish), but also the common and the scientific name for each species reported. He submitted these figures, along with the date the net was hauled, its owner, and its approximate location, to the Fish Commission every month that pound nets operated—roughly from April to November.

Edwards's reports, when analyzed using modern marine ecological tools, present another picture of how Cape Cod's inshore marine animal communities changed around Woods Hole when weir fishing expanded. Again, one

Table 6.2
Trophic Levels and Food Consumption Rates for Select Species*

"Bait species"	Trophic level	Diet trophic level range
Menhaden		
(*Brevoortia tyrannus*)	2.3	2.2–2.79
Alewife		
(*Alosa pseudoharengus*)	3.5	2.2–2.79
Blue-black herring		
(*Alosa aestivalis*)	3.6	2.8+
Mackerel		
(*Scomber scombrus*)	3.7	2.8+
"Food fish"		
Tautog		
(*Tautoga onitis*)	3.3	2.8+
Squeteague or weakfish		
(*Cynoscion regalis*)	3.8**	2.8+
Scup		
(*Stenotomous chrysops*)	3.9	2.8+
Bluefish		
(*Pomatomous saltatrix*)	4.5	2.8+

*These estimates are derived from default values taken from FishBase.org and are not appropriate for every population.
**Based on an 1882 study of the Acushnet River population diets, squeteague also were placed at trophic level 4.1.

way to see possible changes is to compare changing CPUE rates over time. For the Woods Hole pound, daily catch-per-haul calculations offer the most striking results. Between 1886 and 1895, and from 1907 to 1914, these figures reveal a marked decline in alewife, menhaden, scup, tautog, and sea bass—the same species in hook fishermen's complaints in 1872.

Except for mackerel, pound fishermen saw their catches of most of the small forage fish—including alewives and menhaden—decline dramatically. Alewife catches fell by a third, from 136 per haul to about 51. Menhaden suffered similarly: 108 to 70. Fishermen also watched their average landings of some food fish decline. Scup landings fell from an average of over 2,200 per haul to just under 200—over 91 percent. Sea bass dropped from 12 to 6 per haul, and tautog fell from 12 to 2. While numbers of mackerel and bluefish landed rose, those increases pale by comparison to the dramatic declines fishermen saw in other species they were more concerned about.

Table 6.3

Catch and Catch per Haul Figures, Woods Hole Area Traps, 1886–95, 1898, and 1907–14

Species landed	Daily catch/haul 1886–95 (2,108 hauls)	Total catch 1886–95	Daily catch/haul 1907–14 (1,068 hauls)	Total catch 1907–14	Percent change in catch/haul
Menhaden	108.3	228,308	69.9	74,622	35.5
Alewives	136.0	286,655	50.8	54,284	62.6
Mackerel	56.1	118,341	219.0	233,878	290.1
Scup	2,264.0	4,772,602	192.5	205,608	91.5
Tautog	12.0	25,358	2.1	2,293	82.2
Squeteague	21.6	45,561	50.2	53,633	132.3
Sea bass	11.7	24,737	5.6	5,963	52.4
Bluefish	3.2	6,642	15.0	15,997	375.4

Source: "List of Fish Taken in Fish Traps & Pounds," 1885–1914, Vinal Edwards Manuscript Collection, RG 370, Records of National Oceanic and Atmospheric Administration, Box 8: Monthly Fish Reports, NRAB-99-33, National Archives and Records Administration, Waltham, Mass.

All these catch-rate comparisons indicate that across the Cape, pound nets experienced marked declines in the numbers of fish they landed. For pound men, such declines were likely invisible, given the vast quantities of fish they landed. For hook-and-line fishermen, however, who took fish a few at a time, the ecological response to intensified weir fishing added an ecological squeeze to an already unbearable economic one. If pound nets were not destroying breeding stocks of fish, as hook-and-line fishermen contended, they were certainly disrupting the availability of food fish along the coast.

For hook-and-line fishermen, these ecological responses to human fishing activities had disastrous repercussions, as consequences of expanded pound fishing affected local economies and ecologies alike. Studies of ecosystem change rarely consider more than the changing circumstances for different species of fish. But as every fisherman's economic prospects were linked directly to the value of marine organic material in the marketplace, fishermen and their communities were as closely tied to the health of the inshore marine ecosystem as were marine animals. In short, pound nets, by taking more inshore fish, and making them scarcer in the ocean and cheaper in the market, affected fishermen and their families and communities almost as much as they affected populations of fish themselves.

Most significantly, pounds and declining inshore stocks fundamentally changed the labor of fishing. Despite the fact that more fish were landed than ever before, such catches were taken by fewer and fewer fishermen, who worked on very different terms from the inshore fishermen who had supplied local markets until the 1860s. First and foremost, pounds glutted local markets with cheap fish. Frederick True, in writing his report of the Atlantic pound-net fisheries for George Brown Goode in 1887, commented, "Few forms of fishery apparatus are more effective in gathering in all kinds of fish . . . than the great pound-nets of Massachusetts. Hook-and-line fishers, and even the majority of seine fisheries, do not compare with the pound fisheries in the magnitude of their results."[16] Fish landed on the outer Cape were either shipped to New York by smack or taken to the railhead at Dennisport for icing and export. With a terminus at Woods Hole after 1871, fish caught in Vineyard Sound and Buzzards Bay joined the rivers of fish streaming into cities far from Cape Cod's shores. With so much fish, caught so cheaply, moving through so many Cape Cod towns, by the 1880s there was simply no way for an independent hook-and-line fisherman to earn enough on his own hook to provide for his family.

As collapsing fish prices squeezed hook-and-line fishermen out of the fishery, expanded pound fishing offered some options for relief, provided fishermen were willing to accept fundamental changes. True reported that "while most forms of [fishing] apparatus imply very considerable skill in the fisherman, the pound-net requires none. It operates by constant peculiarities of tides and fishes, which remain in force whether the fishermen be awake or asleep."[17] While this may be an extreme statement—situating and setting up traps required considerable skills and local ecological knowledge—True correctly diagnosed that this capital-intensive technology changed the relationships between labor and capital in the fisheries.

> In the larger companies . . . the number of stockholders is often not less than ten or twelve, and the majority do not take an active part in the real work of the company, but simply invest their money here as they would do in any enterprise. . . . In favorable years the investment is a profitable one. The more impecunious fishermen look with envy upon the wealthy weir owners, and many regard them as at once the destroyers of their financial prosperity and of the fishes from which it derived.[18]

Clearing pound nets was a relatively simple, if physically demanding, process. Shoveling fish from a shore pound into a horse cart simply required more brawn and less brains than fishing on one's own hook. While this meant that fishermen could live by a more regular routine, it also meant that pound fishing concentrated the profits, management, and direction into the hands of a relative few, who then employed only a few more to work the rig. For operations on the north side of Cape Cod, for example, four to five men owned the net, who then paid wages to two or three others to clear and maintain it during the summerlong season, and hired another to act as bookkeeper. On the south side, companies targeted more remote waters. As a result, each pound required a base camp and a crew of ten to twelve, along with two cooks and a bookkeeper. Generally, pound fishermen earned wages, and not shares as in the banks fishery. According to True, these wages amounted to about fifty dollars a month on Cape Cod.[19] Wages did protect fishermen from the notoriously variable earnings of a notoriously variable fishery. Wage work on pound nets, however, also fully excluded fishermen from both management decisions and any prospects for windfall earnings. As pound fishing began to employ the hook-and-line fishermen squeezed out of local inshore fisheries, it did so under new rules, new expectations, and new values that marginalized the skills and sweat equity of a fishing crew.

Again, however, it was the ecological effects of pound fishing that really undercut hook-and-line fishermen. Simply put, pounds made it more difficult for hook-and-line fishermen to find the fish on which they subsisted—let alone sold. With banks fishing and independent inshore fishing waning, True was forced to report that the time when a hardworking fishermen could support his family was drawing to an end: "While the vessel fishery has forever disappeared from many of the towns [along the Cape], the weir fishery has taken its place to a considerable extent. We may, however, with the old fisherman, look somewhat regretfully upon a change which has taken the profits of labor from the many and bestowed them upon the few."[20]

Ecological responses to increased removals of alewives and other forage fish imposed upon independent hook-and-line fishermen a dire choice: either remain in one's home and among one's family and struggle against ecology and economy to make ends meet, or abandon home and homestead and leave the Cape for better opportunities elsewhere—be that out west, or just across Buzzards Bay in the growing industrial cities of Fall River and New Bedford. For many Cape Codders, leaving the Cape represented the better option. Between 1865 and 1895 the Cape Cod population dropped from 34,610 to 27,654—more than 20 percent. While Provincetown gained population from the consolidation of what fishing remained, most former centers of fishing—both inshore and banks fishing—lost heavily. During this period, Eastham, for example, despite its growing numbers of pounds, lost over 37 percent of its population. Chatham, long one of the Cape's most active fishing ports, lost over 31 percent. Harwich, next door, shed over 28 percent. Wellfleet, once a center of the highly profitable and well-respected mackerel fishery, suffered the most: the failure of that fishery by 1895 forced nearly 58 percent of the town's residents—1,328 of 2,296 people—to leave.[21] If pound fishing made the economics of inshore hook-and-line fishing untenable, its ecological consequences undermined the fisheries that had long allowed Cape people to at least subsist.

As a response to changing ecologies, then, the emigration of Cape Cod's hook-and-line fishermen was in its way as logical as the changing migration patterns of the food fish on which they had once relied.

By 1895, the effects of Cape Cod's declining fisheries finally attracted the attention of state legislators. At the behest of former Cape resident Charles H. Rogers and supported by the Episcopalian Brotherhood of the Carpenter, the Massachusetts legislature tasked the state's Bureau of Statistics of Labor to investigate the allegation that Cape Cod's decline was driven by an influx of Portuguese immigrants. Conducted between 1895 and 1896, and despite nativist fears of the influx of un-American immigrants, the investigations found that actually only about 11 percent of Cape Cod's population came from the major fishing nations of Canada, Britain, and Portugal (and its colony, the Azores). Furthermore, and much to the consternation of the anti-immigrationists calling for the study, the Portuguese fishing families on the Cape actually represented one of the few instances of successful fishing. "Here [on Cape Cod] there is opportunity [for Portuguese immigrants]; and industry, with the frugality to which they are accustomed, meets an adequate reward. The abandoned lands upon Cape Cod, cheap, near the shore, and near the point of arrival, give them a foothold far superior to that at home, notwithstanding the differences of climate; and there is employment in the fisheries."[22]

Despite the alleged adaptability and resourcefulness of Portuguese immigrants, however, Cape Cod still suffered from an overall decline in the fisheries that hit the local population and the local economy hard. Even in towns such as Provincetown, the state investigators found evidence of decline. There, the community once claimed a variety of fisheries besides the banks cod fishery: mackerel catchers, small boats supplying the fresh-fish market, whaling. These fisheries in turn supported a variety of other industries that processed, packaged, and shipped catches, or that built, maintained, and repaired vessels. These support industries themselves employed numerous skilled workers, each of whom spread the wealth of the fisheries throughout the town. That wealth was now disappearing. "Now, in place of all this activity, we find the fleets absent, the wharves fast going to decay, and two of the three marine railways rotting and falling down; the third, recently sold for taxes, must eventually share the same fate. . . . The failure of fishing firms has caused the loss of much capital, resulting in depriving many of employment."[23]

For inshore hook-and-line fishermen, the situation was worse. "The numerous small boats, which have furnished so large a number of native-born men, now find their opportunity gone." At least part of the blame was attributed to an all-too-familiar source. "This year and the last have been failures [for the inshore mackerel run]. This is attributed to the use of fish traps, as large quantities of small fish are destroyed every year. These traps line the shores so thickly that no fish escape."[24]

Edwards H. Rogers, a shipbuilder and longtime resident of the outer Cape, explained one tie between marine animal communities and human communities most clearly. Addressing the Massachusetts Bureau of Statistics of Labor in 1896, Rogers highlighted the human consequences of marine resource decline in terms of simple cause and effect. For him, "The main cause [for the decline of the mackerel fishery] is to be found in the desertion of our coast by this shy fish. . . ." The effect was indirect, but clear to him: To maintain catches in the face of declining local stocks, the mackerel fishermen had had to turn to purse seines. These large, bulky, but more efficient nets had been adopted beginning in the 1850s in a shift that also fundamentally changed fishing and who could be part of the process. "With the introduction of [purse] seines, the opportunity for the employment of boys in mackerel catching ceased. The spreading and management of nets . . . require the skill and strength of men; boys are useless in such circumstances, and this fact has contributed powerfully to the exodus of youths from the Cape to the mainland."[25]

If in the late 1860s Charles Nordhoff could paint a love story of a Cape girl torn between two fishing brothers with promising futures, a generation later those brothers would have little chance to marry that belle of Cape Cod. As

Rogers explained, failing fisheries even changed marriage patterns in Cape Cod communities. "The favor of young women, and, indeed, of their parents, in respect to marriage, was extended much more freely to landsmen than to fishermen or sailors. . . . It has become evident that the dangers of the coast fishery far outweighed the precarious advantages of the calling, and the eyes of young women, as well as the young men, were sharply directed toward every avenue which opened a way of escape from its awful exposure."[26] Rogers's testimony revealed that weirs were not only restructuring communities of fish along Cape Cod shores, but also restructuring communities of fishermen.

In a series of accounts, the report's other findings also illustrated how Cape towns, in their efforts to survive, turned to other marine resources as the fin fisheries collapsed. In Brewster, "What little fishing remains now consists mostly of quahaugs." Barnstable, too, had to shift over to marine animals further down the food web: "There is very little fishing in this town, although there is some considerable oyster and shell fishing carried on at Cotuit." In Orleans, fishing was so bad that residents resorted to harvesting marine plants: "A new industry has spring up, that of collecting seaweed for the purpose of making paper . . . used [as wall insulation] in the building industry." Certainly, regional fish populations were not as low as they would be a century later. Locally, however, when facing declining local stocks of food fish, Cape Cod fishermen turned to lower-order organisms to keep money coming in.[27]

Ultimately, investigators' findings showed that collapsed fisheries forced people to abandon lands, homes, industries, and communities. In Yarmouth, for example, "There is very little fishing owing to there being no good harbor. A great deal of real estate is owned by non-residents who keep their houses closed the year round."[28] Furthermore, what little immigration Cape Cod experienced represented a result of a larger outmigration: "The comparative cheapness of real estate, due to the departure of the original inhabitants, [is] making it easy [for Portuguese, Irish, and English immigrants] to establish homes."[29] By 1895, Cape Cod land had become so cheap that investigators reported that some legislators had alluded to "the possibility of aiding the unemployed or needy work-people in the State to take up unoccupied land on the Cape, or land that has been abandoned as to cultivation, on account of the death or removal of former residents."[30]

Between 1872 and the end of the nineteenth century, Baird's findings, and the loose state regulations that were enacted afterward, facilitated the removal of both fish and fishermen from Cape Cod. Once the hook-and-line fishermen were removed from management decisions, pound owners found themselves absolved from any responsibility for declines in inshore stocks of fish. Without the need to answer for their actions to local communities, and free to expand and grow as much as they wished, pound owners took full advantage of the favorable regulatory climate to sweep as many fish as they could from Cape Cod's inshore waters. In doing so, they also swept fishermen and their families away. This represented more than an economic transformation, however. Even with falling market prices, as long as hook-and-line fishermen could still find fish on which to subsist, as their predecessors had for generations, they would not have to abandon homes, property, and communities. But ecological consequences of expanded stationary net fishing made even subsistence a more difficult prospect. And in the end, hook-and-line fishermen were forced by both economics and ecology to leave Cape Cod.

Only occasional visitors traveled to Cape Cod before the Civil War. What few that did visit came on angling trips, for religious retreats, or more typically to pass through en route to the more popular island vacation spots developing on Martha's Vineyard and Nantucket.[31] Cape Cod did not have the novel industrial developments that attracted visitors to areas in upstate New York, it did not have the social cachet of a resort like Newport, nor, finally, did it offer many amenities to attract tourists.[32] Simply put, Cape Cod's fishing industry effectively insulated Cape communities from tourism for the first two-thirds of the nineteenth century. It did this in two ways. First, before 1870, fishing provided a stable-enough income for families to get by without opening their homes to boarders. Secondly, fishing represented nothing new: while images of vibrant fishing ports carried important allegorical symbolism to viewers before the Civil War, the industry was still smelly, dirty, and omnipresent along the New England shore. Therefore, fishing in and of itself held nothing worth seeing for East Coast urban residents seeking an escape from similar smells and sights in the cities. As a result, for most of the century so few tourists were attracted to Cape Cod that no major tourist hotels were built there before the 1870s.[33] Supported by thriving fisheries, both inshore and off, Cape residents simply did not have much reason to accommodate tourists, who themselves had little reason to come.

After 1872, however, that changed. As fishing failed, and as families faced harder economic times, local residents had to choose to stay or go. Many left. Into the void they created stepped tourists, who could take advantage of the easy rail connections to Boston and New York. After 1872, more and more summer resort communities opened for business. The first was established in 1872 in Falmouth Heights sitting on a bluff overlooking one of the pound nets Vinal Edwards routinely visited. Immediately following, other resort communities opened in Hyannisport, Wianno, and Osterville, effectively announcing that tourist interest in the Cape was there to stay.[34] Those tourists who wished to summer regularly on Cape Cod, however, also took advantage of the collapsing land prices that were driven down by fishing families fleeing the economic and ecological bind they faced. Fishing families' homes were soon purchased on the cheap by wealthier urban vacationers and turned into quaint summer cottages. Thus, as fishermen fled the Cape, they were replaced by tourists who redefined Cape Cod, its coastlines, and its working past.

Such a dramatic transformation did not happen immediately. Guidebooks and gazetteers reveal that initially, tourist writers highlighted Cape Codders' tenacity and success in pulling wealth from the sea, as much as they promoted the area's climate and convenience. An 1870 *Advocate of Peace* article, for example, claimed that Provincetown certainly offered urban dwellers "a relief to escape from the prolonged heat of the city, where the wall of brick and granite intercept the ocean breezes[,] and enjoy the invigoration of salt-water air." Far from depicting a seaside resort, however, the authors were struck by the scale and prosperity of a community with little useful land at its disposal. "It is sustained by the fishing business including that of whaling. . . . Provincetown, however, does not depend upon the land but the ocean to sustain it. . . . It is a place of wealth and intelligence."[35]

A work published four years later by Elias Nason also highlighted Barnstable County's unmistakable ties to the fisheries. In his *Gazetteer of the State of Massachusetts*, Nason described the region's increasing number of tourist accommodations. But after reviewing the tourist hotels and attractions, Nason went on to include the natural resources and products of each town's major industries. In describing Dennis, for example, Nason noted how both traditional fishing industries and the town's appeal to tourists profitably combined. "By the last State Report, 48 vessels, with 722 men, were employed in the cod and mackerel fisheries, and the capital invested was $117,000. . . . The amount of alewives, shad, bass, and bluefish, taken here, is very large; and thus, with its income from land and sea, together with its railroad-accommodation and its healthful ocean-breezes, Dennis may be set down as a very prosperous and happy town."[36]

In an 1877 two-part feature article appearing in *Potter's American Monthly*, Oramel Senter invited his readers to see that Cape Cod's very underdevelopment made it a more attractive option to Newport: "Here one can enjoy the purest ocean breezes, the best bathing facilities, and any amount of healthful recreation, at the very minimum of expense, an important consideration in these times . . . of financial asphyxia."[37] Easily tied to Boston and New York by rail, and hosting a climate desirable among many urban dwellers, "the Cape Cod region embraced all the seaside resorts that we could visit in the allotted time, and more than we could describe within the limits of a single article." In addition to its financial advantages, Cape Cod offered visitors a view of a unique working past that only added to the region's appeal. "As a whole, you look at this part of Massachusetts and wonder how it ever became settled, and how the people live who are still there. . . . As a comment upon this, we state the fact that the day we reached Provincetown, two of her fishermen caught a thousand bluefish, worth a round hundred dollars." Like visitors before the war, Senter could claim that "everywhere in our travels on 'The Cape' we saw thrift, intelligence, and a cheerful content remarkable for the times, and nowhere did we meet a single case of begging or drunkenness." To Senter, much of this continued prosperity and civility derived from ocean resources, for, "To the inhabitants of Cape Cod, the ocean is their granary, their meat-barrel, and their money-chest."

But the area was changing, as increasingly tourism elbowed its way into Cape Cod's fishing economy. After arriving at night in Provincetown, Senter wrote, "Judge to our surprise when the morning light revealed to us, instead of a few fishermen's huts, as we supposed it would, a large place—a solid and noble town, built among the sand-hills . . . abounding in fine stores, good houses—some of them elegant—and the whole place having an air of comfort and prosperity in marked contrast with many communities surrounded by far greater natural advantages." In truth, Cape Cod's working coasts and working people were adapting to new economic trends that brought in more money through tourism than from fishing. "Every part of this coast, we say, is dotted more or less continuously with seaside resorts, hamlets, hotels, and fishermen's huts or far-houses, where one can enjoy the sports and sanitary benefits of the ocean to his heart's content." Nor were tourism and fishing (or at least seafaring) mutually exclusive. As Senter's account reveals, and as was made explicit in his passage that opened this chapter, tourists were drawn to Cape Cod's natural beauty, its communities' rural distinctiveness, and to the unique opportunities for recreation such combinations offered.[38] After all, where else could you hire a sailboat for a day, and along with it enjoy the services of a veteran mariner? In short, before 1880, fishermen and tourists could share the beach for work and play, even as both visions of the Cape were undergoing dramatic redefinition.

By the early 1880s, however, those uses were coming into conflict. As pounds popped up along every stretch of beach, they made it increasingly difficult for anyone to envision the Cape as pristine nature. In response, artists and writers began to recast earlier visions of Cape Cod's natural, social, and economic distinctiveness. In articles and in artworks, writers and artists coming to southern New England's coastal regions began removing—through omission, erasure, or downright censorship—any signs of the expanding pound fishery lining Cape Cod's shores, in attempts to accommodate their prospective clients' desires to experience pristine nature. For example, writing for the *Century Illustrated Magazine* in 1883, author F. Mitchell encouraged readers to see the Cape not as a place where admirable people earned a living from a unique combination of land and sea resources; instead, he saw the Cape as untouched nature, where a sublimely powerful sea was kept at bay by beaches and dunes that sheltered a bucolic interior. "With all the grandeur of wildness that has seized upon a great part of the outer coast, from Provincetown to Chatham, speaking in every line of storms, of surf, of wrecks, of bodies heaved up by the sea, a quiet inland beauty nestles still in the shelter of Cape Cod." To see Mitchell's vision of Cape Cod's "wildness," however, the reader needed to erase all signs of the Cape's working people:

> Shut your eyes to the sand-hills, to all the neglected acres white with daisies or gay with golden rod; clothe the seventy miles of curving peninsula, except the broad salt-marshes, with forest trees; think of the numberless bays and ponds and streams that light up the country still; picture here and there an Indian clearing, a cluster of wigwams, and a sachem with his followers; fill the woods with deer and wolves and foxes, and you see Cape Cod as it lay on that November morning when the plunge of the Mayflower's anchor broke the stillness.

Mitchell's illustrations furthered the idea of Cape Cod as a wild place bypassed by modern life. Labeled as "Wellfleet Ancient Wharves," "An Old

Inhabitant," "Old Hallett House," and "The Old Mill" (twice: once portrayed from a railroad car), these images helped the reader see Cape Cod as
an area that once had been vital and alive with energy and industry but that
now, with the exception of a few places, lay quiet, its people gone, leaving
only relics and artifacts. More than just a reflection upon old-timers following
old ways, Mitchell's account avoided contemporary fisheries almost altogether. Only twice did he invoke them, and then only to entertain the reader
with local color. The first time, Mitchell retold a story of a retired fishing
captain correcting a grammar-book illustration of a mackerel fishing vessel.
In the second instance, Mitchell commented upon how local home decor
reflected a familiarity with the sea. For Mitchell's readers, Cape Cod's fisheries were past, leaving behind quaint and piquant relics of former glory, and
Cape Cod fishermen were almost completely absent, replaced by empty nature or quaint rustics who found shelter in Cape Cod's wild womb. In short,
Cape Cod's tranquility was as timeless and insulated from humanity as
the sea that surrounded it. "While this current of city visitors disturbs to
some extent the natural charm of simplicity of the villages, still the people of
the Cape, already familiar with the outside world, are not disturbed as most
communities would be." Ultimately, "although in landscape this region has
nothing like the richness of the Beverly shore, it has, nevertheless, not a little
rural beauty with a wild, peculiar charm that is all its own."[39]

Mitchell's artwork falls into a genre that used images of a lost past to ap-
pease viewers' nostalgia for a perceived prewar innocence. Following the
Civil War, many Americans yearned to return to more-rural existences in response to the social and moral aftermath of the Civil War and as industrialization redefined community relationships in cities and towns. Through a
network of publishing outlets and popular images—magazines, stories, and
artwork appearing across American culture—authors such as Mitchell responded to those cravings by creating images of New England as a national
"memory bank," where bygone and idyllic rural lives could be found again,
often as part of tourist travel.[40] In response, people looked to images of New
England farming and fishing as fading bastions against the tides of social
change.[41] Pieces like Mitchell's satisfied these emotional desires for an idealized past, however, only at the expense of the working present. Fishermen,
fishing communities, the reality of expanding pound operations, and the
social and economic consequences of expanded shore fishing all had to be
erased if representations of Cape Cod were to meet the emotional needs of

prospective buyers and clients. Thus, in appealing to the romantic yearnings of tourists, writers and painters sanitized—or worse, simply ignored—the hard realities of the ecological, social, and economic changes that laid the foundations for Cape Cod's tourist industry in the first place.

The need to erase coastal fishing and all its consequences becomes even clearer in artistic representations of the southern New England shore following the Civil War. Nineteenth-century art and the nascent tourist industry shared common roots in America. Many nineteenth-century artists seeking the sublime beauty of nature brought images of majestic vistas back to wealthy urban patrons, who in turn traveled to see those sights for themselves.[42] American painters helped popularize vacation spots in such areas as Niagara Falls, the Adirondacks, the White Mountains, and along the Maine coast. The southern New England shore had pockets of similar appeal: Newport attracted armies of tourists every summer who enjoyed viewing or even purchasing the painted scenes that either reminded them of a pleasant vacation or inspired them to travel to areas of distinct natural beauty.

Artists' portrayals of the southern New England shore produced after the Civil War were far different from those painted before, however. Instead of producing the pastoral images celebrating the harmonious union of human labor and abundant natural resources, postwar painters tried to portray nature as nature itself, and in ways that emphasized light and atmosphere more than didactic relationships between humans and nature. Labeled by scholars "luminism," paintings exploring the effects of light and ambience began attracting popular interest before the Civil War. Indeed, Fitz Henry Lane's work, while celebrating coastal New England's workspaces, also received acclaim for its representation of light and atmosphere. After 1865, however, painters focused more exclusively upon light as nature itself. While this marked a dramatic new direction for American art, it also had a tremendous impact upon how people envisioned the coastlines. As painters paid more attention to nature—one that excluded humanity—their canvases increasingly omitted the human energy, activity, and industry that had been such important subjects in the 1830s, 1840s, and 1850s. As Barbara Novak has argued, "In contrast to the operatic landscapes, luminism . . . discovered, possibly in Dutch painting, structural epigones which it then transformed. In this transformation, the myth of a pristine nature could be recovered convincingly. It was largely recovered, not so much in the new West as in New England."[43] As painters concentrating on southern New England seascapes began excluding human elements—be they fishermen, mariners, shipwrecks, or lighthouses—they also omitted from popular view the fundamental changes shaping that stretch of coast. In doing so, they not only turned people's attention to light and atmosphere, but also erased from larger view social and economic change and all its consequences. If Cape Cod's coasts underwent fundamental economic and ecological change following the Civil War, most people outside Cape Cod did not see any signs of it, nor did they want to.

Works by the popular and acclaimed painters John Frederick Kensett, Thomas Worthington Whittredge, and Martin Johnson Heade best exemplify how changes in American aesthetic tastes erased signs of southern New England's ecological decline and attendant social dislocation. The first thing that set these painters apart from southern New England prewar pastoralists was that none of them had the personal ties to working waterfront communities that had inspired their predecessors. To them, the ports and coasts served only as a place to play out new artistic techniques. Martin Johnson Heade, for example, was born in Bucks County, Pennsylvania, and began painting portraits and genre scenes before moving to New York in 1858. There he established a modest reputation as a landscapist, and he painted his first seascape in 1859. While some of his earliest works included allegorical fishermen—for example in *Approaching Thunder Storm* (1859)—by the early 1860s he had turned to symbolic suggestions of human presence, such as a barrel, distant sails, or abandoned boats. By the 1870s, when he enjoyed significant critical acclaim, though not necessarily from the artistic community, his marine paintings of southern New England and Long Island Sound highlighted the region's natural beauty itself and were almost devoid of any anecdotal human figures.[44]

If Heade's depopulated paintings of the coast enjoyed popular attention in the 1860s, so too did a contemporary whose work gained more widespread acclaim. John Frederick Kensett was born in Cheshire, Connecticut, and developed his artistic talents through engraving. After training in Europe and painting mountain landscapes in the 1840s and '50s, Kensett turned to seascapes around 1859.[45] To develop his signature treatment of light and atmosphere, he de-emphasized human activity and removed human elements to focus the viewer's attention on the ambience of nature itself. This calculus is best revealed though a series of three studies of Beacon Rock, Rhode Island, that Kensett painted between 1855 and 1864.[46] In the first rendition, *Entrance to Newport Harbor* (1855), Kensett included small fishermen and lapping waves to give energy and action to the scene. Toward the left of the canvas, a small fishing boat with two or three fishermen works the inshore waters, as smaller sails in the distance likely represent other people doing the same. In the 1857 version, *Beacon Rock, Newport Harbor*, Kensett slowed the energy down considerably. Waves lap more lazily on the shore, and the small inshore fishing boat is replaced with a single, solitary angler dipping his line into the calm waters. He also removed the two smallest sailboats, substituting instead a single, more distant vessel. Finally, in *Marine off Big Rock* (1864), Kensett produced a picture of absolute calm and devoid of any immediate human presence: no waves lap the shore, and the single sailing vessel, offering only a contrasting splash of white against the gray and blue horizon line, minimizes any human presence in the painting.[47]

Combined, these three works demonstrate that in refining his technique with light, Kensett erased the fishermen, focusing instead on painting an empty seascape he felt was more desirable to larger audiences. His subsequent seascapes continued to omit people working along the coast. Neither *Newport Coast* (1865–70) nor *On the Beverly Coast* (1863) contained any human figures. In his 1869 paintings *Coast at Newport* and *Coast Scene with Figures*, Kensett did bring people back to the shore, but then only as tourists. In his last summer's work—that of 1872—Kensett produced a series of scenes that highlighted his mastery of light and atmosphere and that for many art historians represents the culmination of his life's work and style. In producing these studies of nature and ambience, however, Kensett chose to exclude all human beings from the canvas—workers and tourists alike (Fig 6.6). If Kensett's 1872 studies reveal a master of luminism at work, they also represent the establishment of a new cultural vision of the coast as a place devoid of people, including the fishermen who were increasingly working on the same shores.[48]

Thomas Worthington Whittredge's painted coast scenes similarly erased fishermen and any signs of their presence. Like Kensett, Whittredge was born inland—in Ohio—and studied art formally through extended travels in Europe. He moved to New York in 1859, where he continued painting landscapes, and traveled west with Albert Bierstadt in the 1860s. By the 1870s he was in Newport, where, like his other luminist colleagues, he painted beach scenes in which people, if present at all, were there to reconnect with nature. This appears most clearly in his *Second Beach at Newport* (1878–80), where he decided to include people walking along the beach in contemplative relax-

FIG. 6.6 John Frederick Kensett, *Eaton's Neck* (1872). Gift of Thomas Kensett, 1874. The Metropolitan Museum of Art, New York. Image © The Metropolitan Museum of Art / Art Resource, New York

ation (Fig 6.7). From the greenery and the prominent rock formation, called Bishop's Seat, in the background, it is clear that Whittredge made his sketches during the spring or summer months while sitting on the western end of the beach. If this is true, then according to Rhode Island Fish and Game reports, Whittredge would have seen far more than just solitary figures strolling along the surf. Based upon an 1880 map of fish trap and pound locations for the 1870s, and upon Frederick True's 1887 report that Rhode Island fishermen kept gear working all summer, at least one, and possibly two, pounds nets or traps would have cluttered Whittredge's view on the eastern end of the beach.[49]

The canvas Whittredge ultimately produced reflected one of two conscious decisions: he either chose to simply omit the gear from his final work, or he framed the painting in such a way as to leave out the poles and netting that would have come onshore. In either event, *Second Beach at Newport* reflected his deliberate decision to create an image of the coast cleansed of human industry and commercial development. Like Kensett and Heade before him, Whittredge was interested not in reproducing a portrait of humanity's commercial relationship to the sea, but rather one revealing a pristine, imagined nature nurturing symbolic figures walking along the shore.

Certainly not all seascape painters omitted fishermen from their views. Many works produced after the 1870s included figures working alongshore. Those artists depicting coastal workers in their art, however, had roots among earlier painters with direct ties to working coasts. Robert Swain Gifford, dis-

FIG. 6.7 Thomas Worthington Whittredge, *Second Beach, Newport* (c. 1878–80).
Bowdoin College Museum of Art. Museum purchase, Florence C. Quinby Fund, in memory
of Henry Cole Quinby, Honorary Degree, 1916

cussed earlier, continued to produce coastal working scenes in paint and later
in etchings until his death in 1905. Similarly, a boatbuilder's son named Lemuel Eldred, who studied under William Bradford, painted coastal scenes that
gained him national recognition through the National Academy of Design.
Finally, Albert Bierstadt, between trips out west, also produced works that
explored people's working relationship with the coastal environment, such
as his *Fishing Station, Watch Hill, Rhode Island*, which featured a shore
menhaden seine drying on a net spool on the beach. But these represented
older forms typically produced by artists from a previous generation and
working in older styles. For the most part, new aesthetic tastes favored artists
who re-imagined the southern New England coast—and people's relationship to it—as one more piece of pristine American nature where humanity
could rebuild intimate ties to the natural world.

    This shift in aesthetics helped redefine the southern New England shore
from a workspace to a tourist destination. By omitting fishing gear and fishermen from the beaches, artists, like their literary colleagues, created images of
the coast as untouched and pristine that consciously ignored the almost omnipresent evidence of large-scale fishing. For a growing number of middle-class

urban dwellers, these images promised a place where, if they had the means, they could escape social pressures of the city and reconnect with the power and beauty of the natural world. But such representations emerged at the same time that inshore weirs and pounds proliferated along the coast and consequently challenged writers' and painters' visions. In order to create for viewers the impression that Cape Cod was a place where modern people could commune with nature, all evidence of changing fisheries and eroding fishing communities had to be omitted.

The tension between coast as workspace and as pristine wilderness appeared in more explicit forms than just changing aesthetic tastes, however. In Massachusetts courtrooms in the 1880s and 1890s, tourists and resort owners battled with their fishing neighbors as both sides sought to legally establish whose vision of the Cape Cod shore—tourists' or fishermen's—would define fisheries management issues. Beginning in 1887, debates over the effects of weir fishing reemerged with renewed vigor, and once again they landed fishermen in courtrooms to testify over fish abundances and behavior. The questions remained the same as in the 1872 investigations, and weir men again found themselves on the defensive. This time, however, their opponents were not fellow working fishermen. Instead, anglers and sportsmen championed the campaign to end weir fishing and defended the rights of recreational fishermen to enjoy the bounty of the coastal wilderness. These hearings revealed not only how much Cape Cod's communities had changed since the 1870s, but also how far the Cape had already been converted into a resort area that favored recreation over industrial development.

Even after the conclusion of Spencer Baird's investigations in 1872, petitions calling for bans on weirs and pounds continued to arrive at the statehouse throughout the 1870s and 1880s.[50] While anti-weir advocates pushed this legislative agenda, local authorities in towns lining Buzzards Bay jointly agreed to refuse to issue weir licenses. By 1886, anti-weir proponents felt they had accumulated enough support and new evidence to again attempt to establish a statewide ban.

On February 3, fish merchant George H. Palmer renewed the attack on weirs, traps, pounds, seines, and other nets in testimony presented before the state commissioners of fisheries.[51] Palmer launched a two-pronged offensive. First, he attacked the 1870–72 findings, highlighting Lyman and Atwood's inconsistencies and their railroading of the proceedings. He also noted the expansion of weir fishing, and introduced updated catch data and more sophisticated interpretations to support claims of fisheries decline. Palmer argued, "Knowing as we do of the fecundity of fish, we should naturally suppose that, unless interfered with in an unusual way, the number of fish and their size would be almost the same year by year." Following the reasoning of those fisheries scientists who rejected Huxley's conclusions of inexhaustible fish stocks, Palmer argued that "reasoning forwards, we should say that whatever hinders or prevents the natural increase of fish would tend to exhaustion. Reasoning backwards, if we find fishes of any genera becoming annually scarcer, we should say that something had occurred to prevent their natural increase."[52] Furthermore, Palmer contended that simple presence and absence of important species was not the same as historical abundances: "It is not enough that a few straggling specimens be found feeding upon the shoals and around rocks. They only serve to call bitterly to mind the days when we *used* to go a fishing, and the great store of fish which we *used* to catch. They only remind us of the glory which once was, and the wretched means which have caused it to depart."[53] This was a bold position, one that not only challenged pound fishermen's early assertions of authority, but also questioned the scientific premise of inexhaustible fish populations.

Armed with such a critique of the 1870–72 investigations, Palmer recognized, however, that data and new interpretations alone would not win the day. The second prong of his attack linked local weir fishing to larger concerns gripping the entire nation. Drawing upon Rhode Island citizens' rights to free fishing—which played a prominent role in both the Rhode Island and the Massachusetts hearings in the 1870s—Palmer argued that weir fishing represented a monopoly. "No sufficient means can be assigned why a few men with an extensive apparatus should be permitted to absorb the common wealth of the sea."[54] As such, weir fishing represented a political, social, and even moral affront.

Palmer was no reincarnation of the hook-and-line fishermen from the 1870s, however. Rather, he represented sportsmen and anglers who came to Cape Cod seeking the relaxation, rejuvenation, and adventure that recreational fishing promised. "It is no answer to say, even if it were true, which it is not, that the traps will furnish [fish] cheaper than the hook-and-line. We prefer to catch them ourselves. We like the excitement which it produces, and the health of the body and mind it ensures." Like other middle-class recreationists in the late nineteenth century, Palmer and his supporters saw fishing as an encounter with wilderness that bolstered mind, body, and masculinity.[55] By taking all the local fish, weirs threatened to alienate anglers from the positive moral and physical benefits, as well as from the recreational pleasures, that fishing offered to modern men. "The weary day, the longing expectation, the disappointment, the wet jacket, the empty basket, and the hungry stomach; these are what are left to us, while the trap is overflowing to him for whom the sea was forced to yield up its treasures, while he was sleeping in his bed."[56]

Weir fishermen were well-prepared to fend off this new effort, however. They had learned from their rearguard action in the 1870s to have resources at the ready for when another fight developed. Through the 1870s and into the 1880s, weir fishermen united across state lines and enlisted financial and political support from southern New England businessmen tied to the weir fishery. At the center of this movement stood Pacific Guano Company chemist and fishing weir investor Azariah F. Crowell, who by the 1880s had emerged as an organizing figure within the weir-fishing community. In 1886, as pressures mounted for a renewed assault on fish weirs, Crowell began calling upon regional weir fishermen to fund their defense. Weir men from around the region responded. Moses Rogers, from Noank, Connecticut, wrote Crowell, "Yours of the 14 instant at hand . . . [;] please find the amount enclosed as payment for the pounds as statement in your letter[; I] hope the question will be decided favorably to the fishermen."[57] Similarly, Charles C. Chuck, of New Bedford, rallied weir men from across Buzzards Bay to Crowell's cause. "I will raise what money I can from the Cuttyhunk traps," he reported after identifying the owners of the island's seven installation. He also listed the owners of weirs at New Bedford, Martha's Vineyard, Woods Hole, and Noank, Connecticut, with whom he communicated and who presumably would also provide funds to support the cause. Chuck's letter also indicated that some owners balked, however, suggesting that not all weir men supported Crowell's efforts: "Peter Davis, New Bedford, I have seen and he says he will not give a cent."[58] Others' efforts, however, were more successful. In February 1887 one agent in South Dartmouth wrote to Crowell, "Find enclosed check for one hundred and sixty four dollars. [I] expect to get another $20 or $25 more as there is three of the fishermen that have not subscribed as yet."[59] Daniel Vincent induced Squibnockett weir owners to donate thirty-five dollars, and they held out the promise of more: "Should your friends be short, let us hear from you later. Should hope to be able to do something more."[60] This was no fleeting response to a sudden legal conflict;

weir fishermen were ready and able to enter into another protracted legal fight over their right to fish.

Weir men's organization went beyond fund-raising. Local allies also kept close tabs on anti-weir petitioners' activities and the data they would use to support their case. For example, on February 6, 1886, just three days after Palmer had reopened the weir debate, Crowell received word from an ally who happened to be at the right place at the right time. On the way home on the Boston–New Bedford train, Fairhaven selectman Daniel W. Deane sat "just behind [weir opponent] Noah Hammond of Matta[poisett] who, like myself, occupied a seat alone." After a time, another weir opponent, this time Wareham representative Handy, joined Hammond, apparently taking no notice of Deane behind them. "Handy of Wareham came and sat down with him, [and] of course the question of fish was at once introduced by Hammond." Deane was soon joined by another weir supporter named Bonney, who recognized an opportunity to get some inside information. After Bonney struck up a conversation to create the impression to their opponents in front of them that they could speak freely, Deane recounted, "I heard distinctly Handy say to Hammond 'what I was most afraid of was, that some man from our place would go as a witness, and begin talking about our catch of herrings.' Hammond just then cautioned him to be careful by pointing over his shoulder at me." That slip identified to Deane a potential weakness that Crowell could exploit. "I think we ought to look up [the herring catch]."[61] With a functioning network of friends within government, weir men enjoyed both formal and informal advantages over their opponents.

Weir men also drew upon the observations of their friends across the region. In December 1886, for example, New Bedford fish dealer William A. Bassett took time to inform Crowell of important new information. "Our enemy's [sic] are exceedingly busy, see Sunday's *Boston Herald* and read the piece under items of news from New Bedford[.] The catch as given there don't look as though fish was dying out very fast in Buzzards Bay." Not only were correspondents forwarding information—they were actively enacting their own plans. Bassett continued, "I am glad they did not find out the doings of our meeting [which] the Herald calls . . . a secret meeting[.] Have seen some of the Vineyard pound fishermen they seem to be willing to help the cause."[62] Ultimately, when Palmer reopened the debates about weirs, he faced well-organized and well-funded opponents all across the region and within government ready to stave off assaults.

As a result of their fund-raising, weir men were able to hire the prominent Cape Cod lawyer George Augustus King to defend them once the conflict flared again. A friend of Louis Agassiz, former state senator, member of the state judiciary committee, and well connected to Boston elite, King laid out a defense that brought into clear focus how the weir debate had turned into a proxy battle over whose vision of the coast would direct Cape Cod's future development. Skillfully attacking Palmer's desire to preserve coastal resources for angling, King contended that conflict really existed between "the welfare of the toiling millions of this country, in the necessity that they should have food cheap and abundant, and the 'we' who desire the pleasurable excitement of catching fish by hook and line, even though they prevent the people of the country getting their supply of this kind of food." For King, the renewed effort to ban weirs represented an affront to efficiency and to democracy: "It is no answer to them to say that the people of this country get fish abundantly and cheaply by means of these weirs; they are to be abolished, thrown out of existence, in order that the select few have the pleasure of catching them by hook and line."[63] In short, King countered Palmer's indictment of the ecological consequences of weir fishing with a populist argument that pitted urban elite against honest coastal workingmen.

Once again, both sides presented testimonies, data, observations, and arguments about the benefits and costs of weir fishing, and each side reprinted legal arguments for mass distribution to those unable to attend the hearings. In 1887 and throughout the subsequent hearings in 1889 and 1892, King's defense remained consistent: petitions to ban weirs were put forward by gentlemen tourists seeking to remove the hardworking locals from their working coastlines. In the 1892 hearings, in fact, both parties had refined their arguments to rest upon the firmest, most appealing legal and ideological foundations. In redeploying older arguments about private and public fishing rights, progressive lawyer Charles F. Chamberlayne, who joined Palmer in his attack on weirs, embraced the contemporary antitrust crusade and argued that weirs should be banned because they benefited the privileged few at the expense of the many. "The fisheries of the coast belong . . . to the people of the shore. They are entitled to such a preservation of the same as will give them all they require for food and for their prosperity. We further contend that such rights are paramount, and that to eliminate the natural advantage of one section for the benefit of another . . . is, simply, spoliation."[64]

In response, King claimed, without irony, the backing of history. Ignoring the relatively recent development of the larger commercial weirs in dispute, King argued that weirs, far from novel machines of social and environmental destruction, actually represented Cape Cod's fishing traditions. "[Weirs] are no new thing. They are as old as the country. They were used as a means of taking fish by the Indians, and by the early colonists. . . . And the fish weirs to-day are but the natural outgrowth and development of those early and primitive ones." Admittedly, these were not the same operations that had been used in the past. "They have simply grown in magnitude and in the skill with which they are constructed and used with the general growth in other industries." As such, Cape Cod weirs, in providing a domestic supply of bait for the banks fleets, played an important role as tensions between American fishermen and Canadian bait suppliers intensified in the late nineteenth century. "In any international complication with Great Britain, the Gloucester and Provincetown fishermen are liable to be thrown for their [bait] supply entirely upon the weirs upon our shores." Ultimately, however, weirs were not the tools by which monopolists robbed coastal peoples of their fish. Instead, weirs served the larger community, be it along the shores or in the national interior. "[Weirs] have been tried and used with great benefit to the people. They have supplied the community with food fish in abundance. They have carried the wealth of the waters back from the shore line into the country, in our own State and into the far West. . . . The supply has been certainly as cheap, if not cheaper, than it ever was before." Faced with challenges from middle-class recreationists, weir men defended themselves by appealing to their utility to the larger community of working people.[65]

Beyond the repetitive charges and countercharges, these renewed legal proceedings highlighted the extent to which Cape Cod's maritime community had changed in just under two decades. Where thousands of inshore fishermen had signed petitions to ban traps in 1870, Chamberlayne called no hook-and-line fishermen to take the stand. Instead, he called Cape Cod's new residents—summer vacationers and resort owners—as witnesses to the health of the coastal ecosystem. As King sardonically pointed out, "The petitioners have not called here . . . one single fisherman whose business it was to follow his calling by hook and line, or by weir, season in and season out,— one that is dependent upon that calling for a living, and knows what he is talking about." Instead, Chamberlayne called the Wareham town assessor, another town official from Fairhaven, the hotel keeper of the Quissett Harbor House, the counsel for the Buzzards Bay Boatmen's Association, and a representative of the sportsman's club, the Southeastern Massachusetts Fish and Game League.[66] Nowhere on the petitioners' witness list appeared one of the thousands of independent hook-and-line fishermen who signed petitions twenty years prior.

The absence of Cape Cod's independent fishermen allowed weir men to claim, in a bitter twist of irony, that they were the traditional fishing people of the coast. As King summarized, "I took great pride in putting Prince M. Stewart upon the stand. . . . He fishes with a weir as long as the weir fishing [is] of value, and then he takes to his hook and line, and follows out the season. This he has done . . . for a living,—not one of your *dilettante* Southern Massachusetts Fish and Game Association style of fishing by any means."[67] Pitted against such experience, King contended, were "men who fish a little, some retired shipmaster who goes out for a day's sport,—some boatman who takes a party who goes out for a day's sail, —a few men of that sort, who have no special knowledge of the matter they are testifying about."[68] The desire of those "dilettantes" to have unspoiled recreation along Cape Cod's shores not only undermined the working uses of the coastline, but represented an unmanly relationship to nature: "Then we have our friend down there, who keeps the hotel at Quissett. His sensibilities were greatly disturbed by some dead scup lying upon the shore. Mr. Chairman and gentlemen, that man is too delicately constituted for this rude world. The rough sights and odors of the seashore he ought not to be called upon to endure. I think he should be taken and wafted away to some land where the roses and violets are in perpetual bloom, and where the odor of decaying fish will never reach him more."[69] Unlike the robust and hardy weir-men, the opposition were effeminates, King implied, seeking to purge the coast of honest working people serving the common good. "It is no use to disguise it, gentlemen. These members of the Massachusetts Fish and Game Association [are] . . . fellows that get rigged up in a blazer and get bandaged about the stomach with a woman's scarf, are men who are annoyed at the soiled garments of the men who catch fish for a living; they don't want to see them; they want them got out of the way."[70]

Nor was there any new scientific element to the disputes of the 1880s and 1890s. With data so closely monitored and quickly criticized, neither side bothered to enlist the support of working naturalists, fisheries scientists, or fisheries managers, as they had in 1871 and 1872. Instead, both teams deferred to Baird's 1872 findings, catch statistics supplied to the state fish commission, and subsequent fish commission reports. In contrast to the 1870 hearings, which at least had tried to enlist the aid of state-of-the-art science, the only live scientific presence in the entire hearing was that of U.S. Fish Commission specimen collector Vinal Edwards, whom Chamberlayne called upon to testify regarding Buzzards Bay's role as a spawning ground and its recent depletion. But Edwards's testimony and his years of experience sampling, collecting, and classifying in Buzzards Bay received little of the respect that Atwood's or Lyman's observations had received earlier. King, in his closing arguments, challenged Edwards's testimony, arguing that "he bears the same relation to the men of science that the bod carrier bears to the architect. He cannot give you any intelligent information about it, because he doesn't have it, any more than a bod carrier can tell you about the mathematical questions relating to the construction of this State House."[71] As for the preserved fish samples Edwards presented as evidence, King dismissed them as a "rag-and-bottle shop for the purpose of bolstering up the assertion [that all fish spawn in Buzzards Bay]. I didn't know what my friends were at here, whether they were going to set up a drug store or serve up a fish chowder for the Committee." More tellingly, King even dismissed the credibility of scientific information and the method by which it was generated. "With their bottles of spawn and with their witnesses, they assert that fish of all kinds spawn in Buzzards Bay. Do they suppose that we are so ignorant as not to know that bottles of spawn can be collected in any bay from Maine to Florida?"[72]

Tactics aside, the absence of inshore fishermen from these proceedings reflected another consequence of changing ecosystems. After fifteen years of commercial and ecological pressure, Cape Cod's independent hook fishermen were nowhere to be seen—or at least heard. Those interests had now been co-opted, like the coastline itself, by sportsmen, vacationers, and anglers more interested in transforming Cape Cod into a tourist destination.

Ultimately, in the final round of hearings in 1892, the weir issue came to rest not on the question of whether weirs were destroying the fisheries and the fishing communities, but rather how the new and expanding tourist industry—which sold a vision of an untainted coastal wilderness—could accommodate the very weirs, pounds, and traps that made it clear that the shore was anything but wild and pristine. In closing, Chamberlayne argued that local tourism represented local property, and therefore the age-old tenet, the protection of property, needed to be adapted to the new commercial realities. "Our people used to lead a seafaring life. The sea is no longer open to our ships. . . . Our sandy, sterile soils cannot compete on staple crops with the fertility of the West. Of recent years, the Cape towns, have largely and seriously entered upon the business of entertaining summer guests."[73] With these new realities acknowledged, tourism had to be defended, just as any previous industry had been before: "Any legitimate business which furnishes livelihood to a community is entitled to the protection of the law so far as to insure it such a development as is consistent with the rights of others. No sneer about 'sport' or 'dudes'; no attempt to waken class prejudices or social distinctions can alter the fact that the business, practically the *sole* business, of our Buzzards Bay towns lies in making themselves attractive to outsiders, and rendering an equivalent in honest toil for the money so received."[74]

What was different was how business was conducted. No longer were Cape Cod's fishing communities (save for the weirs) interested in producing fish for a market—few could earn a living by those means by the 1890s. Instead, tourism rested as much upon the appearance of natural abundance as it did its actuality. "Good fishing makes a long season. . . . Good fishing means a long stop and money spent in our towns over a longer period. Poor fishing means a short season, or none at all. . . . If fishing is poor, property is not rapidly sold, improvements or repairs are not made, new houses are not built. It is a check to our growth. It may be said that good fishing is a sentimental feeling; if so, sentiment means cold, hard dollars for all of us."[75]

In the end, and despite their financial support, political organizing, and hard-hitting defense, the weir men lost some ground to the recreationists. After 1892, while weirs in the rest of the state were allowed to remain operating, Buzzards Bay weir fishing bans grew to cover the entire bay and would remain in effect until weir fishing itself began to fade after World War I. The renewed weir dispute highlighted the removal of fish and small, independent fishermen from the coastal ecosystem. It also highlighted the removal of scientific investigation from the management process. The battle over the effects of weir fishing eventually devolved into a mere proxy battle over whose outside interests—the wholesale fish exporters' or the tourists'—would dominate how Cape Cod coasts would be used.

The hearings also revealed that, like the travel writers and seascape painters, tourists—in particular sportsmen and anglers—effectively removed working people from the management of the coastline. In their place, tourists created a vision of the Cape as a coastal wilderness that could ease the pressures of modern life. To do so, they had to ignore weir fishing itself and the very clear evidence of the economic and ecological consequences of weir fishing. In ignoring the consequences, and indeed consciously overlooking them to sell a distinctly different image, writers, artists, and tourists played as active a role in the decline of Cape Cod's inshore fisheries as did the weirs and weir men they ignored. Both weirs and the fishermen they displaced challenged new visions of the Cape as unspoiled and natural; and in order for tourists to continue to come to the Cape, that industry and those displaced people needed to be hidden from view. In omitting from view what was changing the coastline, as well as how that coastline changed, images of Cape Cod allowed their consumers to remain either ignorant of social and ecological change, or to rationalize away the negative effects of new economic regimes.

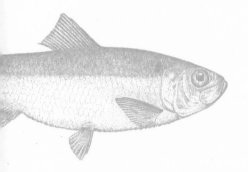

Conclusion

In the 1920s two publications appeared that encapsulated, unintentionally, how changing inshore ecosystems, science, and cultural attitudes toward the coast had affected Cape Cod's people. In the first, a report on the state alewife fisheries, Massachusetts state biologist David Belding reported, "While in some streams the alewife fishery has held its own or even improved, it has in others to such an extent been [in] a serious decline." Quite simply, Cape Cod people had ceased paying attention, or even noticing, these once-essential fish. "Laxity in town oversight and apathetic indifference on the part of the townspeople" had brought about a collapse in the once important alewife fishery.[1] Armed with a camera, Belding went out into the field to document and photograph alewife runs filled with refuse, branches, pollution, or in some cases filled in with dirt. More than a report on the health of a fishery, Belding's 1921 *Report on the Alewife Fishery of Massachusetts* represented an archaeological autopsy of a past union between people and their local fisheries.[2]

In a similar picture of emptiness and apathy, in 1928 author Henry Beston published *The Outermost House*, wherein he appealed to his readers' desires to return to a more authentic existence with nature. Beston fled civilization and spent a year just inside the dunes that formed the outer, easternmost land of Cape Cod. There he reflected upon "a great ocean beach [that] runs north and south unbroken, mile lengthening into mile. Solitary and elemental, unsullied and remote, visited and possessed by the outer sea, these sands might be the end or the beginning of a world."[3] At Nauset, Beston built a house distant and separated from one and all. And over the course of a year, this patch of Cape Cod, far from the vibrant fishing and farming community that it had been when Thoreau passed through seventy years earlier, served

Beston as the touchstone of wilderness where he could reflect upon his modern life. Without small fish or small fishermen, Cape Cod was neither wasteland nor workspace. It was now an iconic wilderness, used by urban people—ignorant of the cascading ecological and economic dislocations that preceded—for restorative recreation.

Together, these two publications capture well how much Cape Cod had changed between 1818 and 1920. From a region where balanced resource use and economic underdevelopment worked together to support communities of fish and fishermen, it had become by century's end a place where wealthy tourists found communities of local residents desperate to cater to their vacation needs, albeit at a pretty profit. But Belding's and Beston's works also reveal how little people knew or cared about the region's past, which speaks to how few remained of those who had once understood how important inshore fish runs were to local communities and local survival. Not until the 1960s, with John Hay's *The Run*, did Cape residents, who now viewed the tourist economy as Cape Cod's traditional industry, take new interest in the fish and their fish runs that still remained. By then, though, the damage had been done, and the once-bountiful runs were so weak that even the open streams could support very little fishing.

Unlike anywhere else on the eastern seaboard, Cape Cod's finite terrestrial resources, its people's understandings of the marine ecosystem, its communities' push to commercialize those resources, and its visitors' treatment of the changing shoreline reveal people's complex responsibilities for, and responses to, ecological decline. As the preceding pages argue, natural knowledge is both a blessing and a curse: it can empower people to better preserve their resources, and it can also empower them to more efficiently exploit them. Similarly, people's love of and yearning for pristine nature, too, pushed them to contradictory goals. In the twentieth and twenty-first centuries, such love has fueled conservation movements at international, national, and regional levels. It also fueled the grassroots campaigns of the 1960s and 1980s to restore Cape Cod's alewife runs. But such love and yearning, in the late nineteenth century, also allowed people to overlook how resources were being used. Instead of seeing the weirs and traps that lined Cape Cod's shores by 1900, beach- and nature-loving visitors simply averted their eyes, seeking instead only to see what they believed to be pockets of pristine nature. In the end, it all came down to interpretation: how changing ecosystems were interpreted, how the beach itself was interpreted. In both cases, those imbued with the authority to present those interpretations were able to direct people's use and abuse of local marine resources.

Ironically, local fishermen's knowledge and interpretations of their changing marine ecosystems now offers "new" insights that scientists and managers believe could help restore the fishery for the future. Recent investigations by fisheries scientists, anthropologists, and historians have begun to suggest that fishers have in their collective memory important information about past ecosystem function now needed to preserve the long-term health of the world's fish populations. Announcing the integration, or reintegration, of fishermen's knowledge in fisheries science, a 2007 United Nations Educational, Scientific, and Cultural Organization (UNESCO) publication introduced to the scientific community new ways to include information from fishermen.[4] Many contributing authors contained therein turned to indigenous cultures around the globe to see what traditional ecological knowledge could offer to modern managers. Among those researchers, however, Ted Ames looked to old Gulf of Maine fishermen to locate cod spawning grounds never previously known to scientists. Ames's work, along with all the other research presented, challenged scientists to ask a simple question: what if fishermen were really interested in the long-term preservation of their fisheries resources? What if their information could be used? How could the inclusion of this vocational knowledge improve management policies? In the early twenty-first century, what had once formed the foundation for environmental understanding has reemerged as a radical new approach to fisheries management and restoration.

In another piece of irony, weir fishing may also offer solutions for the future preservation of fish stocks—including river herring. The four families that still operate weirs on Cape Cod run their stations very differently from their nineteenth-century predecessors. Instead of operating from April until November, weir owners put down their nets for only a few weeks in the early spring. Once the bluefish arrive, the season, successful or not, is over, and the fishermen return to other work, whether that is fishing, building, or painting. Weir owners in different towns also have changed how they operate their weirs. In Provincetown, for example, weir men in the 1960s and 1970s took whole catches to shoreside processing plants for culling. Those fish with market value were shipped, the rest relegated to fertilizer or bait or simply thrown away. Chatham weir men, however, culled their catch live at the net—releasing more or less unharmed those fish they did not wish to send to market. This represented an expensive choice, for it meant that crews spent more time at each net and could therefore clear fewer nets each day. Yet they recognized that this was important for the long-term survival of their fisheries, and in their ability to live cull, weirs represent an optimistic future direction in an industry facing the consequences of the wastefulness of modern deep-sea fishing. Weirs remove, almost completely, the problems of "ghost gear" and bycatch. Longlines and gill nets, if lost by the fishermen setting them, can become the so-called ghost gear that continues to kill fish until the weight of the carcasses pulls them to the ocean floor. Weirs do not pose that problem. As for bycatch—the fish hauled to the surface but discarded for market or regulatory reasons—weirs offer more possibilities. Furthermore, unlike otter trawls, weirs allow fishermen to take only those species desired at market and release the rest back into the ocean. As Daniel Pauly and Jay Maclean have argued, the future of fishing may rest not in the capital-intensive, large-scale, industrial fishing vessels, but in intentionally less efficient, small-scale, locally based operations like weirs. By removing the costs of the vessel and fuel, weirs can still be profitable, while taking fewer fish and better rewarding fishermen's efforts.[5] In short, these former agents of ecological, social, and economic change may offer new directions for the future restoration of communities of both fish and fishermen alike.

Irony aside, the fact remains that by 1900, Cape Cod hosted more tourist resorts than fishing communities. Three decades of social, economic, ecological, and cultural change had ensured that small fish and hook-and-line fishermen were cleared from the coasts. Similarly, the memories of the thriving communities of fish and hook-and-line fishermen that had made the region their home were also allowed to fade away. Unlike more conventional stories of industrialists displacing artisans, these removals had more to do with the region's ecological dynamism and cultural representation than with concentrated capital and worker resistance. As the inshore ecosystem responded to changing fishing patterns, and as artists and writers erased the realities and legacies of those changes, both small fish and small fishermen left the Cape, and in a short amount of time, memories of both left, too.

The ties between ecology and culture, ties that pass through economic and scientific realms, played an unusually powerful role in Cape Cod's transformation, complicating our attempts to understand how people and local marine resources related to—and failed to relate to—one another. At this story's core lies an inshore marine environment not just receiving human actions, but responding to them actively and dynamically, and in turn shaping the human communities onshore.

As important as the story is of how changing ecology shaped Cape Cod's cultural representation, of just as much importance to modern readers is how those changes came to be forgotten. The economic, ecological, and social changes that presaged Cape Cod's tourist economy did not simply slip from local memory. Tourist promoters, painters, and writers used, acknowledged, and handled those changes and their legacies to turn Cape Cod into a place where weary urban residents could find a convenient reconnection to pristine nature. Thus, as much as this is a story of change, it is also a story of understanding and memory: when Cape Cod residents failed to pay attention to their local environment as their predecessors had done, all suffered; but such suffering posed unpleasantness to a burgeoning tourist industry, and so it had to go.

These changes were made more concrete by forces far beyond the coastlines and fish nets, however. Considered in isolation from the larger cultural context, this story is one of greedy fishermen taking too many fish. Yet those fishermen, their communities, and their families lived within a larger environment, one that included Cape Cod's unique agricultural limitations, changing scientific understandings, changing regulatory and commercial visions, and changing cultural visions of the coast. Responsibility for the decline of Cape Cod's inshore fishery and fishing communities, and all the attendant social, economic, and cultural changes, rests as much with the readers, painters, tourists, anglers, and recreationists as it does with the fishermen, the scientists, and the regulators who stood at the forefront of the conflicts. Whether we see ecological change, and how such change is viewed by the larger community, plays an important role in legitimating fishing. The visitors, painters, writers, and correspondents may have been removed from the immediate process by which fish were taken from the sea, but they ate the fish, praised, ignored, or ignorantly damned the fishermen, and reconfigured the role the coastline played within the larger society; and as such, they—and we—too, share responsibility for creating and then ignoring decline.

Cape Cod's nineteenth-century transformation reveals to us all that labor, environment, science, culture, and ecology are intimately intertwined. Fishermen were part of a larger ecological, social, and cultural context that also affected how and how intensely they took fish. Only by examining the intersections of natural systems, natural knowledge, cultural representations of nature, and the social history of those dependent upon nature can we see the complexity of historical forces that shape how people use their natural resources. This study also reveals that the responsibility for taking fish and for ignoring resultant changes lies with many more than the fishermen working the weirs, pounds, traps, seines, and hand lines. Fishermen respond to demand from the larger community, and they in part see their work through the eyes of those who see them. How the larger community perceived fishing and its consequences had as much to do with undermining Cape Cod's inshore fishery as the fishermen themselves. By celebrating fishing, and then by ignoring the attendant social and ecological fallout that ensued, artists and writers, and the public that purchased their works, played an active role in interpreting—and not interpreting—changing coastal conditions.

Notes

Introduction

1. The first modern manifestation of this line came from McEvoy in 1986, but his approach has been followed by many others since. See Arthur F. McEvoy, *The Fisherman's Problem: Ecology and the Law in California Fisheries, 1850–1980* (Cambridge, U.K.: Cambridge University Press, 1986); Richard White, *The Organic Machine: The Remaking of the Columbia River* (New York: Hill & Wang, 1995); Joseph E. Taylor, *Making Salmon: An Environmental History of the Northwest Fisheries Crisis* (Seattle: University of Washington Press, 1999); George A. Rose, *Cod: The Ecological History of the North Atlantic Fisheries* (St. John's, Newfoundland: Breakwater Press, 2007); Connie Chiang, *Shaping the Shoreline: Fisheries and Tourism on the Monterey Coast* (Seattle: University of Washington Press, 2008); W. Jeffrey Bolster, "Putting the Ocean in Atlantic History: Maritime Communities and Marine Ecology in the Northwest Atlantic, 1500–1800," *American Historical Review* 113 (2008): 19–47.

2. Bolster, "Putting the Ocean in Atlantic History."

3. In New England, much of this work has focused on competition over riparian resources with the advent of industrialization. Studies by Theodore Steinberg, Gary Kulick, Richard Judd, and Daniel Vickers have all looked at how competing visions of human relations to the environment shaped responses to the construction of mill dams and the consequent effects upon river fisheries. For most of these scholars, those tensions revealed important lessons about the advent of industrial capitalism and the decline of traditional common resource access rights. Only recently, however, have investigations included agency of the environment itself. Brian Donahue, for example, shows how the riparian environment responded to dam construction, and how those responses, in turn, affected the ways farmers transferred nutrients from the river to more upland fields. See Theodore Steinberg, *Nature Incorporated: Industrialization and the Waters of New England* (Amherst: University of Massachusetts Press, 1991); Gary Kulick, "Dams, Fish and Farmers: Defense of Public Rights in Eighteenth-Century Rhode Island," in *The Countryside in the Age of Capitalist*

Transformation: Essays in the Social History of Rural America, edited by Steven Hahn and Jonathan Prude (Chapel Hill: University of North Carolina Press, 1985), 25–50; Richard Judd, *Common Lands, Common People: The Origins of Conservation in Northern New England* (Cambridge, Mass.: Harvard University Press, 1997); Richard Judd, "Reshaping Maine's Landscape: Rural Culture, Tourism and Conservation, 1890–1929," *Forest History* 32 (October 1988): 180–90; Daniel Vickers, "Those Dammed Shad: Would the River Fisheries of New England Have Survived in the Absence of Industrialization?" *William and Mary Quarterly*, 3rd ser., 61 (2004): 685–712; Brian Donahue, "'Dammed at Both Ends and Cursed in the Middle': The 'Flowage' of the Concord River Meadows, 1798–1862," *Environmental Review* 13 (1989): 46–67; Brian Donahue, *The Great Meadow: Farmers and the Land in Colonial Concord* (New Haven, Conn.: Yale University Press, 2004).

4. As Dona Brown has argued, tourism came late to the Cape, emerging as a major industry only after the early 1870s. But unlike her work, and that of others exploring tourism during the same period, this study hopes to shed light on the reasons why those communities being "toured" chose to embrace what many fishermen viewed as a degraded field of labor and one to which many did not take to kindly. Like Judd's work on Maine, this study shows that only as the local resources declined could tourism gain a foothold in what had previously proved to be a region where traditional work—farming or fishing—made tourism appear a poor economic substitute. This work also differs from others exploring the role of the romanticized rustic in the advent of tourism in the twentieth century. Unlike Ian McKay's work on early twentieth-century Nova Scotia, for example, this study maintains that few saw Cape Cod fishermen as a regional "folk" embodying the moral center and embryo for national culture. As I will argue, few after 1880 took any interest in idealizing, celebrating, or communing with Cape Cod fishermen. Furthermore, Cape Cod "rustics" were not, as Blake Harrison argues for Vermont, present at their own creation as a nostalgic, rural antithesis to industrializing cities. Unlike the Nova Scotian and Vermont cases, late nineteenth-century tourists were eager to move Cape Cod fishermen out of the way—or erase them altogether—so they could get to a beach they saw as untrammeled, pristine, and timeless nature. See Dona Brown, *Inventing New England: Regional Tourism in the Nineteenth Century* (Washington, D.C.: Smithsonian Institution Press, 1995); Ian McKay, *The Quest of the Folk: Antimodernism and Cultural Selection in Twentieth-Century Nova Scotia* (Montreal: McGill–Queen's University Press, 1994); Blake Harrison, *The View from Vermont: Tourism and the Making of an American Rural Landscape* (Burlington: University of Vermont Press, 2006), 29–36.

1. *Wastelands*

The opening epigraph to this chapter is from Helen Vanderhoop Manning, with Jo-Ann Eccher, *Moshup's Footsteps: The Wampanoag Nation Gay Head / Aquinnah,*

The People of First Light (Aquinnah, Mass.: Blue Cloud Across the Moon Publishing Company, 2001), 22–23. The second epigraph is from Wampanoag Tribe of Gay Head, "Other Stories and Information," http://www.wampanoagtribe.net/Pages/Wampanoag_Way/other.

1. Robert N. Oldale, *A Geologic History of Cape Cod* (Washington, D.C.: U.S. Geological Survey, 1980); Robert N. Oldale, *Cape Cod and the Islands: the Geologic Story* (East Orleans, Mass.: Parnassus Imprints, 1992); Arthur N. Strahler, *A Geologist's View of Cape Cod* (Garden City, N.Y.: Natural History Press, 1966).

2. Strahler, *Geologist's View of Cape Cod*, 92–93. See also W. J. Latimer et al., *Soil Survey of Norfolk, Bristol, and Barnstable Counties, Massachusetts* (Washington, D.C.: Government Printing Office, 1924), 1033–1119; U.S. Department of Agriculture, *The Changing Fertility of New England Soils*, Agricultural Information Bulletin No. 1333 (Washington, D.C.: Government Printing Office, December 1954); and Peter Fletcher, *Soil Survey of Barnstable County, Massachusetts* (Washington, D.C.: U.S. Department of Agriculture, 1993).

3. Strahler, *Geologist's View of Cape Cod*, 93–94.

4. Frederick J. Dunford, "Paleoenvironmental Context for the Middle Archaic Occupation of Cape Cod, Massachusetts," in Mary Anne Levine, Kenneth E. Sassaman, and Michael S. Nassaney, eds., *The Archaeological Northeast* (Westport, Conn.: Bergin & Garvey, 1999), 39–47.

5. Simon Jennings, Michael J. Kaiser, and John D. Reynolds, *Marine Fisheries Ecology* (Oxford: Blackwell Science, 2001), 34–35.

6. Bruce B. Collette and Grace Klein-MacPhee, eds., *Bigelow and Schroeder's Fishes of the Gulf of Maine*, 3rd ed. (Washington, D.C.: Smithsonian Institution Press, 2002), 228–35.

7. Dunford, "Paleoenvironmental Context," 49–53.

8. Elizabeth A. Little and Margaret J. Schoeninger, "The Late Woodland Diet on Nantucket Island and the Problem of Maize in Coastal New England," *American Antiquity* 60 (1995): 351–68; William A. Ritchie, *The Archaeology of Martha's Vineyard* (Garden City, N.Y.: Natural History Press, 1969); J. Clinton Andrews, "Indian Fish and Fishing off Coastal Massachusetts," *Bulletin of the Massachusetts Archaeological Society* 47 (1986): 42–46; Elizabeth A. Little, "Three Kinds of Indian Land Deeds at Nantucket, Massachusetts," in William Cowan, ed., *Papers of the Eleventh Algonquian Conference*, 61–70, as cited in Kathleen Bragdon, *Native People of Southern New England, 1500–1650* (Norman: University of Oklahoma Press, 1996), 63.

9. David J. Bernstein, "Prehistoric Seasonality Studies in Coastal Southern New England," *American Anthropologist*, New Series 92 (1990): 96–115; Kevin A. McBride, "Archaic Subsistence in the Lower Connecticut Valley: Evidence from Woodchuck Knoll," *Man in the Northeast* 78 (1978): 124–32; Mark Tveskov, "Maritime Settlement and Subsistence along the Southern New England Coast: Evidence from

Block Island, Rhode Island," *North American Archaeologist* 18 (1997): 343–61; Jordan E. Kerber, "Where Are the Woodland Villages in the Narragansett Bay Region?" *Bulletin of the Massachusetts Archaeological Society* 49 (1988): 66–71.

10. Little and Schoeninger, "Late Woodland Diet," 351–68.

11. Bragdon, *Native People of Southern New England*, 55–79.

12. Ibid., 35–36.

13. On Champlain's early description of specific Cape Cod locations see H. Roger King, *Cape Cod and Plymouth Colony in the Seventeenth Century* (Lanham, Md.: University Press of America, 1994), 1–7.

14. Samuel de Champlain, *Voyages of Samuel de Champlain*, trans. Charles Pomeroy Otis, vol. 2 (Boston: Prince Society, 1878), 81.

15. Ibid., 2:83.

16. Ibid., 2:90.

17. John R. Stilgoe, "A New England Coastal Wilderness," *Geographical Review* 71 (1981): 33–50.

18. "Letter of Isaack des Rasieres to Samuel Blommaert, 1628 (?)," in J. Franklin Jameson, ed., *Narratives of New Netherland, 1609–1664* (New York: Charles Scribner's Sons, 1909), 110.

19. William Bradford, *Bradford's History "Of Plimouth Plantation"* (Boston: Wright & Potter, 1898), 94. Spellings and grammar modernized by the author.

20. On the challenges and significance of New Englanders' learning how to use small craft—from canoes to boats—see Daniel Vickers, *Young Men and the Sea: Yankee Seafarers in the Age of Sail* (New Haven, Conn.: Yale University Press, 2005), 7–24.

21. John Brereton, "Briefe and True Relation of the Discoverie of the North Part of Virginia in 1602," in George Parker Winship, ed., *Sailors Narratives of the New England Coast* (Boston: Houghton Mifflin, 1905), 39.

22. Martin Pring, "A Voyage from the Citie of Bristoll . . . for the discoverie of the North part of Virginia, in the yeere 1603, under the command of me, Martin Pring," in Samuel Purchas, ed., *Hakluytus Posthumous, or, Purchas, His Pilgrimes*, Part IV (London: H. Fetherstone, 1625), 1656.

23. For the Europeans' wonder with the New World, see Stephen Greenblatt, *Marvelous Possession: The Wonder of the New World* (Chicago: University of Chicago Press, 1991).

24. Brereton, "Briefe and True Relation," 39.

25. Pring, "Voyage from the Citie of Bristoll," 1655–56.

26. Champlain, *Voyages of Samuel de Champlain*, 2:80.

27. Ibid., 2:82.

28. John Smith, *A Description of New England* (London: Robert Clerke, 1616), 9–10.

29. See, for example, Lorenzo Sabine, *Report of the Principal Fisheries of the*

American Seas (Washington, D.C.: Robert Armstrong, 1853); Spencer Fullerton Baird, *Report on the Condition of the Sea Fisheries of the South Coast of New England in 1871 and 1872*, Part I (Washington, D.C.: Government Printing Office, 1873), 149–72; Raymond McFarland, *A History of the New England Fisheries* (New York: University of Pennsylvania Press, 1911); Samuel Eliot Morison, *Maritime History of Massachusetts* (Boston: Houghton Mifflin, 1921); Daniel Vickers, *Farmers and Fishermen: Two Centuries of Work in Essex County, Massachusetts, 1630–1850* (Chapel Hill: University of North Carolina Press, 1994); Theodore Steinberg, *Down to Earth: Nature's Role in American History* (New York: Oxford University Press, 2002); Bolster, "Putting the Ocean in Atlantic History," 19–47.

30. Martin Pring, "A Voyage Set out from the Citie of Bristoll, at the Charge of the Chiefest Merchants and Inhabitants . . . For the Discouerie of the North Part of Virginia, in the Yeere 1603. Vnder the Command of Me Martin Pring," in David B. Quinn and Alison M. Quinn, eds., *The English New England Voyages* (London: Hakluyt Society, 1983), 226. It is not certain what Pring meant by "Creuises."

31. Rosier, James, "A True Relation of Waymouth's Voyage, 1605," in Henry S. Burrage, ed., *Early English and French Voyages, Chiefly from Hakluyt, 1534–1609* (New York: Barnes & Noble, 1906), 363–94.

32. Smith, *Description of New England*, 30.

33. John Smith, *The Generall Historie of Virginia, New-England, and the Summer Isles* . . . (London: I. D. and I. H. for Michael Sparkes, 1624), 212–16.

34. For a discussion of providential deliverance and historical representation in Bradford's histories see David Read, "Silent Partners: Historical Representation in William Bradford's *Of Plymouth Plantation*," *Early American Literature* 33 (1998): 291–314.

35. Carolyn Merchant, *Ecological Revolutions: Nature, Gender, and Science in New England* (Chapel Hill: University of North Carolina Press, 1989), 31.

36. *Mourt's Relation: A Journal of the Pilgrims at Plymouth* (Cambridge, Mass.: Applewood Books, 1986), 15.

37. Bradford, *Bradford's History*, 93.

38. *Mourt's Relation*, 17.

39. Ibid., 24.

40. Ibid., 16.

41. Ibid., vii–xvi.

42. Ibid., 18.

43. Ibid., 20.

44. George Morton, *A Relation or Journal of the Beginning and Proceeding of the English Plantation Settled at Plymouth in New England* (London: John Bellamie, 1622), 39, 85.

45. Bradford, *Bradford's History*, 95.

46. Ibid., 121.

47. For more on the challenges and economies of farm building see, among many, Daniel F. Vickers, *Farmers and Fishermen: Two Centuries of Work in Essex County, Massachusetts, 1630–1850* (Chapel Hill: University of North Caroline Press, 1994) and Brian Donahue, *The Great Meadow: Farmers and the Land in Colonial Concord* (New Haven, Conn.: Yale University Press, 2004).

48. For Native American use of alewives for fertilizer see Stephen A. Mrozowski, "The Discovery of a Native American Cornfield on Cape Cod," *Archaeology of Eastern North America* 22 (1994): 47–62.

49. Bradford, *Bradford's History*, 121.

50. Ibid., 94–95.

51. Ibid., 128.

52. Edward Johnson, *A History of New England* (London: Nath. Brooke [1653]), 49–54.

53. William Morrell, *New England, or, A Briefe Narration of the Ayre, Earth, Water, Fish and Fowles of that Country* (London: I. D[awson], 1625), 16.

54. Council for New England, *An Historicall Discoverie and Relation of the English Plantations in New England* (London: John Bellamie, 1627), n.p.

55. [Edward Winslow], "Good News from New England," in Edward Arber, ed., *The Story of the Pilgrim Fathers, 1606–1623 A.D.* (Boston: Houghton Mifflin, 1897), 530.

56. William Wood, *New England's Prospect* (London: John Bellamie, 1634), 32–36.

57. Such extrapolations represent dually risky assumptions. First, the historian must assume that a name given to a particular fish corresponds to what that fish is currently called. In this regard there is some help, as fisheries scientists today maintain lists of historically used common names. The second assumption is more troubling—modern fisheries information has been developed from populations of fish that have faced unprecedented and perhaps even cataclysmic fishing pressure. Biologists are beginning to understand that under such pressure, fish spawning and migration patterns may change. To accommodate this possibility, information for the species mentioned here comes from Bigelow and Schroeder's 1953 edition of *Fishes of the Gulf of Maine*. By referring to these findings, and not research performed subsequently when Gulf of Maine stocks faced even greater fishing pressure, I can more accurately represent the southern New England inshore the settlers first encountered.

58. Wood, *New England's Prospect*, 32–36.

59. Thomas Morton, *New English Canaan* ([London]: Charles Greene, 1632), 86–91.

60. See entries 2a–d for "commodity" in online *Oxford English Dictionary*, 2nd ed., 1989: http://dictionary.oed.com/cgi/entry/50045094?single=1&query_type=word &queryword=commodity&first=1&max_to_show=10.

61. Morton, *New English Canaan*, 86–91.

62. John Josseleyn, *New England's Rarities Discovered* (London: C. Widdowes, 1675).

2. Management

1. H. Roger King, *Cape Cod and Plymouth Colony in the Seventeenth Century* (Lanham, Md.: University Press of America), 51–53.

2. For more on cartographic omissions and "silences" see J. B. Harley, "Silences and Secrecy: The Hidden Agenda of Cartography in Early Modern Europe," *Imago Mundi* 40 (1988), 57–76.

3. King, *Cape Cod and Plymouth Colony*, 177.

4. R. R. Cook and Peter J. Auster, *A Bioregional Classification of the Continental Shelf of Northeastern North America for Conservation Analysis and Planning Based on Representation*, Marine Sanctuaries Conservation Series NMSP-07-03 (Silver Spring, Md.: U.S. Department of Commerce, National Oceanic and Atmospheric Administration, National Marine Sanctuary Program, 2007).

5. Daniel Vickers, *Farmers and Fishermen: Two Centuries of Work in Essex County, Massachusetts, 1630–1850* (Chapel Hill: University of North Carolina Press, 1994), 91–99.

6. Andrew A. Rosenberg et al., "The History of Ocean Resources: Modeling Cod Biomass Using Historical Sources," *Frontiers in Ecology and the Environment* 3 (2005), 84–90; Collette and Klein-MacPhee, *Bigelow and Schroeder's Fishes*, 228.

7. Henry B. Bigelow and William C. Schroeder, *Fishes of the Gulf of Maine*, Fishery Bulletin 74 of the Fish and Wildlife Service, Volume 53 [Contribution No. 592, Woods Hole Oceanographic Institution], (Washington, D.C.: Government Printing Office, 1953), 182, 199, 213.

8. Sharon R. Turner, "Salting Fish," Virginia Tech Sea Grant, Commercial Fish and Shellfish Technologies Notes (URL http://www.cfast.vt.edu/Publications/salting.shtml).

9. Ibid.

10. Bo Poulsen, *Dutch Herring: An Environmental History, c. 1600–1800* (Amsterdam: Aksant Academic Publishers, 2009).

11. Bolster, "Putting the Ocean in Atlantic History," 19–47.

12. Josseleyn, *New England's Rarities Discovered*, 23–37.

13. "Notes of Mr. Bennet, 1740," in Justin Winsor, ed., *Memorial History of Boston*, vol. 2 (Boston: James R. Good and Co., 1881), 464.

14. "The Journal of a Captive, 1745–1748," in Isabel M. Calder, ed., *Colonial Captivities, Marches, and Journeys* (New York: MacMillan, 1935), 134–35.

15. François Alexandre Frédéric, duc de La Rochefoucault-Liancourt, *Travels through the United States of North America, 1795–97*, vol. 2 (London: R. Phillips, 1800), 138.

16. Timothy Dwight, *Travels in New York and New England*, Barbara Miller Solomon and Patricia King, eds., vol. 3 (Cambridge, Mass.: Harvard University Press, 1969), 33.

17. Caroline Hazard, ed., *Nailer Tom's Diary: The Journal of Thomas B. Hazard, 1778–1840* (Boston: Merrymount Press, 1930).

18. On the capitalist nature of Rhode Island's river fisheries see Vickers, "Those Dammed Shad," 685–712; Peter E. Pope, *Fish into Wine: The Newfoundland Plantation in the Seventeenth Century* (Chapel Hill: University of North Carolina Press, 2004).

19. Ruth Lynn Friedman, "Governing the Land: An Environmental History of Cape Cod, Massachusetts, 1600–1861" (doctoral dissertation, Brandeis University, 1993), 63–127.

20. Secretary of the Commonwealth of Massachusetts, comp., *Laws Relating to Inland Fisheries in Massachusetts, 1623–1886* (Boston: Wright & Potter, 1887), 3.

21. Secretary of the Commonwealth, *Laws Relating to Inland Fisheries*, 3.

22. King, *Cape Cod and Plymouth Colony*, 209–11.

23. Ibid.

24. Secretary of the Commonwealth, *Laws Relating to Inland Fisheries*, 4.

25. Ibid.

26. Ibid., 4–6.

27. Collette and Klein-MacPhee, *Bigelow and Schroeder's Fishes*, 379.

28. King, *Cape Cod and Plymouth Colony*, 212.

29. Collette and Klein-MacPhee, *Bigelow and Schroeder's Fishes*, 124.

30. Sandwich Town Records, vol. 1 (1650/1–1692); March 12, 1650/1; March 1681; and April 14, 1687. Sandwich Town Archives, Sandwich, Mass.

31. See Theodore Steinberg, *Nature Incorporated: Industrialization and the Waters of New England* (Amherst: University of Massachusetts Press, 1991); and Gary Kulick, "Dams, Fish and Farmers: Defense of Public Rights in Eighteenth-Century Rhode Island," in *The Countryside in the Age of Capitalist Transformation: Essays in the Social History of Rural America*, edited by Steven Hahn and Jonathan Prude (Chapel Hill: University of North Carolina Press 1985), 25–50. Nor was this just a local policy. In 1741 the Massachusetts General Court enacted colonywide legislation that also favored spring fish runs over industrial development.

32. Sandwich Town Records [typescripts], April 10, 1719, and March 10, 1728/9. Sandwich Public Library, Sandwich, Mass.

33. Secretary of the Commonwealth, *Laws Relating to Inland Fisheries*, 9–14.

34. [Samuel Sewall], "Letter-Book of Samuel Sewall," *Massachusetts Historical Society Collections*, Sixth Series, vol. 1 (Boston, 1886), 37–112.

35. William Douglass, *A Summary, Historical and Political, of the First Settlements, Progressive Improvements, and Present State of the British Settlements in North America*, vol. 1 (London: 1760).

36. "Records of the Boston Customs District, 1768," *Proceedings of the Massachusetts Historical Society* 62 (1925): 424.

37. Sandwich Town Records [typescripts], March 28, 1734.

38. Ibid., May 2, 1743, and March 13, 1743/4.

39. Ibid., May 16, 1745.

40. Rochester Proprietor's Records, vol. 1, 71–72. Rochester Town Hall, Rochester, Mass.

41. Sandwich Town Records [typescripts], May 26, 1752.

42. Rochester Proprietor's Records, vol. 1, 138.

43. Sandwich Town Records [typescripts], May 17, 1764.

44. Ibid., March 29, 1780.

45. Harwich Town Records, vol. 2, 328 (April 1787). Harwich Town Hall, Harwich, Mass.

46. Falmouth Town Records, microfilm, March 18, 1788. Falmouth Public Library, Falmouth, Mass.

47. Massachusetts Division of Fish and Game, Department of Conservation, *A Report upon the Alewife Fisheries of Massachusetts* (Boston: Wright & Potter, 1921), 40–45.

48. Commonwealth of Massachusetts to Joseph Palmer, [April 9, 1802]. Falmouth Town Records Herring Fishery, oversize box, Falmouth Historical Society, Falmouth, Mass.

49. [Arrest Warrant for Barnabas Hinckley], May 4, 1804. Falmouth Town Records Herring Fishery.

50. William Holmes to James Hinckley, May 17, 1802, Falmouth Town Records Herring Fishery.

51. Helen Rozwadowski, *Fathoming the Ocean: The Discovery and Exploration of the Deep Sea* (Cambridge, Mass.: Harvard University Press, 2004). See also Keith R. Benson, Helen Rozwadowski, and David van Keuren, introduction to *The Machine in Neptune's Garden*, Helen Rozwadowski and David van Keuren, eds., (Sagamore Beach, Mass.: Science History Publications, 2004).

52. D. Graham Burnett, *Trying Leviathan* (Princeton, N.J.: Princeton University Press, 2007).

53. Committee of the Town of Falmouth to the Massachusetts Senate and House of Representatives, [n.d.] labeled #164–#11. Falmouth Town Records Herring Fishery.

54. Despite these hearings, Hinckley's case ran through petitions, court hearings, and more petitions as the town worked every angle to pin Hinckley down. Ultimately, however, it was not politics but tragedy that put the divisive issue into perspective and let cooler heads develop a resolution. In September 1805 twenty-seven-year-old Thomas Gifford set out to make a statement about how this controversy over the

fisheries affected his town and community. One morning on or before midmonth, he pulled onto the village green an old field piece and rammed down a powder charge. On top of the charge he filled the barrel with herring, and then fired. When the gun went off, the back pressure from the herring caused the weakened iron barrel to burst, sending fish and iron shrapnel in every direction, including into Gifford himself. He died of his wounds a few days later, taking with him to the grave whatever statement he wanted to make about the Revolution and fish. In the aftermath of the tragedy, Falmouth's Herring War appears to have been put to an end. In the middle of Madison's 1807 embargo, a town meeting was called to remove obstructions from the river in cooperation with local residents. Hinckley appears to have gone along, as no protest or any other controversy emerged in town records.

55. Steinberg, *Nature Incorporated*.

56. "Description of Cape Cod, and the County of Barnstable," *Massachusetts Magazine*, February 1791.

57. Rev. Mellen, "A Topographical Description of the Town of Barnstable," *Collections of the Massachusetts Historical Society* 3 (1810): 12–17.

58. Ibid.

59. Anonymous, "A Topographical Description of Truro," *Collections of the Massachusetts Historical Society* 3 (1810): 195–200.

60. Levi Whitman, "A Topographical Description of Wellfleet," *Collections of the Massachusetts Historical Society* 3 (1810): 117–21.

61. Dwight, *Travels*, 52.

62. Ibid., 59

63. Ibid., 65.

64. Ibid., 67.

65. Edward Augustus Kendall, *Travels through the Northern Parts of the United States in the Years 1807 and 1808* (New York: I. Riley, 1809), 148.

66. Ibid., 162.

67. Ibid., 163–64.

68. Ibid., 164–65.

3. *Workspace*

1. Raymond McFarland, *A History of the New England Fisheries* (New York: University of Pennsylvania, 1911); Samuel Eliot Morison, *The Maritime History of Massachusetts* (Boston: Houghton Mifflin, 1921); Harold A. Innis, *The Cod Fisheries: The History of An International Economy* (Toronto: University of Toronto Press, 1940 [1985]); Wayne M. O'Leary, *Maine Sea Fisheries: The Rise and Fall of a Native Industry, 1830–1890* (Boston: Northeastern University Press, 1996).

2. William Leavenworth, "Opening Pandora's Box: Tradition, Competition, and Technology on the Scotian Shelf, 1852–1860," in David J. Starkey and James E. Can-

dow, eds., *The North Atlantic Fisheries: Supply, Marketing and Consumption, 1560–1990. Studia Atlantica* 8 (2006): 29–49.

3. Stephen Higginson to John Adams, March 25, 1790, *Annual Report of the American Historical Association* I (1897): 719–78, as printed in John C. Pearson, ed., *The Fish and Fisheries of Colonial North America, Part II: The New England States*, NOAA Report No. 72040302, (Springfield, Va.: National Technical Information Services, 1972), 395.

4. George Brown Goode and J. W. Collins, "The George's Bank Cod Fishery," in George Brown Goode, ed., *The Fisheries and Fishery Industries of the United States, Section V: History and Methods of the Fisheries* I (Washington, D.C.: Government Printing Office, 1887), 197–98.

5. McFarland, *New England Fisheries*, 161.

6. Collette and Klein-MacPhee, eds., *Bigelow and Schroeder's Fishes*, 523–25.

7. McFarland, *New England Fisheries*, 160–97.

8. Anon., "The Mackerel Fishery," *The Friend: A Religious Literary Journal*, May 1, 1852.

9. George Brown Goode and J. W. Collins, "The Mackerel Hook Fishery," in George Brown Goode, ed., *The Fisheries and Fishery Industries of the United States, Section V: History and Methods of the Fisheries* I (Washington, D.C.: Government Printing Office, 1887), 278, n. 2.

10. Goode and Collins, "The Mackerel Hook Fishery," 280.

11. Ibid., 277; Howard I. Chapelle, *The National Watercraft Collection* (Washington, D.C.: Museum of History and Technology of the United States National Museum, 1960), 167–68.

12. Oscar E. Settee and A. W. H. Needler, *Statistics of the Mackerel Fishery off the East Coast of North America, 1804–1930*. U.S. Department of Commerce, Bureau of the Fisheries, Investigational Report No. 19 (Washington, D.C.: Government Printing Office, 1934), 32.

13. McFarland, *New England Fisheries*, 187–89.

14. Henry C. Kittredge, *Cape Cod: Its People and Their History* (Boston: Houghton Mifflin, 1930 [1968]), 190–92.

15. Andrew A. Rosenberg et al., "The History of Ocean Resources: Modeling Cod Biomass Using Historical Records," *Frontiers in Ecology and the Environment* 3 (2005): 84–90. Leavenworth, "Opening Pandora's Box," 29–49. For more on the technological revolutions in the nineteenth-century fishery, see O'Leary, *Maine Sea Fisheries*, chapters 6 and 7. While O'Leary's assessment provides a detailed overview of new material designs in fishing technologies, he omits fishermen's expertise and ability to use the ecosystem itself as part of their technological innovations.

16. O'Leary, *Maine Sea Fisheries*, 160–63.

17. Leavenworth, "Opening Pandora's Box." Leavenworth also argues that the

transition from hand lines to dory hand lines to tub trawls effectively cleared fish from local areas and undermined cod populations on the Scotian Shelf.

18. Truro and Wellfleet data from John Hayward, *The New England Gazetteer* (Concord, N.H.: Boyd & White, 1839); Massachusetts data from Sabine, *Principal Fisheries*, 189.

19. U.S. Department of the Census, *Compendium of the Enumeration of the Inhabitants and Statistics of the United States* (Washington, D.C.: Government Printing Office, 1841), 10.

20. Sabine, *Principal Fisheries*, 189.

21. Anon., "The Mackerel Fishery."

22. U.S. Department of the Census, *Heads of Families at the First Census of the United States Taken in the Year 1790: Massachusetts* (Washington, D.C.: Government Printing Office, 1908), 9; Hayward, *New England Gazetteer*; U.S. Department of the Census, *Abstract of the Returns of the Fifth Census . . .* (Washington, D.C.: Government Printing Office, 1832), 5; U. S. Department of the Census, *Compendium of the Enumeration of the Inhabitants and Statistics of the United States . . .* (1841), 10; *Statistical View of the United States . . . Compendium of the Seventh Census* (Washington, D.C.: Government Printing Office, 1854), 254; U.S. Department of the Census, *Population of the United States in 1860* (Washington, D.C.: Government Printing Office, 1864), 219.

23. For mackerel hook-and-line finances, see the John Hopkins Papers, Mss. 44, Series A; Kendall Institute, New Bedford Whaling Museum, New Bedford, Mass.

24. Goode and Collins, "Mackerel Hook Fishery," 280–83.

25. Ibid., 287.

26. Ibid., 283.

27. Hand-lining vessels tended to cast a gill net off the stern at night to catch passing fish to use as bait the next day. See Leavenworth, "Opening Pandora's Box."

28. *Cape Ann Advertiser*, February 23, 1877, as cited in R. Edward Earll, "The Frozen Herring Industry," in George Brown Goode, ed., *The Fisheries and Fishery Industries of the United States, Section V: History and Methods of the Fisheries* I (Washington, D.C.: Government Printing Office, 1887), 440. For uses of clam bait, see George Brown Goode and J. W. Collins, "The Bank Hand-line Cod Fishery," in George Brown Goode, ed., *The Fisheries and Fishery Industries of the United States, Section V: History and Methods of the Fisheries* I (Washington, D.C.: Government Printing Office, 1887), 127.

29. Earll, "The Frozen Herring Industry," 441.

30. See O'Leary, *Maine Sea Fisheries*, 173–74, for how bait increased overhead costs of tub trawling.

31. George Brown Goode and J. W. Collins, "George's Bank Cod Fishery," in

George Brown Goode, ed., *The Fisheries and Fishery Industries of the United States, Section V: History and Methods of the Fisheries* I (Washington, D.C.: Government Printing Office, 1887), 193.

32. Goode and Collins, "The Bank Trawl-Line Cod Fishery," in George Brown Goode, ed., *The Fisheries and Fishery Industries of the United States, Section V: History and Methods of the Fisheries* I (Washington, D.C.: Government Printing Office, 1887), 151.

33. Goode and Collins, "Bank Trawl-Line Cod Fishery," 151.

34. Goode and Collins, "George's Bank Cod Fishery," 193.

35. George Brown Goode and J. W. Collins, "The Haddock Fishery of New England," in George Brown Goode, ed., *The Fisheries and Fishery Industries of the United States, Section V: History and Methods of the Fisheries* I (Washington, D.C.: Government Printing Office, 1887), 236–37.

36. Goode and Collins, "Mackerel Hook Fishery," 287.

37. D. Humphrey Storer, "A Report on the Fishes of Massachusetts," *Boston Journal of Natural History* II (1839): 290.

38. Ibid., 291.

39. Ibid., 330.

40. Nathaniel E. Atwood, "Autobiography of Capt. N. E. Atwood," in George Brown Goode, ed., *The Fisheries and Fisheries Industries of the United States, Section IV,* (Washington, D.C.: Government Printing Office, 1887), 162–67.

41. Hayward, *New England Gazetteer*, entry for "Barnstable County, Mass."

42. Ibid., entry for "Truro, Massachusetts."

43. William B. Fowle and Asa Fitz, *An Elementary Geography for Massachusetts Children* (Boston: Fowle and Capen, 1845), 136.

44. Leo Marx, *The Machine in the Garden: Technology and the Pastoral Ideal in America* (New York: Oxford University Press, 1964, 2000), chapter 3.

45. Sarah Burns, *Pastoral Inventions: Rural Life in Nineteenth-Century American Art and Culture* (Philadelphia: Temple University Press, 1989), 32.

46. Ibid.

47. Barbara Novak, *Nature and Culture: American Landscape and Painting, 1825–1875*, rev. ed. (New York: Oxford University Press, 1995), 7.

48. Roger B. Stein, *Seascape and the American Imagination* (New York: Clarkson N. Potter, 1975), 35–51.

49. Ibid., 67–84.

50. John Wilmerding, *American Marine Painting* (New York: Harry N. Abrams, 1987); Stein, *Seascape*.

51. Ralph Waldo Emerson, *The American Scholar / Self Reliance / Compensation*, Orren Henry Smith, ed., (New York: American Book Co., 1893, 1911), 42.

52. John Ruskin, "The Harbours of England," in E. T. Cook and Alexander Wedderburn, eds., *The Complete Works of John Ruskin*, vol. 13 (London: George Allen, 1904), 13.

53. Ibid., 11–25.

54. Ibid., 24.

55. *The Crayon*, November 1856, 335.

56. Angela Miller, *Empire of the Eye: Landscape Representation and American Cultural Politics, 1825–1875* (Ithaca, N.Y.: Cornell University Press, 1993), 14.

57. Ibid., 47–48.

58. Joseph Conforti, *Imagining New England* (Chapel Hill: University of North Carolina Press, 2001), 124–50.

59. John Wilmerding, *Fitz Hugh [Henry] Lane, 1804–1865: American Marine Painter* (Salem, Mass.: Essex Institute, 1964).

60. Marx, *Machine in the Garden*, 363.

61. For images of these works, and for a biography of Gifford, see Elton W. Hall, "R. Swain Gifford," in *Robert Swain Gifford, 1850–1905* (New Bedford, Mass.: Old Dartmouth Historical Society, 1974).

62. Mary Jean Blasdale, *Artists of New Bedford* (New Bedford, Mass.: Old Dartmouth Historical Society, 1990), 96.

63. Ibid., 196.

64. On the effect of landscape and pastoral painting on tourism see Barbara Bloemink et al., *Frederic Church, Winslow Homer, and Thomas Moran: Tourism and the American Landscape* (Washington, D.C.: Smithsonian Institute Press, 2006). On the appeal of industrial development to tourism see Dona Brown, *Inventing New England: Regional Tourism in the Nineteenth Century* (Washington, D.C.: Smithsonian Institution Press, 1995), 27–31.

65. On the rise of Newport as a tourist destination see Jon Sterngass, *First Resorts: Pursuing Pleasure at Saratoga Springs, Newport & Coney Island* (Baltimore: Johns Hopkins University Press, 2001).

66. Henry David Thoreau, *Cape Cod* (New York: Penguin Books, 1987), 74.

67. Ibid., 21.

68. Ibid., 32.

69. Ibid., 33.

70. Ibid., 92.

71. Ibid., 26–27.

72. Ibid., 67.

73. Ibid., 93–116.

74. Ibid., 185–86

75. Ibid.

76. Ibid.

77. Ibid., 252

78. Ibid., 217–18.

79. Robert Pinsky, introduction to *The Writings of Henry David Thoreau: Cape Cod* (Princeton, N.J.: Princeton University Press, 2003), xvii.

80. Pinsky, introduction, xviii.

4. *Prosperity*

1. Charles Nordhoff, "Mehetabel Rogers's Cranberry Swamp," *Harper's New Monthly Magazine*, February 1864, 367–77.

2. Sandwich Town Records, vol. 2, March 5, 1765; vol. 3, March 9, 1773, March 11, 1779, March 29, 1780, March 14, 1782, March 5, 1783, March 11, 1784, March 18, 1788, May 10, 1789, March 11, 1790, March 17, 1791, March 15, 1792, March 20, 1794, March 17, 1795, March 14, 1796; vol. 4, March 7, 1797, March 15, 1798. Sandwich Public Library, Sandwich, Mass.

3. Rochester Town Records, vol. 3, December 28, 1789 [back of p. 191], March 17, 1794 [p. 66]; vol. 4, pp. 21, 35, 44, 129, 136, 162; vol. 5, pp. 120, 152. Rochester Town Hall, Rochester, Mass. Relative values based upon unskilled wage rate comparisons and relative share of GDP calculations. See Samuel H. Williamson, "Six Ways to Compute the Relative Value of a U.S. Dollar Amount, 1790 to Present," Measuring-Worth, 2009, http://www.measuringworth.com/uscompare/.

4. Harwich Town Records, vol. 3, Part I, March 9, 1814, March 3, 1818, March 5, 1821. Harwich Town Hall, Harwich, Mass. Massachusetts Division of Fisheries and Game, Department of Conservation, *Report upon the Alewife Fisheries of Massachusetts* (Boston: Wright & Potter, 1921), 41.

5. *Report upon the Alewife Fisheries*, 42–45.

6. Town of Rochester, Massachusetts, *Reports of the School Committee, Selectmen and Herring Inspectors of the Town of Rochester . . . 1861–1867* (New Bedford, 1860–68).

7. Matthew G. McKenzie, "Baiting Our Memories: The Impact of Offshore Technology Change on the Species around Cape Cod, 1860–1895," in David Starkey, Poul Holm, and Michaela Barnard, eds., *Oceans Past: Management Insights from the History of Marine Animal Populations Project* (London: Earthscan Press, 2008), 77–89.

8. Secretary of the Commonwealth, *Laws Relating to Inland Fisheries*, 198–290.

9. Ibid., 220.

10. Ibid., 222.

11. Ibid., 223.

12. "Marstons Mills Fishing Company Records, 1867–1879." Nickerson Room, Cape Cod Community College, Barnstable, Mass.

13. Secretary of the Commonwealth, *Laws Relating to Inland Fisheries*, 239.

14. Ibid., 293; *Report upon the Alewife Fisheries*, 102.

15. Spencer Fullerton Baird, *Report on the Condition of the Sea Fisheries of the*

South Coast of New England in 1871 and 1872, Part I (Washington, D.C.: Government Printing Office, 1873), xxv.

16. Baird, *Sea Fisheries*, 261–62.

17. Brian Payne, "George Brown Goode and the Technological Development of the Fisheries." Paper presented at the Middle-Atlantic New England Council for Canadian Studies, October 2002.

18. George Brown Goode and A. Howard Clarke, "The Menhaden Fishery," in George Brown Goode, ed., *The Fisheries and Fishery Industries of the United States, Section V: History and Methods of the Fisheries*, I (Washington, D.C.: Government Printing Office, 1887), 342.

19. Ibid.

20. Frederick W. True, "The Pound Net Fisheries of the Atlantic States," in George Brown Goode (prep.), *The Fisheries and Fishery Industries of the United States, Section V: History and Methods of the Fisheries*, I (Washington, D.C.: Government Printing Office, 1887), 595–610.

21. Baird, *Sea Fisheries*, 173, 177.

22. Secretary of the Commonwealth, *Laws Relating to Inland Fisheries*, 210–74.

23. Francis DeWitt, *Statistical Information Relating to Certain Branches of Industry in Massachusetts for the Year Ending June 1, 1855* (Boston: William White, 1856), 4.

24. Baird, *Sea Fisheries*, 7. For more details surrounding the testimony see chapter 5.

25. "Map of the Coast of Massachusetts and Rhode Island to Accompany the Report of the U.S. Commissioner of Fish and Fisheries, showing the locations of Traps and Pounds as also the Explorations of the Commission in 1871," in Baird, *Sea Fisheries*, inserted map.

26. It is essential to present these figures with a caveat: all numbers generated in the past need to be approached cautiously, and these figures represent no exception. As the chief of the state Bureau of Labor and Statistics reported in the 1875 Massachusetts census, the fisheries figures were "not satisfactory." The problem lay in the fact that "the difficulty in the way of correct returns of fisheries is that the census is taken at the very same time of year when our fishermen are the most active, their vessels are away, and no adequate means of obtaining the facts remaining." There is little reason to suppose that previous censuses did not suffer similar shortcomings. That said, however, the figures—as questionably comprehensive as they are—do offer some idea of the magnitude of the inshore fisheries and how they compared to one another. Moreover, if any branch of the fisheries was likely to be more accurately represented, it would have been those that kept fishermen inshore, close to home, and easily contacted by census takers.

27. DeWitt, *Statistical Information*.

28. True, "Pound Net Fisheries," 595–610.

29. For more about similar efforts to "enclose" the inshore commons see Bonnie McCay, *Oyster Wars and the Public Trust: Property, Law, and Ecology in New Jersey History* (Tucson: University of Arizona Press, 1998), and more specifically, Bonnie McCay, "Historical Observation on Old and New World Fisheries," in Bonnie McCay and James Acheson, eds., *The Question of the Commons: The Culture and Ecology of Communal Resources* (Tucson: University of Arizona Press, 1990).

30. Baird, *Sea Fisheries*, 19–29.

31. Ibid., 48.

32. Ibid., 53.

33. Ibid., 49.

34. Ibid.

35. Ibid., 71.

36. Ibid.

37. Ibid., 39.

38. Ibid., 36.

39. Ibid., 39.

40. Ibid., 70–71. Details of the Brightman's story come from U.S. census records for Westport, Massachusetts, for 1860 and 1870.

41. Baird, *Sea Fisheries*, 49.

42. Ibid., 50.

43. Ibid., 52. Handy was listed in the 1860 census as a manufacturer of lightning rods.

44. Baird, *Sea Fisheries*, 52.

45. Ibid., 48.

46. Ibid., 52.

5. *Abstractions*

1. Baird, *Sea Fisheries*, 20.

2. Ibid., viii–ix. Despite the lieutenant governor's electoral loss, the Rhode Island legislature seated him in office anyway. Will Bryant, "'The Strength of the Scup Ticket': The Politics of Fishery Management in Rhode Island, 1870–1872." Paper presented at the North Atlantic Fisheries History Association Annual Meeting, Old Dominion University, Norfolk, Va., August 2009.

3. Baird, *Sea Fisheries*, 104.

4. Ibid., 104–6.

5. Ibid., 106–7.

6. Ibid., 50.

7. Ibid., 71.

8. Ibid., 52.

9. D. Hamilton Hurd, *History of Bristol County, Massachusetts* (Philadelphia: J. W. Lewis & Co., 1883), 10–11.

10. Massachusetts Commissioners of Inland Fish and Game, *Sixth Annual Report of the Commissioners of Inland Fisheries* (Boston: Wright & Potter, 1872), 17.

11. Information based on 1865 census reports. See Oliver Warner, *Statistical Information Relating to Certain Branches of Industry in Massachusetts for the Year Ending May 1, 1865* (Boston: Wright & Potter, 1866).

12. See Atwood Company Records, Pilgrim Monument Museum, Provincetown, Mass.

13. Massachusetts Commissioners of Inland Fish and Game, *Sixth Annual Report*, 17.

14. Baird, *Sea Fisheries*, 117.

15. Ibid. 117–18.

16. Ibid., 118–24

17. Ibid., 122.

18. Ibid., 120.

19. Ibid., 123.

20. Secretary of the Commonwealth, *Laws Relating to Inland Fisheries*, 321, 335.

21. Massachusetts Commissioners of Inland Fish and Game, *Sixth Annual Report*, 18.

22. Ibid., 26.

23. Ibid.

24. Massachusetts Commissioners of Inland Fisheries, *Massachusetts Senate No. 193: Reports of the Commissioners of Inland Fisheries, May 1857* (Boston: Wright & Potter, 1857), 8–9.

25. *Report of the Commissioners of Fisheries* (Wright & Potter: Boston, 1868), 7.

26. Ibid., 6.

27. Massachusetts Commissioners of Inland Fish and Game, *Sixth Annual Report*, 27. For more discussion of Lyman's critique of Baird's work see Smith, *Scaling Fisheries*, 48–51.

28. H. P. Bowditch, *Biographical Memoir of Theodore Lyman, 1833–1897, Read before the National Academy of Sciences April 23, 1903* (Washington, D.C.: Judd and Detweiler, 1903), 145–46.

29. Massachusetts Commissioners of Inland Fish and Game, *Sixth Annual Report*, 17.

30. Ibid., 28.

31. Ibid.

32. Ibid., 29, 31.

33. Ibid., 32.

34. Ibid., 37.

35. For a more detailed account of those negotiations see Dean C. Allard, *Spencer Fullerton Baird and the U.S. Fish Commission* (New York: Arno Press, 1978), 69–86. For a fuller study of Baird's negotiations and the culture of scientific research in Baird's Washington, D.C., see Smith, *Scaling Fisheries*, 38–51.

36. Baird, *Sea Fisheries*, xvii.

37. Ibid., xiv.

38. Ibid., 137–38.

39. Ibid., xviii.

40. Tim Smith, *Scaling Fisheries: The Science of Measuring the Effects of Fishing, 1855–1955* (Cambridge, U.K.: Cambridge University Press, 1994), 9, 70–71.

41. Allard makes an explicit argument about Baird's vision of his investigations as much about politics of federally funded science as about discovering natural systems. See Allard, *Spencer Fullerton Baird*.

42. Baird, *Sea Fisheries*, xix–xx.

43. David Starr Jordan, "Spencer Fullerton Baird and the United States Fish Commission," *The Scientific Monthly* 17 (1923), 97–107. E. F. Rivinius and E. M. Youssef, *Spencer Baird of the Smithsonian* (Washington, D.C.: Smithsonian Institution Press, 1994), 170–72.

44. Baird, *Sea Fisheries*, xxii.

45. Ibid., 127

46. Dean C. Allard argues that Baird was more interested in securing federal funding for natural science than he was in conserving fish, or fishermen, for that matter. See Allard, *Spencer Fullerton Baird*. For more on Baird's role in applying fisheries science to immediate management policies see Smith, *Scaling Fisheries*, chapter 2; Jennifer Hubbard, *A Science on the Scales: The Rise of Canadian Atlantic Fisheries Biology, 1898–1939* (Toronto: University of Toronto Press, 2006), 43.

47. Spencer Fullerton Baird, "Conclusions as to Decrease of Cod-Fisheries on the New England Coast," 1874," *Report of the U. S. Commissioner of Fish and Fisheries for 1872–1873* (1874): xi.

48. For example, daily trap landings taken by Vinal Edwards in Woods Hole in the early 1880s showed that no landings were recorded for Sundays throughout the season. Sundays were also a day of rest on banks hand-lining vessels, at least through the 1860s. See "List of Fish Taken in Fish Traps & Pounds," 1885–1914, Vinal Edwards Manuscript Collection, RG 370, Records of National Oceanic and Atmospheric Administration, Box 8: Monthly Fish Reports, NRAB-99-33, National Archives and Records Administration, Waltham, Mass.

49. Massachusetts Commissioners on Inland Fisheries, *Thirteenth Annual Report of the Commissioners on Inland Fisheries* (Boston: Rand, Avery & Co., 1879), 49.

50. Ibid., 48. Emphasis in original.

51. For more on the shift from commercial optimization and conservation within the U.S. Fish Commission and its subsequent derivations see Michael L. Weber, *From Abundance to Scarcity: A History of U.S. Marine Fisheries Policy* (Washington, D.C.: Island Press, 2002).

6. Removals

1. Massachusetts Commission of Inland Fisheries, *Thirteenth Annual Report of the Commissioners of Inland Fisheries* (Boston: Rand, Avery & Co., 1879), 49–61.

2. Carroll D. Wright, ed., *The Census of Massachusetts: 1885. Vol 2: Manufactures, the Fisheries, and Commerce* (Boston: Wright & Potter, 1888), 1369–1405.

3. Horace G. Wadlin, ed., *Census of the Commonwealth of Massachusetts: 1895. Vol. 6: The Fisheries, Commerce, and Agriculture* (Boston: Wright & Potter, 1899), 93–131.

4. Massachusetts Bureau of Statistics of Labor, "Social and Industrial Changes," 50–52.

5. McFarland, *New England Fisheries*, 289.

6. Andrew A. Rosenberg et al., "The History of Ocean Resources: Modeling Cod Biomass Using Historical Records," *Frontiers in Ecology and the Environment* 3 (2005): 84–90. Leavenworth, "Opening Pandora's Box: Tradition, Competition, and Technology on the Scotian Shelf, 1852–1860," in David J. Starkey and James Candow, eds., *The North Atlantic Fisheries: Supply, Marketing and Consumption, 1560–1990, Studia Atlantica* 8 (2006): 29–49; Glenn M. Grasso, "What Appeared Limitless Plenty: The Rise and Fall of the Nineteenth-Century Atlantic Halibut Fishery," *Environmental History* 13, 1 (January 2008): 66–91.

7. McFarland, *New England Fisheries*, 292.

8. The 1889 census appears to have suffered from some confusion about what Cape Codders referred to as a "herring" and its relationship to the more distinct alewife fishery. As in the eighteenth century, locals referred to all alewives (*Pomolobus pseudoharengus* [1953], currently *Alosa pseudoharengus*) and blue-backs (*Pomolobus aestivalis* [1953], currently *Alosa aestivalis*) as river herring or, more confusingly, just "herring." Given the low numbers of alewives and the high number of herring reported landed by inshore traps, it is likely that USFC inspectors mistakenly included fishermen's reported "herring" landings with sea herring (*Clupea harengus*) catches, and not with alewife landings, which Massachusetts inland fisheries inspectors had done previously. Furthermore, sea herring shy away from the beaches lining Cape Cod, preferring open waters; when they come inshore to spawn, they prefer pebbly or rocky bottoms and not the long stretches of sandy beach lining Cape Cod. Bigelow and Schroeder claimed in 1953 that "nor has [sea] herring spawn ever been reported as cast up by the surf on the beaches of New England." See Bigelow and Schroeder, *Fishes of the Gulf of Maine*, Fishery Bulletin 74 of the Fish and Wildlife Service 53 (Washington, D.C.: Government Printing Office, 1953), 91. Supporting

sea herring's aversion to Cape Cod's inshore waters, Vinal Edwards counted only 65,000 sea herring from 1885 to 1895 and from 1905 to 1915. During that same period Falmouth traps landed 341,000 alewives and about 2,000 blue-black herring. See "List of Fish Taken in Fish Traps & Pounds," 1885–1914, Vinal Edwards Manuscript Collection, RG 370, Records of National Oceanic and Atmospheric Administration, Box 8: Monthly Fish Reports, NRAB-99–33, National Archives and Records Administration, Waltham, Mass.

9. The 1865 Massachusetts industrial census provides data to suggest that each barrel contained five hundred alewives. Given that these were cured fish, the more conservative figure of three hundred fish per barrel accommodates differences between headed and gutted fish and those left whole. See Oliver Warner, *Statistical Information Relating to Certain Branches of Industry in Massachusetts for the Year Ending May 1, 1865* (Boston: Wright & Potter, 1866). See accounting of alewives taken by Sandwich fishermen.

10. *Bulletin of the United States Fish Commission* X (1892): 136.

11. According to Bigelow and Schroeder, alewives weigh on average eight to nine ounces and blue-backs seven ounces each. The figures presented above are derived from an assumed average weight of eight ounces, which may be on the heavy side. Bigelow and Schroeder also point out that the 16.4 million alewives landed in 1898 weighed 8.8 million pounds, or roughly half a pound each. See Bigelow and Schroeder, *Fishes of the Gulf of Maine*, 101 and 107.

12. Species listed come from testimony collected by Baird in 1871 and 1872 and represent those species fishermen claimed were declining. See Baird, *Sea Fisheries,* 7–72. For species typically used as bait, see chapter 3.

13. Values determined from Fishbase.org's "Life History Tool" for each species identified. Garrison and Link's studies of differing trophic position at varying stages of development further reinforce the relative roles played by species discussed here. See Lance P. Garrison and Jason S. Link, "Dietary Guild Structure of the Fish Community in the Northeast United States Continental Shelf Ecosystem," *Marine Ecology Progress Series* 202 (August 28, 2000): 231–40.

14. Another study broke down populations of select northwest Atlantic species by relative size and preferred food to present similar conclusions. Medium alewives and all mackerels preferred plankton, thus making these fish crucial conduits by which nutrients from the base of the food web are transferred up to higher-order animals. All bluefish, large and extra-large cods, and medium and small squeteague (weakfish) were piscivores—that is, they prefer smaller fish, such as alewives and mackerel, for prey. See Lance P. Garrison and Jason S. Link, "Dietary Guild Structure of the Fish Community in the Northeast United States Continental Shelf Ecosystem," *Marine Ecology Progress Series* 202 (August 28, 2000): 231–40.

15. See "List of Fish Taken in Fish Traps & Pounds," 1885–1914, Vinal Edwards

Manuscript Collection. For a discussion of the effects of fishing upon marine animal communities and populations see Jennings, Kaiser, and Reynolds, *Marine Fisheries Ecology*, 245–57. For historical consequences see Jeremy Jackson et al., "Historical Overfishing and the Recent Collapse of Coastal Ecosystems," *Science* 293 (July 27, 2001): 629–38. See also James A. Estes et al., eds., *Whales, Whaling, and Ocean Ecosystems* (Berkeley: University of California Press, 2006). For fish communities and trophic cascades see A. S. Brierley, "Fisheries Ecology: Hunger for Shark Fin Soup Drives Clam Chowder off the Menu," *Current Biology* 17, 14 (July 17, 2007): R555–R557; John F. Bruno and Mary I. O'Connor, "Cascading Effects of Predator Diversity and Omnivory in a Marine Food Web," *Ecology Letters* 8, 10 (October 2005): 1048–56; A. Bundy and L. P. Fanning, "Can Atlantic Cod (*Gadus morhua*) Recover? Exploring Trophic Explanations for the Non-Recovery of the Cod Stock on the Eastern Scotian Shelf, Canada," *Canadian Journal of Fisheries and Aquatic Sciences* 62, 7 (2005): 1474–89; Kenneth T. Frank, Brian Petrie, Jae S. Choi, and William C. Leggett, "Trophic Cascades in a Formerly Cod-Dominated Ecosystem," *Science* 308, 5728 (June 10, 2005): 1621–23.

16. True, "Pound Net Fisheries," 597.

17. Ibid.

18. Ibid., 601.

19. Payne, "George Brown Goode"; True, "Pound Net Fisheries," 603.

20. True, "Pound Net Fisheries," 599.

21. Massachusetts Bureau of Statistics of Labor, "Social and Industrial Changes in the County of Barnstable," *27th Annual Report of the Bureau of Statistics of Labor of Massachusetts*, Part I (Boston: Wright & Potter, 1897), 5–7.

22. Ibid., 61–62.

23. Ibid., 57.

24. Ibid.

25. Ibid., 79.

26. Ibid., 81.

27. This pattern reflects an earlier manifestation of what modern marine ecologists have noticed happens to marine food webs as larger animals are removed. Daniel Pauly et al., "Fishing Down Marine Foodwebs," *Science*, New Series, 279, 5352 (February 2, 1998): 860–63.

28. Bureau of Statistics of Labor, "Social and Industrial Changes," 55.

29. Ibid., 30.

30. Ibid., 89.

31. Brown, *Inventing New England*; James C. O'Connell, *Becoming Cape Cod* (Hanover, N.H.: University of New Hampshire and University Press of New England, 2003), 3–10.

32. Brown, *Inventing New England*, 3–4; Jon Sterngass, *First Resorts: Pursuing*

Pleasure at Saratoga Springs, Newport & Coney Island (Baltimore: Johns Hopkins University Press, 2001), 40–74.

33. O'Connell, *Becoming Cape Cod,* 3–26.

34. Ibid., 13–20.

35. "Provincetown, Mass.," *Advocate of Peace,* September 1870, 283.

36. Elias Nason, *A Gazetteer of the State of Massachusetts* (Boston: B. B. Russell, 1874), 179–80.

37. Oramel Senter, "Civic and Scenic New England," *Potter's American Monthly,* August 1877, 81–95.

38. In this regard, Cape Cod was no different from other rural areas in New England where urban vacationers went seeking to reconnect with an idealized rural past. See Blake Harrison, *The View from Vermont: Tourism and the Making of an American Rural Landscape* (Burlington: University of Vermont Press, 2006); and Ian McKay, *Quest for the Folk: Antimodernism and Cultural Selection in Twentieth-Century Nova Scotia* (Montreal: McGill-Queen's University Press, 1994).

39. F. Mitchell, "Cape Cod," *Century Illustrated Magazine,* September 1883.

40. Roger B. Stein, "After the War: Constructing a Rural Past," in William B. Truettner and Roger B. Stein, eds., *Picturing Old New England: Image and Memory* (New Haven, Conn.: Yale University Press, 1999), 37.

41. Bruce Robertson, "Perils of the Sea," in Truettner and Stein, *Picturing Old New England,* 143.

42. That pattern was well established in areas outside southern New England by the 1840s. See Gail S. Davidson, "Landscape Icons, Tourism, and Land Development in the Northeast," in Gail S. Davidson et al., eds., *Frederic Church, Winslow Homer, and Thomas Moran: Tourism and the American Landscape* (Washington, D.C.: Smithsonian Institute Press, 2006), 3–6.

43. Novak, *Nature and Culture,* 32–33.

44. Karen E. Quinn, "Seascapes," in Theodore E. Stebbins Jr., ed., *Martin Johnson Heade* (New Haven, Conn.: Yale University Press, 1999), 11–28. On Heade's popularity see Theodore E. Stebbins Jr., "Picturing Heade: The Painter and His Critics," in Stebbins, *Martin Johnson Heade,* 141–68.

45. For a biographical outline of Kensett see John K. Howat, "Kensett's World," and John Paul Driscoll, "From Burin to Brush: The Development of a Painter," both in John Paul Driscoll and John K. Howat, *John Frederick Kensett: An American Master* (New York: W. W. Norton, 1985).

46. For the images and a more technical analysis of the development of Kensett's use of light see Driscoll and Howat, *John Frederick Kensett,* 99–136.

47. For images and comparison of these three works see Driscoll and Howat, *John Frederick Kensett,* 106–9.

48. Driscoll and Howat, *John Frederick Kensett,* 99–136.

49. *Ninth Annual Report of the Commissioners of Inland Fisheries* [of Rhode Island], (Providence: Freeman & Co., 1880). True, "Pound Net Fisheries," 604–6.

50. George Augustus King, *Argument of Hon. George A. King before the Committee on Fisheries and Game of the Legislature of Massachusetts, February 24, 1887* (Boston: Fred W. Barry, 1887), 1.

51. George H. Palmer, *The Exhaustion of the Food Fishes on the Seacoast of Massachusetts by Destructive Methods of Fishing* . . . (Boston: Addison C. Getchell, 1887).

52. Ibid., 10.

53. Ibid., 20.

54. Ibid., 10.

55. Bill Parenteau, "'A Very Determined Opposition to the Law': Conservation, Angling Leases, and Social Conflict in the Canadian Atlantic Salmon Fishery, 1867–1914," *Environmental History* 9, 3 (July 2004): 436–63.

56. Palmer, *Exhaustion of the Food Fishes*, 21.

57. Moses Rogers to Azariah F. Crowell, February 15, 1886. Pacific Guano Co. Records, Box 2, Folder 27 [Trap Fishermen in Opposition to Legislative Bill, 1886–1887], Baker Library, Harvard Business School, Cambridge, Mass.

58. Charles C. Chuck to Azariah F. Crowell, December 20, 1886. Pacific Guano Co. Records.

59. Anonymous to Azariah F. Crowell, February 5, 1887. Pacific Guano Co. Records.

60. Daniel A. Vincent to Azariah F. Crowell, March 14, 1887. Pacific Guano Co. Records.

61. Daniel W. Deane to Azariah F. Crowell, February 6, 1887. Pacific Guano Co. Records, Box 2, Folder 26.

62. William A. Bassett to Azariah F. Crowell, December 13, 1886. Pacific Guano Company Records, Box 2, Folder 27.

63. King, *Argument*, 2.

64. Charles F. Chamberlayne, *Is It Sport or Business for the Buzzards Bay Towns? An Argument of Charles F. Chamberlayne* . . . *for the Abolition of Weirs, Pounds, Traps, etc., from Buzzards Bay* (Boston: Rockwell and Churchill, 1892), 8.

65. King, *Argument*, 1–2. For more on the changes in American access to bait supplies in the northwest Atlantic, see Brian Payne, *Fishing a Borderless Sea: Environmental Territorialism in the North Atlantic, 1818–1910* (East Lansing: Michigan State University Press, 2010).

66. Chamberlayne, *Sport or Business*, 39.

67. King, *Argument*, 14.

68. Ibid., 6.

69. Ibid., 5.

70. Ibid., 21.

71. George Augustus King, *Fish Weirs: Argument before the Committee on Fisheries and Game . . . March 15, 1892* (n.p.: [1892]), 7. A bod carrier is a laborer who carries heavy masonry supplies to bricklayers and masons working on scaffolding.

72. King, *Fish Weirs*, 6.

73. Chamberlayne, *Sport or Business*, 14.

74. Ibid.

75. Ibid., 26–27.

Conclusion

1. Massachusetts Division of Fish and Game, Department of Conservation, *A Report upon the Alewife Fisheries of Massachusetts* (Boston: Wright & Potter, 1921).

2. For more on the application of the concept of autopsies on fisheries, see Tim D. Smith and Jason S. Link, "Autopsy Your Dead . . . and Living: A Proposal for Fisheries Science, Fisheries Management and Fisheries," *Fish and Fisheries* 6 (2005): 73–87.

3. Henry Beston, *The Outermost House: A Year of Life on the Great Beach of Cape Cod* (New York: Henry Holt, 1928, [1988]), 2.

4. Nigel Haggan, Barbara Neiss, and Ian G. Baird, eds., *Fisher's Knowledge in Fisheries Science and Management* (Paris: United Nations Educational, Scientific, and Cultural Organization, 2007).

5. Daniel Pauly and Jay Maclean, *In a Perfect Ocean: The State of Fisheries and Ecosystems in the North Atlantic Ocean* (Washington, D.C.: Island Press, 2003).

Bibliography

Archival Collections

Atwood Company Records. Pilgrim Monument Museum. Provincetown, Massachusetts.

Falmouth Town Records. Herring Fishery. Falmouth Historical Society. Falmouth, Massachusetts.

Falmouth Town Records microfilm. Falmouth Public Library. Falmouth, Massachusetts.

Harwich Town Records. Harwich Town Hall. Harwich, Massachusetts.

John Hopkins Papers. Mss. 44, series A. Kendall Institute, New Bedford Whaling Museum. New Bedford, Massachusetts.

Marstons Mills Fishing Company Records, 1867–79. Nickerson Room. Cape Cod Community College. Barnstable, Massachusetts.

Pacific Guano Company Records. Baker Library, Harvard Business School. Cambridge, Massachusetts.

Rochester Proprietors' Records. Rochester Town Hall. Rochester, Massachusetts.

Rochester Town Records. Rochester Town Hall. Rochester, Massachusetts.

Sandwich Town Records [typescripts]. Sandwich Public Library. Sandwich, Massachusetts.

Sandwich Town Records. Sandwich Public Library. Sandwich, Massachusetts.

———. Sandwich Town Archives. Sandwich, Massachusetts.

Vinal Edwards Manuscript Collection. RG 370, Records of National Oceanic and Atmospheric Administration. NRAB -99-33. National Archives and Records Administration. Waltham, Massachusetts.

Published Primary Sources

Atwood, Nathaniel E. "Autobiography of Capt. N. E. Atwood." In *The Fisheries and Fisheries Industries of the United States, Section IV,* edited by George Brown Goode, 149–68. Washington, D.C.: Government Printing Office, 1887.

Baird, Spencer Fullerton. *Report on the Condition of the Sea Fisheries of the South Coast of New England in 1871 and 1872*, Part 1. Washington, D.C.: Government Printing Office, 1873.

———. "Conclusions as to Decrease of Cod-Fisheries on the New England Coast," 1874." *Report of the U. S. Commissioner of Fish and Fisheries for 1872–1873* (1874): xi–xiv.

Beston, Henry. *The Outermost House: A Year of Life on the Great Beach of Cape Cod.* New York: Henry Holt & Co., 1928, [1988].

Bowditch, H. P. *Biographical Memoir of Theodore Lyman, 1833–1897, Read before the National Academy of Sciences April 23, 1903.* Washington, D.C.: Judd and Detweiler, 1903.

Bradford, William. *Bradford's History "Of Plimouth Plantation."* Boston: Wright & Potter, 1898.

Brereton, John. "Briefe and True Relation of the Discoverie of the North Part of Virginia in 1602." In *Sailors* [sic] *Narratives of the New England Coast*, edited by George Parker Winship, 30–49. Boston: Houghton, Mifflin & Co., 1905.

Chamberlayne, Charles F. *Is It Sport or Business for the Buzzards Bay Towns? An Argument of Charles F. Chamberlayne . . . for the Abolition of Weirs, Pounds, Traps, etc., from Buzzards Bay*. Boston: Rockwell and Churchill, 1892.

Champlain, Samuel de. *Voyages of Samuel de Champlain*, vol. 2. Translated by Charles Pomeroy Otis. Boston: Prince Society, 1878.

Council for New England. *An Historicall Discoverie and Relation of the English Plantations in New England*. London: John Bellamie, 1627.

"Description of Cape Cod, and the County of Barnstable." *Massachusetts Magazine*, February, 1791.

DeWitt, Francis. *Statistical Information Relating to Certain Branches of Industry in Massachusetts for the Year Ending June 1, 1855*. Boston: William White, 1856.

Douglass, William. *A Summary, Historical and Political, of the First Settlements, Progressive Improvements, and Present State of the British Settlements in North America*, I. London: 1760.

Dwight, Timothy. *Travels in New York and New England*, vol. 3, edited by Barbara Miller Solomon and Patricia King. Cambridge, Mass.: Harvard University Press, 1969.

Earll, R. Edward. "The Frozen Herring Industry." In *The Fisheries and Fishery Industries of the United States, Section V: History and Methods of the Fisheries*, vol. 1, edited by George Brown Goode, 439–58. Washington, D.C.: Government Printing Office, 1887.

Emerson, Ralph Waldo. *The American Scholar/ Self Reliance/ Compensation*, edited by Orren Henry Smith. New York: American Book Company, 1893, [1911].

Fowle, William B., and Asa Fitz. *An Elementary Geography for Massachusetts Children*. Boston: Fowle and Capen, 1845.

Goode, George Brown and A. Howard Clarke. "The Menhaden Fishery." In *The Fisheries and Fishery Industries of the United States, Section V: History and Methods of the Fisheries*, vol. 1, edited by George Brown Goode, 327–415. Washington, D.C.: Government Printing Office, 1887.

Goode, George Brown and J. W. Collins. "The Bank Hand-line Cod Fishery." In *The Fisheries and Fishery Industries of the United States, Section V: History and Methods of the Fisheries*, vol. 1, edited by George Brown Goode, 123–33. Washington, D.C.: Government Printing Office, 1887.

———. "George's Bank Cod Fishery." In *The Fisheries and Fishery Industries of the United States, Section V: History and Methods of the Fisheries*, vol. 1, edited by George Brown Goode, 187–98. Washington, D.C.: Government Printing Office, 1887.

———. "The Bank Trawl-Line Cod Fishery." In *The Fisheries and Fishery Industries of the United States, Section V: History and Methods of the Fisheries*, vol. 1, edited by George Brown Goode, 148–87. Washington, D.C.: Government Printing Office, 1887.

———. "The Haddock Fishery of New England." In *The Fisheries and Fishery Industries of the United States, Section V: History and Methods of the Fisheries*, vol. 1, edited by George Brown Goode, 234–41. Washington, D.C.: Government Printing Office, 1887.

———. "The Mackerel Hook Fishery," in, *The Fisheries and Fishery Industries of the United States, Section V: History and Methods of the Fisheries*, vol. 1, edited by George Brown Goode, 275–94. Washington, D.C.: Government Printing Office, 1887.

Hay, John. *The Run*. Boston: Beacon Press, 1959.

Hayward, John. *The New England Gazetteer*. Concord, N. H.: Boyd & White, 1839.

Hazard, Caroline, ed. *Nailer Tom's Diary: The Journal of Thomas B. Hazard, 1778–1840*. Boston: The Merrymount Press, 1930.

Hurd, D. Hamilton. *History of Bristol County*. Philadelphia: J. W. Lewis & Co., 1883.

Johnson, Edward. *A History of New England*. London: Nath. Brooke [1653].

Jordan, David Starr. "Spencer Fullerton Baird and the United States Fish Commission." *The Scientific Monthly*, 17 (1923): 97–107.

Josseleyn, John. *New England's Rarities Discovered*. London: C. Widdowes, 1675.

"The Journal of a Captive, 1745–1748." In *Colonial Captivities, Marches, and Journeys*, edited by Isabel M. Calder, 3–136. New York: MacMillan Co., 1935.

King, George Augustus. *Argument of Hon. George A. King before the Committee on Fisheries and Game of the Legislature of Massachusetts, February 24, 1887*. Boston: Fred W. Barry, 1887.

———. *Fish Weirs: Argument before the Committee on Fisheries and Game . . . March 15, 1892* [1892].

La Rochefoucauld-Liancourt, François Alexandre Frédéric, duc de. *Travels through the United States of North America, 1795–97*, vol. 2. London: R. Phillips, 1800.

"Letter of Isaack des Rasieres to Samuel Blommaert, 1628 (?)." In *Narratives of New Netherland, 1609–1664*, edited by J. Franklin Jameson, 102–15. New York: Charles Scribner's Sons, 1909.

"The Mackerel Fishery." *The Friend: A Religious Literary Journal*, May 1, 1852.

Manning, Helen Vanderhoop. *Moshup's Footsteps: The Wampanoag Nation Gay Head / Aquinnah, The People of First Light*. Aquinnah, Mass.: Blue Cloud Across the Moon Publishing Co., 2001.

Massachusetts Bureau of Statistics of Labor. "Social and Industrial Changes in the County of Barnstable," *27th Annual Report of the Bureau of Statistics of Labor of Massachusetts*, part 1. Boston: Wright & Potter, 1897.

Massachusetts Commissioners of Inland Fish and Game. *Sixth Annual Report of the Commissioners of Inland Fisheries*. Boston: Wright & Potter, 1872.

Massachusetts Commissioners of Inland Fisheries. *Massachusetts Senate No. 193: Reports of the Commissioners of Inland Fisheries, May 1857*. Boston: Wright & Potter, 1857.

———. *Report of the Commissioners of Inland Fisheries for the Year Ending January 1, 1875*. Boston: Wright & Potter, 1875.

———. *Thirteenth Annual Report of the Commissioners on Inland Fisheries*. Boston: Rand, Avery & Co., 1879.

Massachusetts Division of Fish and Game, Department of Conservation. *A Report upon the Alewife Fisheries of Massachusetts*. Boston: Wright & Potter, 1921.

Mellen, Reverend. "A Topographical Description of the Town of Barnstable." *Collections of the Massachusetts Historical Society* 3 (1810): 12–17.

Mitchell, F. "Cape Cod," *Century Illustrated Magazine*, September 1883.

Morrell, William. *New England, or, A Briefe Narration of the Ayre, Earth, Water, Fish and Fowles of that Country*. London: I. D[awson], 1625.

Morton, George. *A Relation or Journal of the Beginning and Proceeding of the English Plantation Settled at Plymouth in New England*. London: John Bellamie, 1622.

Morton, Thomas. *New English Canaan*. [London]: Charles Greene, 1632.

Mourt's Relation: A Journal of the Pilgrims at Plymouth. Cambridge, Mass.: Applewood Books, 1986.

Nason, Elias. *A Gazetteer of the State of Massachusetts*. Boston: B. B. Russell, 1874.

Nordhoff, Charles. "Mehetabel Rogers's Cranberry Swamp," *Harper's New Monthly Magazine*, February 1864.

"Notes of Mr. Bennet, 1740." In *Memorial History of Boston*, vol. 2, edited by Justin Winsor. Boston: James R. Good and Co., 1881.

Palmer, George H. *The Exhaustion of the Food Fishes on the Seacoast of Massachusetts by Destructive Methods of Fishing . . .* Boston: Addison C. Getchell, 1887.

Pring, Martin. "A Voyage Set out from the Citie of Bristoll, at the Charge of the Chiefest Merchants and Inhabitants . . . For the Discouerie of the North Part of Virginia, in the Yeere 1603. Vnder the Command of Me Martin Pring." In *The English New England Voyages*, edited by David B. Quinn and Alison M. Quinn. London: Hakluyt Society, 1983.

———. "A Voyage from the Citie of Bristoll . . . for the discoverie of the North part of Virginia, in the yeere 1603, under the command of me, Martin Pring." In *Hakluytus Posthumous, or, Purchas, His Pilgrimes*, part 4, edited by Samuel Purchas, 1654–56. London: H. Fetherstone, 1625.

"Provincetown, Mass." *Advocate of Peace*, September 1870.

"Records of the Boston Customs District, 1768." *Proceedings of the Massachusetts Historical Society* 62 (1925).

[Rhode Island Commissioners of Inland Fisheries]. *Ninth Annual Report of the Commissioners of Inland Fisheries* [of Rhode Island]. Providence: Freeman & Co., 1880.

Rochester, Massachusetts, Town of. *Reports of the School Committee, Selectmen and Herring Inspectors of the Town of Rochester . . . 1861–1867* (New Bedford, 1860–68).

Rosier, James. "A True Relation of Waymouth's Voyage, 1605." In *Early English and French Voyages, Chiefly from Hakluyt, 1534–1609*, edited by Henry S. Burrage. New York: Barnes & Noble, 1906.

Ruskin, John. "The Harbours of England." In *The Complete Works of John Ruskin*, vol. 13, edited by E. T. Cook and Alexander Wedderburn, 1–33. London: George Allen, 1904.

Sabine, Lorenzo. *Report of the Principal Fisheries of the American Seas*. Washington, D.C.: Robert Armstrong, 1853.

Secretary of the Commonwealth of Massachusetts, comp. *Laws Relating to Inland Fisheries in Massachusetts, 1623–1886*. Boston: Wright & Potter Printing Co., 1887.

Senter, Oramel. "Civic and Scenic New England." *Potter's American Monthly*, August 1877, 81–95.

[Sewall, Samuel]. "Letter-Book of Samuel Sewall." *Massachusetts Historical Society Collections*, 6th ser., vol. 1 (1886): 37–112.

Smith, John. *A Description of New England*. London: Robert Clerke, 1616.

———. *The Generall Historie of Virginia, New-England, and the Summer Isles . . .* London: I. D. and I. H. for Michael Sparkes, 1624.

John C. Pearson, ed. *The Fish and Fisheries of Colonial North America, Part II: The New England States*. NOAA Report No. 72040302. Springfield, Va.: National Technical Information Services, 1972.

Storer, D. Humphrey. "A Report on the Fishes of Massachusetts." *Boston Journal of Natural History* II (1839): 289–570.

Thoreau, Henry David. *Cape Cod*. New York: Penguin Books, 1987.

———. *Cape Cod*. Edited by Joseph J. Moldenhauer. Princeton, N.J.: Princeton University Press, 1988.

"A Topographical Description of Truro." *Collections of the Massachusetts Historical Society* 3 (1810): 195–200.

True, Frederick W. "The Pound Net Fisheries of the Atlantic States." In *The Fisheries and Fishery Industries of the United States, Section V: History and Methods of the Fisheries*, vol. 1, edited by George Brown Goode, 595–610. Washington, D.C.: Government Printing Office, 1887.

United States Department of the Census. *Abstract of the Returns of the Fifth Census*. Washington, D.C.: Government Printing Office, 1832.

———. *Compendium of the Enumeration of the Inhabitants and Statistics of the United States*. Washington, D.C.: Government Printing Office, 1841.

———. *Heads of Families at the First Census of the United States Taken in the Year 1790: Massachusetts*. Washington, D.C.: Government Printing Office, 1908.

———. *Population of the United States in 1860*. Washington, D.C.: Government Printing Office, 1864.

———. *Statistical View of the United States. . . .Compendium of the Seventh Census*. Washington, D.C.: Government Printing Office, 1854.

Wadlin, Horace G., ed. *Census of the Commonwealth of Massachusetts: 1895. Vol. 6: The Fisheries, Commerce, and Agriculture*. Boston: Wright & Potter, 1899.

Warner, Oliver. *Statistical Information Relating to Certain Branches of Industry in Massachusetts for the Year Ending May 1, 1865*. Boston: Wright & Potter, 1866.

Whitman, Levi. "A Topographical Description of Wellfleet." *Collections of the Massachusetts Historical Society* 3 (1810): 117–21.

[Winslow, Edward]. "Good News from New England." In *The Story of the Pilgrim Fathers, 1606–1623 A.D.*, edited by Edward Arber. Boston: Houghton Mifflin, 1897.

Wood, William. *New England's Prospect*. London: John Bellamie, 1634.

Wright, Carroll D. ed. *The Census of Massachusetts: 1885. Volume II: Manufactures, the Fisheries, and Commerce*. Boston: Wright & Potter, 1888.

Kendall, Edward Augustus. *Travels through the Northern Parts of the United States in the Years 1807 and 1808*. New York: I. Riley, 1809.

Secondary Sources

Allard, Dean C. *Spencer Fullerton Baird and the U. S. Fish Commission*. New York: Arno Press, 1978.

American Paradise: The World of the Hudson River School. New York: Metropolitan Museum of Art, 1987.

Anderson, Katharine. "Does History Count?" *Endeavour* 30 (2006): 150–55.

Andrews, J. Clinton. "Indian Fish and Fishing off Coastal Massachusetts." *Bulletin of the Massachusetts Archaeological Society* 47 (1986): 42–46.

Benson, Keith R., Helen Rozwadowski, and David van Keuren. Introduction to *The Machine in Neptune's Garden*, edited by Helen Rozwadowski and David van Keuren. Sagamore Beach, Mass.: Science History Publications, 2004.

Bernstein, David J. "Prehistoric Seasonality Studies in Coastal Southern New England." *American Anthropologist*, new ser., 92 (1990): 96–115.

Bigelow, Henry B., and William C. Schroeder. *Fishes of the Gulf of Maine*. Fishery Bulletin 74 of the Fish and Wildlife Service, vol. 53 [Contribution No. 592, Woods Hole Oceanographic Institution]. Washington, D.C.: United States Government Printing Office, 1953.

Blasdale, Mary Jean. *Artists of New Bedford*. New Bedford, Mass.: Old Dartmouth Historical Society, 1990.

Bolster, W. Jeffrey. "Opportunities in Marine Environmental History." *Environmental History* 11 (2006): 567–97.

———. "Putting the Ocean in Atlantic History: Maritime Communities and Marine Ecology in the Northwest Atlantic, 1500–1800." *American Historical Review* 113 (2008): 19–47.

Brierley, A. S. "Fisheries Ecology: Hunger for Shark Fin Soup Drives Clam Chowder off the Menu." *Current Biology* 17 (2007): R555–R557.

Brown, Dona. *Inventing New England: Regional Tourism in the Nineteenth Century*. Washington, D.C.: Smithsonian Institution Press, 1995.

Brown, Richard D. "Microhistory and the Postmodern Challenge." *Journal of the Early Republic* 23 (2003): 1–20.

Bruno, John F., and Mary I. O'Connor. "Cascading Effects of Predator Diversity and Omnivory in a Marine Food Web." *Ecology Letters*, 8 (October, 2005): 1048–56.

Bryant, Will. "'The Strength of the Scup Ticket': The Politics of Fishery Management in Rhode Island, 1870–1872." Paper presented at the North Atlantic Fisheries History Association Annual Meeting, Old Dominion University, Norfolk, Va., August 2009.

Bundy, A., and L. P. Fanning. "Can Atlantic Cod (*Gadus morhua*) Recover? Exploring Trophic Explanations for the Non-Recovery of the Cod Stock on the Eastern Scotian Shelf, Canada." *Canadian Journal of Fisheries and Aquatic Sciences* 62 (2005): 1474–89.

Burnett, D. Graham. *Trying Leviathan*. Princeton, N.J.: Princeton University Press, 2007.

Burns, Sarah. *Pastoral Inventions: Rural Life in Nineteenth-Century American Art and Culture*. Philadelphia: Temple University Press, 1989.

Bushman, Richard L. "Markets and Composite Farms in Early America." *The William and Mary Quarterly*, 3rd ser., 55 (1988): 351–74.

Chapelle, Howard I. *The National Watercraft Collection*. Washington, D.C.: Museum of History and Technology of the United States National Museum, 1960.

Chiang, Connie Y. *Shaping the Shoreline: Fisheries and Tourism on the Monterey Coast.* Seattle: University of Washington Press, 2008.

Clark, Christopher. *The Roots of Rural Capitalism: Western Massachusetts, 1780–1860.* Ithaca, N.Y.: Cornell University Press, 1990.

Collette, Bruce B., and Grace Klein-Mcphee, eds. *Bigelow and Schroeder's Fishes of the Gulf of Maine.* 3rd ed. Washington, D.C.: Smithsonian Institution Press, 2002.

Conforti, Joseph. *Imagining New England.* Chapel Hill: University of North Carolina Press, 2001.

Cook, R. R., and Peter J. Auster, *A Bioregional Classification of the Continental Shelf of Northeastern North America for Conservation Analysis and Planning Based on Representation.* Marine Sanctuaries Conservation Series NMSP-07-03. Silver Spring, Md.: U.S. Department of Commerce, National Oceanic and Atmospheric Administration, National Marine Sanctuary Program, 2007.

Cronon, William. *Changes in the Land: Indians, Colonists, and the Ecology of New England* (New York: Hill & Wang, 1983).

———. "The Uses of Environmental History." *Environmental History Review* 17 (1993): 1–22.

Davidson, Gail S., Flormae McCarron-Cates, Barbara Bloemink, Sarah Burns, Karal Ann Marling, eds. *Frederic Church, Winslow Homer, and Thomas Moran: Tourism and the American Landscape.* Washington, D.C.: Smithsonian Institute Press, 2006.

———. "Landscape Icons, Tourism, and Land Development in the Northeast." In *Frederic Church, Winslow Homer, and Thomas Moran: Tourism and the American Landscape,* edited by Gail S. Davidson, Flormae McCarron-Cates, Barbara Bloemink, Sarah Burns, Karal Ann Marling, 3–72. Washington, D.C.: Smithsonian Institute Press, 2006.

Donahue, Brian. *The Great Meadow: Farmers and the Land in Colonial Concord.* New Haven, Conn.: Yale University Press, 2004.

Driscoll, John Paul. "From Burin to Brush: The Development of a Painter." In *John Frederick Kensett: An American Master,* edited by John Paul Driscoll and John K. Howat, 46–135. New York: W. W. Norton, 1985.

Dunford, Frederick J. "Paleoenvironmental Context for the Middle Archaic Occupation of Cape Cod, Massachusetts." In *The Archaeological Northeast,* edited by Mary Anne Levine, Kenneth E. Sassaman, and Michael S. Nassaney, 39–47. Westport, Conn.: Bergin & Garvey, 1999.

Estes, James A., Douglas P. Demaster, Daniel F. Doak, Terrie M. Williams, and Robert L. Brownell, eds. *Whales, Whaling and Ocean Ecosystems.* Berkeley: University of California Press, 2006.

Fletcher, Peter. *Soil Survey of Barnstable County, Massachusetts.* Washington, D.C.: U.S. Department of Agriculture, 1993.

Frank, Kenneth T., Brian Petrie, Jae S. Choi, and William C. Leggett. "Trophic Cascades in a Formerly Cod-Dominated Ecosystem." *Science*, vol. 308, no. 5728 (2005): 1621–23.

Friedman, Ruth Lynn. "Governing the Land: An Environmental History of Cape Cod, Massachusetts, 1600–1861." PhD diss., Brandeis University, 1993.

Garrison, Lance P., and Jason S. Link. "Dietary Guild Structure of the Fish Community in the Northeast United States Continental Shelf Ecosystem." *Marine Ecology Progress Series* 202 (August 28, 2000): 231–40.

Grasso, Glenn M. "What Appeared Limitless Plenty: The Rise and Fall of the Nineteenth-Century Atlantic Halibut Fishery." *Environmental History* 13 (January 2008): 66–91.

Greenblatt, Stephen. *Marvelous Possession: The Wonder of the New World*. Chicago: University of Chicago Press, 1991.

Haggan, Nigel, Barbara Neiss, and Ian G. Baird, eds. *Fisher's Knowledge in Fisheries Science and Management*. Paris: United Nations Educational, Scientific and Cultural Organization, 2007.

Hall, Elton W. *Robert Swain Gifford, 1850–1905*. New Bedford, Mass.: Old Dartmouth Historical Society, 1974.

Harley, J. B. "Silences and Secrecy: The Hidden Agenda of Cartography in Early Modern Europe." *Imago Mundi* 40 (1988), 57–76.

Harrison, Blake. *The View from Vermont: Tourism and the Making of an American Rural Landscape*. Burlington: University of Vermont Press, 2006.

Howat, John K. "Kensett's World." In *John Frederick Kensett: An American Master*, by John Paul Driscoll and John K. Howat, 12–46. New York: W. W. Norton, 1985.

Hubbard, Jennifer. *A Science on the Scales: The Rise of Canadian Atlantic Fisheries Biology, 1898–1939*. Toronto: University of Toronto Press, 2006.

Innis, Harold A. *The Cod Fisheries: The History of an International Economy*. Toronto: University of Toronto Press, 1940 [1985].

Jackson, Jeremy, et al., "Historical Overfishing and the Recent Collapse of Coastal Ecosystems." *Science* 293 (July 27, 2001): 629–38.

Jennings, Simon, Michael J. Kaiser, and John D. Reynolds. *Marine Fisheries Ecology* Oxford: Blackwell Science, 2001.

Judd, Richard. *Common Lands, Common People: The Origins of Conservation in Northern New England*. Cambridge, Mass.: Harvard University Press, 1997.

———. "Grass-Roots Conservation in Eastern Coastal Maine: Monopoly and the Moral Economy of Weir Fishing, 1893–1911." *Environmental Review* 12 (Summer 1988): 80–103.

———. "Reshaping Maine's Landscape: Rural Culture, Tourism, and Conservation, 1890–1929." *Forest History* 32 (October 1988): 180–90.

Kerber, Jordan E. "Where are the Woodland Villages in the Narragansett Bay Region?" *Bulletin of the Massachusetts Archaeological Society* 49 (1988): 66–71.

King, H. Roger. *Cape Cod and Plymouth Colony in the Seventeenth Century*. Lanham, Md.: University Press of America, 1994.

Kittredge, Henry C. *Cape Cod: Its People and Their History*. Boston: Houghton Mifflin, 1930 [1968].

Kulick, Gary. "Dams, Fish, and Farmers: Defense of Public Rights in Eighteenth-Century Rhode Island." In *The Countryside in the Age of Capitalist Transformation: Essays in the Social History of Rural America*, edited by Steven Hahn and Jonathan Prude, 25–50. Chapel Hill: University of North Carolina Press, 1985.

Latimer, W. J., E. T. Maxon, H. C. Smith, A. S. Mallory, and O. H. Roberts. *Soil Survey of Norfolk, Bristol, and Barnstable Counties, Massachusetts*. Washington, D.C.: Government Printing Office, 1924.

Leavenworth, William B. "Opening Pandora's Box: Tradition, Competition, and Technology on the Scotian Shelf, 1852–1860." *Studia Atlantica* 8 (2006): 29–49.

———. "The Ship in the Forest: New England Maritime Industries and Coastal Environment, 1630–1850." PhD diss., University of New Hampshire, 1999.

Little, Elizabeth A., and Margaret J. Schoeninger. "The Late Woodland Diet on Nantucket Island and the Problem of Maize in Coastal New England." *American Antiquity* 60 (1995): 351–68.

Marx, Leo. *The Machine in the Garden: Technology and the Pastoral Ideal in America*. New York: Oxford University Press, 1964 [2000].

McBride, Kevin A. "Archaic Subsistence in the Lower Connecticut Valley: Evidence from Woodchuck Knoll." *Man in the Northeast* 78 (1978): 124–32.

McCay, Bonnie. "Historical Observation on Old and New World Fisheries." In *The Question of the Commons: The Culture and Ecology of Communal Resources*, edited by Bonnie McCay and James Acheson, 195–216. Tucson: University of Arizona Press, 1990.

———. *Oyster Wars and the Public Trust: Property, Law, and Ecology in New Jersey History*. Tucson: University of Arizona Press, 1998.

McEvoy, Arthur. *The Fisherman's Problem: Ecology and Law in the California Fisheries, 1850–1980*. Cambridge, U.K.: Cambridge University Press, 1986.

McFarland, Raymond. *A History of the New England Fisheries*. New York: University of Pennsylvania Press, 1911.

McKay, Ian. *Quest for the Folk: Antimodernism and Cultural Selection in Twentieth-Century Nova Scotia*. Montreal: McGill-Queen's University Press, 1994.

McKenzie, Matthew G. "Baiting Our Memories: The Impact of Offshore Technology Change on the Species around Cape Cod, 1860–1895." In *Oceans Past: Management Insights from the History of Marine Animal Populations*, edited by David

Starkey, Poul Holm, and Michaela Barnard, 75–89. London: Earthscan Press, 2008.

Merchant, Carolyn. *Ecological Revolutions: Nature, Gender, and Science in New England*. Chapel Hill: University of North Carolina Press, 1989.

Miller, Angela. *Empire of the Eye: Landscape Representation and American Cultural Politics, 1825–1875*. Ithaca, N.Y.: Cornell University Press, 1993.

Morison, Samuel Eliot. *Maritime History of Massachusetts*. Boston: Houghton Mifflin, 1921.

Mrozowski, Stephen A. "The Discovery of a Native American Cornfield on Cape Cod." *Archaeology of Eastern North America* 22 (1994): 47–62.

Novak, Barbara. *Nature and Culture: American Landscape and Painting, 1825–1875*, rev. ed. New York: Oxford University Press, 1995.

O'Connell, James C. *Becoming Cape Cod*. Hanover, N.H.: University of New Hampshire and University Press of New England, 2003.

Oldale, Robert N. *Cape Cod and the Islands: the Geologic Story*. East Orleans, Mass.: Parnassus Imprints, 1992.

———. *A Geologic History of Cape Cod*. Washington, D.C.: U.S. Geological Survey, 1980.

O'Leary, Wayne M. *Maine Sea Fisheries: The Rise and Fall of a Native Industry, 1830–1890*. Boston: Northeastern University Press, 1996.

Parenteau, Bill. "'A Very Determined Opposition to the Law': Conservation, Angling Leases, and Social Conflict in the Canadian Atlantic Salmon Fishery, 1867–1914." *Environmental History* 9 (July 2004): 436–63.

Pauly, Daniel, and Jay Maclean. *In a Perfect Ocean: The State of Fisheries and Ecosystems in the North Atlantic Ocean*. Washington, D.C.: Island Press, 2003.

Pauly, Daniel, et al. "Fishing Down Marine Foodwebs." *Science*, new ser., 279 (1998): 860–63.

Payne, Brian. *Fishing a Borderless Sea: Environmental Territorialism in the North Atlantic, 1818–1910*. East Lansing: Michigan State University Press, 2010.

———. "George Brown Goode and the Technological Development of the Fisheries." Paper presented at the Middle-Atlantic New England Council for Canadian Studies, October 2002.

Pinsky, Robert. Introduction to *The Writings of Henry David Thoreau: Cape Cod*, edited by Joseph J. Moldenhauer. Princeton, N.J.: Princeton University Press, 2003.

Pope, Peter E. *Fish into Wine: The Newfoundland Plantation in the Seventeenth Century*. Chapel Hill: University of North Carolina Press, 2004.

Poulsen, Bo. *Dutch Herring: An Environmental History, c. 1600–1800*. Amsterdam: Aksant Academic Publishers, 2009.

Quinn, Karen E. "Seascapes." In *Martin Johnson Heade*, edited by Theodore Stebbins Jr., 11–28. New Haven, Conn.: Yale University Press, 1999.

Read, David. "Silent Partners: Historical Representation in William Bradford's *Of Plymouth Plantation.*" *Early American Literature* 33 (1998): 291–314.

Ritchie, William A. *The Archaeology of Martha's Vineyard.* Garden City, N.Y.: Natural History Press, 1969.

Rivinius, E. F., and E. M. Youssef. *Spencer Baird of the Smithsonian.* Washington, D.C.: Smithsonian Institution Press, 1994.

Robertson, Bruce. "Perils of the Sea." In *Picturing Old New England: Image and Memory,* edited by William B. Truettner and Roger B. Stein, 143–70. New Haven, Conn.: Yale University Press, 1999.

Rose, George A. *Cod: The Ecological History of the North Atlantic Fisheries.* St. John's, Newfoundland: Breakwater Press, 2007.

Rosenberg, Andrew A., W. Jeffrey Bolster, Karen E. Alexander, William B. Leavenworth, Andrew B. Cooper, and Matthew G. McKenzie. "The History of Ocean Resources: Modeling Cod Biomass Using Historical Sources." *Frontiers in Ecology and the Environment* 3 (2005): 84–90.

Rothman, Hal K. *Devil's Bargains: Tourism in the Twentieth-Century American West.* Lawrence: University Press of Kansas, 1999.

Rozwadowski, Helen. *Fathoming the Ocean: The Discovery and Exploration of the Deep Sea.* Cambridge, Mass.: Harvard University Press, 2004.

Settee, Oscar E., and A. W. H. Needler. *Statistics of the Mackerel Fishery off the East Coast of North America, 1804–1930.* U.S. Department of Commerce, Bureau of the Fisheries, Investigational Report No. 19. Washington, D.C.: Government Printing Office, 1934.

Smith, Tim D. *Scaling Fisheries: The Science of Measuring the Effects of Fishing, 1855–1955.* Cambridge, U.K.: Cambridge University Press, 1994.

Smith, Tim D., and Jason S. Link. "Autopsy Your Dead . . . and living: A Proposal for Fisheries Science, Fisheries Management and Fisheries." *Fish and Fisheries* 6 (2005): 73–87.

Starkey, David, Poul Holm, and Michaela Barnard, eds. *Oceans Past: Management Insights from the History of Marine Animals Populations Project.* London: Earthscan Press, 2008.

Stebbins, Theodore E. Jr. "Picturing Heade: The Painter and His Critics." In *Martin Johnson Heade,* edited by Theodore E. Stebbins Jr., 141–67. New Haven, Conn.: Yale University Press, 1999.

Stein, Roger B. "After the War: Constructing a Rural Past." In *Picturing Old New England: Image and Memory,* edited by William B. Truettner and Roger B. Stein, 15–42. New Haven, Conn.: Yale University Press, 1999.

———. *Seascape and the American Imagination.* New York: Clarkson N. Potter, 1975.

Steinberg, Theodore. *Down to Earth: Nature's Role in American History.* New York: Oxford University Press, 2002.

———. *Nature Incorporated: Industrialization and the Waters of New England*. Amherst: University of Massachusetts Press, 1991.

Sterngass, Jon. *First Resorts: Pursuing Pleasure at Saratoga Springs, Newport & Coney Island*. Baltimore: Johns Hopkins University Press, 2001.

Stilgoe, John R. *Alongshore*. New Haven, Conn.: Yale University Press, 1994.

———. "A New England Coastal Wilderness." *Geographical Review* 71 (1981): 33–50.

Strahler, Arthur N. *A Geologist's View of Cape Cod*. Garden City, N.Y.: Natural History Press, 1966.

Taylor, Joseph E. "Insert Fact Here: Modeling the Past at Sea." Paper presented at the annual meeting of the American Society for Environmental History, Tallahassee, Fla., February 25 to March 1, 2009.

———. *Making Salmon: An Environmental History of the Northwest Fisheries Crisis*. Seattle: University of Washington Press, 1999.

Turner, Sharon R. "Salting Fish." Virginia Tech Sea Grant, Commercial Fish and Shellfish Technologies Notes (URL http://www.cfast.vt.edu/Publications/salting .shtml).

Tveskov, Mark. "Maritime Settlement and Subsistence along the Southern New England Coast: Evidence from Block Island, Rhode Island." *North American Archaeologist* 18 (1997): 343–61.

U.S. Department of Agriculture, *The Changing Fertility of New England Soils*, Agricultural Information Bulletin No. 333. Washington, D.C.: Government Printing Office, December 1954.

Van Sittert, Lance. "The Other Seven-Tenths." *Environmental History* 10 (2005): 106–9.

Vickers, Daniel. "Those Dammed Shad: Would the River Fisheries of New England Have Survived in the Absence of Industrialization?" *William and Mary Quarterly*, 3rd ser., 61 (2004): 685–712.

———. *Farmers and Fishermen: Two Centuries of Work in Essex County, Massachusetts, 1630–1850*. Chapel Hill: University of North Carolina Press, 1994.

———. *Young Men and the Sea: Yankee Seafarers in the Age of Sail*. New Haven, Conn.: Yale University Press, 2005.

Weber, Michael L. *From Abundance to Scarcity: A History of U.S. Marine Fisheries Policy*. Washington, D.C.: Island Press, 2002.

White, Richard. *The Organic Machine: The Remaking of the Columbia River*. New York: Hill & Wang, 1995.

Wilmerding, John. *American Light: The Luminist Movement, 1850–1875*. New York: Harper & Row, 1980.

———. *American Marine Painting*. New York: Harry N. Abrams, 1987.

———. *American Views: Essays on American Art*. Princeton, N.J.: Princeton University Press, 1991.

———. *Fitz Hugh Lane, 1804–1865: American Marine Painter*. Salem, Mass.: Essex Institute, 1964.

Wilton, Andrew, and Tim Barringer. *American Sublime: Landscape Painting in the United States, 1820–1880*. Princeton, N.J.: Princeton University Press, 2002.

Index

Page numbers in *italics* refer to tables and figures.

Agassiz, Louis, 69
agriculture: and campaign against pound nets
and weirs, 117; and colonists, 22–23, 28;
cranberry farming, 88, 89, 90; development
of, and reliance on sea, 49; in literature,
88–89, 90; onions as commodity, 48; use of
marine resources, 51, 103. *See also* soils
alewives: in colonial period, 26; as export commodity, 32, 34, 40; fishery expansion
attempts, 93, 94; life cycle, 38–39, 43–47;
role as forage fish, 144–45, 201nn13–14;
stocks after Baird recommendations, 140,
141–45, *142–44, 148,* 200–201nn8–9, 201n11;
trophic level, 145–46, *147;* in 20th century,
1, 174; in 21st century, 1. *See also* blue-black
herring
Algonquians, 13
Allard, Dean C., 199n41, 199n46
American Revolution, 41–42, 55–56
"The American Scholar" (Emerson), 54, 72
Ames, Ted, 176
Andrews Fishing Company, 94
archaeology, 13
art: and evocation of rural past, 157–58; iconographical significance, 70–73; prosperity
as harmonious with nature, *76,* 76–82, *77,
78, 80;* and tourism, 82, 157–59, 163–64,
203n42. *See also* seascapes
artificial runs, 92–96
Atwood, Nathaniel E., 69, 111, 117–22, 132, 137

Baird, Spencer Fullerton: congressional
inquiry, 127–35; consequences of recom-

mendations, *136,* 137–39, 140, 140–45,
142–45, 148–49, 200–201nn8–9, 201n11;
and federal funding of science, 199n41,
199n46; on fishery exhaustion, 111; on
pound nets, 97–98
baitfish/bait fisheries: artificial runs constructed,
92–96; and banks fishing industry dependence, 120; bluefish as cause of stocks
decline, 120, 127, 133; economic importance,
140; expansion after Baird recommendations, 140–45, *142–45,* 200–201nn8–9; and
hook-and-line fishermen, 105; innovations,
64–67, 90–91; and mackereling, 58–59,
65–66, 68; markets, 100–101; prepackaged,
67–68; profitability, 102–3, 104, 196n26; and
weir fishing, 96–97. *See also* pound nets/
pound fishing
banks fisheries: and campaign against pound
nets and weirs, 117; dependence on cheap
baitfish, 118, 120; economic impact, 2–3, *33,*
139; fish stocks decline, 139; Georges Banks,
56, 60–61; Grand Banks, 61, 66, 67; profitability, 104; Scotian Shelf, 61, 66
"The Bank Trawl-Line Fishery" (Goode and
Collins), 54
Barber, John, 74–76, *75, 76, 77*
Barnstable, 29, 153
Bassett, C. H., 115
Bassett, William A., 167
Beacon Rock, Newport Harbor (Kensett), 161
Belding, David, 174, 175
Bernstein, David, 13
Beston, Henry, 174–75

Bierstadt, Albert, 163

Bigelow, Henry B., 31

Black Hawk, 61

Blackwell, Michael, 39

blue-black herring: 2005 ban on fishing, 1; defining, 200n8; as export commodity, 32; stocks after Baird recommendations, 201n8, 201n11; trophic level, 145, *147*

bluefish, 120, 127, 133, *147–48*, 201n14

Bolster, Jeff, 2

Bourn, Jonathan, 41

Bradford, William (colonist), 16, 20–21, 22–23, 36

Bradford, William (painter), 77, 79–80, *80, 81*, 81–82

Bragdon, Kathleen, 13

Brereton, John, 16, 17

Brewster, 153

Brightman, Elias, 107

Brightman, Potter, 106–7

Brinley, Francis, 114, 116

Brown, Sam, 113

bultows (longlines) development, 62–63, 191–92n17

Burnett, D. Graham, 45

Burns, Sarah, 71

Cape Cod (Cape James/Cape Mallebar): archaeology, 13; geology, 8–11, *10*; harbor description, 21; names, 15. *See also place names*

capelin, 67

catch per unit of effort (CPUE), 141, *144*, 147

Chamberlayne, Francis, 168, 169–70, 171–72

Champlain, Samuel de, 14–15, 17

Chatham: economics of fishing methods, 104; harbor mouth silting, 139–40; mid-20th century weir fishing, 177; population decline in latter half of 19th century, 151; pound fishing after Baird recommendations, 138, 141–43, *143–44*; settlement, 29

Chuck, Charles C., 166

chum bait, 65–66

"Civic and Scenic New England" (Senter), 137

Clark, William, 37

Cleghorn, John, 131

coastal areas: artistic image as workspaces, 70–73, 76, 87; Colonial knowledge, 29, *30*; as community centers, 74–76, *75, 76*, 77; as

devoid of fishing industry, 157–62, *162*, 203n38; interpretation of, 175–76; as literary symbols of nonconformity, 83, 84; and local investment in artificial runs, 95; and ownership, 168; as wasteland, 49–53, 54–55. *See also* bait fish/bait fisheries; inshore fish/fisheries

coastal ecosystem: bait fisheries development, 91; fisheries scientists as experts, 112–13, 121–22, 128, 132, 172, 199n41; forage fish role, 144–45; local residents as experts, 44–46, 47, 114, 116, 119, 121–22, 132, 176; pound and weir fishermen as experts, 121–22; pound net fishing consequences, 148–49, 150–51, 154; relationship to terrestrial ecosystem, 24–25; responsibility for decline, 178–79; and tourism, 164, 165–66, 169

codfish/codfisheries: bait needs, 66–67, 192n27; commercial value as noted by explorers, 17; employment, 63, 64; Georges Banks, 56, 60–61; increased exploitation, 61–63, *63*, 191–92n17; as premier export commodity, 31–32, 33, 56; water preference, 31

Collins, J. W., 54

colonial period: commercial fishing regulations, 38, 40; domestic vs. commercial use of fish, 25–27; fish exports, 32–33; inshore fisheries and survival during, 23–24, 28–29, 32–33; management of inshore fisheries, 35–38, 39–41, 188n31; Pilgrims, 20–23; settlement pattern, 29, *30*; soils during, 21, 22, 28, 29; terrestrial ecosystem management, 25; use of ecological cycles, 24–25; and Wampanoag, 14

common good vs. private development, 43–47

common man, fisherman as iconographic American, 71–72

Cotuit, 123–27, 153

Council for New England, 24

Coy's Brook Fishing Company, 94

CPUE (catch per unit of effort), 141, *144*, 147

cranberry farming, 88, 89, 90

Crowell, Azariah F., 166

Crowell, David, 46

Davis, Malachi, 45–46

Davis, Peter, 166

Deane, Daniel W., 167

Dennis, 60, 104

domestication of seascapes, 71, 72
domestic markets, 55, 63–64
Donahue, Brian, 181n3
dory hand-lining, 61–62, *62*, *63*, 89, 191–92n17
Douglass, William, 40
Dunford, Frederick J., 13
Dwight, Timothy, 28, 34, 49–51

Eastham, 29, 47, 49, 138
Eaton's Neck (Kensett), *162*
Eccher, Jo-Ann, 7
economy: antebellum prosperity in art, 73–82,
    75, *76*, *77*, *78*, *80*, *81*; and baitfish, 101, 118,
    120–21, 140; and banks fisheries, 2–3, 33,
    139; and collapse in fish prices, 107–9, 149;
    colonial period resource management,
    36–38; community tensions and prosperity,
    89–90; in early 19th century, 49–53;
    employment in cod and mackerel fisheries,
    63, 64; at end of 19th century, 151–52; envi-
    ronmental degradation and prosperity, 6;
    export commodities, 26–27, 31–33, 34,
    39–40, 41, 56; growth after Baird recom-
    mendations, 138–39; and image of U.S.,
    70–71; increasing reliance on marine eco-
    system, 48–50; and inshore fisheries, 6,
    33–35, 93–95, 130, 131; and overfishing due
    to pound nets, 108–10; pound fishing ban
    consequences, 123–24; profitability of different
    fishing types, 102–4, 107, 196n26; prospects
    as seen by explorers, 17–18; regional trade,
    69–70; technological innovations and
    growth, 69; and tourism, 155, 171–72
ecosystems. *See* coastal ecosystem; marine
    ecosystem
Edgartown, 74, 75, *75*, 94, 95
Edwards, Vinal, 146, 171, 199n48, 201n8
Eldred, Lemuel, 163
Eliot, Thomas Dawes, 117
Emerson, Ralph Waldo, 54, 72
Entrance to Newport Harbor (Kensett), 160–61
estuaries formation, 11
European explorers, 14–19
experts: fisheries scientists as, 112–13, 121–22,
    128, 132, 199n41; fisheries scientists rejected
    as, 172; local residents as, 44–46, 47, 116,
    132, 176; local residents marginalized as,
    114; local residents rejected as, 119, 121–22;
    pound and weir fishermen as, 121–22

export commodity, fish as, 26–27, 31–33, 34,
    39–40, 41, 56

Fairhaven, in art, 75, *78*, 79–80, *80*, *81*
Falmouth: Herring War, 43–47, 93–94,
    189–90n54; inshore management, 42,
    93; settlement, 29; soils, 47
Falmouth Heights, 155
farming. *See* agriculture
file form vessels, 60
fish: decline on offshore banks, 139; domestic
    vs. commercial uses in colonial period,
    25–27; life cycles, 12–13, 107; names,
    186n57, 200n8; original abundance of,
    17–19, 21–22; preservability, 32; seasonal
    cycles, 24–25, 31, 36–37; types listed by
    explorers, 19. *See also individual species*
fisheries scientists: as experts, 112–13, 121–22,
    128, 132, 199n41; funding, 132, 134, 199n41,
    199n46; rejection as experts, 172; vision of
    boundless marine resources, 137
Fishing Station, Watch Hill, Rhode Island
    (Bierstadt), 163
Fish Wear Company, 101
Fitz, Asa, 70
food chain, 11–12, 145–46, 153, 201nn13–14,
    202n27
forage fish, 65, 67. *See also* bait fish/bait fisheries
Fowle, William B., 70
French and Indian War, 41

gangings, 62
Gazetteer of the State of Massachusetts (Nason),
    155–56
gear innovations: and cod fishing, 61–63, *63*,
    191–92n17; and mackereling, 57–60, *58*, *59*
gender in fishing communities, 89
geology of Cape Cod, 8–11, *10*
Georges Banks fisheries, 56, 60–61
Gertie Lewis, 61
ghost gear, 177
Gifford, Robert Swain, 77, 80, 81, 117, 162–63
Gifford, Thomas, 189–90n54
Gloucester, 60, 76
Goode, George Brown, 54
Gosnold, Bartholomew, 15, 17
Grand Banks (Newfoundland) fisheries, 61,
    66, 67
Gulf of Maine, 31

Hallett, Almoran, 106

Hammond, Noah, 167

hand-lining, 61–62, *62*, *63*, 66–67, 191–92n17, 192n27

Handy, Hetsel, 108, 116, 167

The Harbours of England (Ruskin), 72–73

Harwich: mackereling, 60; population decline in latter half of 19th century, 151; pound fishing after Baird recommendations, 141–43, *143–44*; regulation of inshore fisheries, 42, 92–93; settlement, 29

Hawes, John A., 118–19, 121

Hay, John, 175

Hayward, John, 63, 69–70

Hazard, Thomas, 34–35

Heade, Martin Johnson, 160

herring, defining, 200n8. *See also* river herring

Herring War, 43–47, 93–94, 189–90n54

Higginson, Stephen, 55–56

Hinckley, Barnabas, 43–47, 189–90n54

Hinckley, James, 47

Hingham, 93

Historical Collections of Massachusetts (Barber), 74–76, *75*, *76*, 77

An Historicall Discoverie and Relation of the English Plantations in New England (Council for New England), 24

Holmes, William, 44–46

hook-and-line fishermen: and Baird proposals, 135, 136, 148–49, 199n48; and congressional inquiry, 127–35; and effects of pound fishing, 105–6; emigration from Cape Cod, 150–51; industry profitability, 103, 104, 107–8; and late 19th-century attack on pound fishing, 169–70, 171; and mackerel, 57–59, *58*, *59*; pound fishing ban campaigns, 111, 113–27; relationship to fish, 112; removal as managers of inshore fisheries, 121–22, 154

hook footprint expansion, 61

Hunter, William, 39

Huxley, Thomas Henry, 120, 130, 132

Hyannisport, 155

industrialization, effects of, 39, 52–53, 181n3, 188n31, 189–90n54

innovations. *See* technology

inshore fish/fisheries: abundance noted by explorers, 18; during colonial period, 23–24, 28–29, 32–33; conditions in mid-19th century, 105; consequences of Baird recommendations, 140–41, 143, 148–49, 200–201nn8–9; and diet of Native Americans, 13–14; and economy, 33–35, 104, 123–24; and industrialization, 181n3; as managed by locals, 35; and pound nets, 96–98, *97*, *99*, 100–101, 106–9; responsibility for decline, 178–79; stock declines, 111, 117–22, 130, 132; and subsistence, 3. *See also* baitfish/bait fisheries; management of inshore fish/fisheries

Jenkins, James, 46

jig improvements, 57–58

Johnson, Edward, 23–24

Josseleyn, John, 27, 33

Judd, Richard, 181n3

Kendall, Edward Augustus, 51–52

Kensett, John Frederick, 160–61, *162*

Kerber, Jordan, 13

King, George Augustus, 168–69, 170, 171

Kulick, Gary, 181n3

Lady Elgin, 61

Lane, Fitz Henry, 77–78, 159

Lankester, Ray, 131

La Rochefoucauld, François, duc de, 34

Late Woodland Native Americans, 13

Laurentide ice sheet, 9

lease system, Plymouth, 36–37

literature, 82–87, 88–90, 158–59

Little, Elizabeth, 13

local residents: awareness of overfishing, 108–9; and baitfish runs, 91–93, 96; and colonial period regulations, 37, 38; as experts, 44–46, 47, 116, 132, 176; marginalization as experts, 114; rejection as experts, 119, 121–22; and Thoreau, 83–86

Long Pond Fishing Company, 94

Loring, Joseph G., 106

Luce, Jason, 101

Lumbert, Henry, 106

luminism, 159–61

Lyman, Theodore: and Agassiz, 69; on Atwood hearings, 118; and Baird, 132; consequences of decisions, 137; on Cotuit petition hearing, 123; on economic potential of fisheries, 123–24; hearings, 125–27; and institutionalization of commercial expediency, 135–36; on pound net usage, 98, 100; and privatization of natural resources, 124–25; on scientific management of fisheries, 135

mackerel/mackerel fisheries: bait, 58–59, 65–66, 68; colonial period management, 36–37; employment, 63, 64; increased exploitation, 57–60, 58, 59; utilization difficulties, 56–57
Maclean, Jay, 177
management of inshore fish/fisheries: during American Revolution, 40–41; during antebellum period, 93–96; Baird proposals, 135, 199n48; during colonial period, 35–38, 39–41, 188n31; during early 19th century, 92–94; and economic health of communities, 130, 131; at end of 18th century, 6, 42–43, 91–92; and knowledge of ecological cycles, 38, 43; local investment in artificial runs, 95; local residents as experts, 44–46, 47, 114, 116, 119, 121–22, 132, 176; and Lyman, 125–26; pound and weir fishermen as experts, 121–22; and pound fishing, 105, 106–9; regulations and seasonal cycles, 36–37; scientists as experts, 112–13, 121–22, 128, 132, 172, 199n41; themes, 37–38, 43; by tourist industry, 172–73; during 21st century, 1
Manning, Helen Vanderhoop, 7
marginal value theorem, 12
marine ecosystem: and bait, 67–68; as boundless, 137; Cape Cod vs. Gulf of Maine, 31; congressional inquiry, 127–35; decline of, and communities' decline, 150–53; degradation, 48; as encouraging indolence, 52; fishermen's role in research, 68–69; increasing economic reliance on, 48–50; needs from, and population, 52; research funding, 132, 136, 199n41, 199n46; resources used in agriculture, 51; responding to and shaping human actions, 177–79; as responsible for decrease in fish, 127, 133; scientific vs. local perspectives, 121–22
Marine off Big Rock (Kensett), 161
Marstons Mills Fishing Company, 95
Martha Burgess, 61
Martha's Vineyard, 8, 9, 93

Marx, Leo, 79
Mashpee, 92
McBride, Kevin, 13
McEvoy, Arthur, 2
"Mehetabel Rogers's Cranberry Swamp" (Nordhoff), 88–90
menhaden, 100, 103, 141, 144–46, 147–48
Merchant, Epes W., 65
Miller, Angela, 71, 73–74
mills for bait, 65–66
Mirror, 61
Mitchell, F., 157–58
Morrell, William, 24
Morton, Thomas, 25–27
Moshup, 7–8, 13, 14
Moshup's Footsteps: The Wampanoag Nation Gay Head / Aquinnah, The People of First Light (Manning and Eccher), 7
Mourt's Relation, 20, 21

Nantucket, 9
Nason, Elias, 155–56
nationalism and art, 71–74, 76, 76–82, 77, 78, 80
Native Americans, 7–8, 13, 14
Nauset, 174–75
navigational hazards, 14–16, 20–21
New Bedford, 75–76, 77, 78–79, 80, 80, 116–17
New Bedford from Fairhaven (van Beest), 79, 80
New-England, or a Briefe Narration of the Ayre, Earth, Water, Fish and Fowles of that Country (Morrell), 24
New England's Rarities Discovered (Josseleyn), 33
Noepe (Martha's Vineyard), 8, 9
Nordhoff, Charles, 88–90
Novak, Barbara, 71, 159

Of Plimoth Plantation (Bradford), 20–21
O'Leary, Wayne, 61–62
Orleans, 101, 153
Osterville, 155
The Outermost House (Beston), 174, 175

Pacific Guano Company, 117, 166
Palmer, George H., 129, 164–66, 167–68
pastoral images, iconographical significance of, 70–71
Pault, Daniel, 177
Pease, Josiah, 101, 107

Pease, Rufus, 107

Pilgrims, 20–23

Pinsky, Robert, 87

Plymouth, 20–23, 36–38

Pocha Pond Meadow and Fishing Company, 95

population: antebellum growth of, 64; at end of 19th century, 138; in latter half of 19th century, 150–51; and privatization of natural resources, 124; and prosperity, 69–70; and resource management, 52

pound nets/pound fishing: Baird proposals, 135, 199n48; congressional inquiry, 127–35; decline in catches, 147, *148*; described, 3, 97–98, *99*; ecological effects, 148–49, 150–51, 154; economics of, 103–4, 107, 149–50; expansion after Baird recommendations, 138–39, 140–45, 200–201nn8–9; and fishermen as managers of inshore fisheries, 121–22; and fishermen's relationship to fish, 112; as future fish stock preserver, 107, 176–77; and growth of baitfish industry, 96–98, *97*, *99*, 100–102; hook-and-line fishermen's campaigns against, 111, 113–27; late 19th-century campaign against, 164–72; local residents' awareness of overfishing, 108–9; as monopoly, 165; and recreational tourist interests, 164; skill requirements, 149–50

poverty as comparative, 50–52

Prence, Thomas, 36

primary production, 11

Pring, Martin, 16, 17, 18

privatization of natural resources, 43–47, 92–96, 124–25

Provincetown: in art, 74–75, *76*; and banks fisheries, 139, 140; importance of cheap baitfish, 118; mackereling, 60; Pilgrims, 21–22; population increase in latter half of 19th century, 150–51; pound nets after Baird recommendations, 138; railroad station, 101; Thoreau on, 86; tourism, 155, 156–57; weir fishing in mid-20th century, 176–77

railroads, 101, 105, 117, 15

Rasieres, Isaack, 15–16

recreationists, 164, 165–66, 172

regulation. *See* management of inshore fish/fisheries

Report of the Condition of the Sea Fisheries of the South Coast of New England in 1871 and 1872 (Baird), 111

Report on the Alewife Fishery of Massachusetts (Belding), 174, 175

Rhode Island, 111, 113–16

river herring: artificial runs, 94; and community management, 91–93; defining, 200n8; knowledge of ecological cycles, 38, 43; life cycle, 39; management during colonial period, 39–41, 188n31; overview of 19th-century decline, 1–2. *See also* blue-black herring

Rochester, 41, 91–92, 93

Rockwell, Henry E., 129

Rogers, Charles H., 151

Rogers, Edward H., 137, 152, 153

Rogers, Moses, 166

Romp, 60

Rosier, James, 18, 19

Rozwadowski, Helen, 44

The Run (Hay), 175

Ruskin, John, 72–73

Sabine, Lorenzo, 64

Sanchachantacket Fishing Company, 94

Sandwich: regulation of inshore fisheries, 39–40, 41–42, 91, 188n31; settlement, 29; soils, 47–48; Thoreau on, 83; tourism in 18th century, 47

Schroeder, William C., 31

Scotian Shelf fisheries, 61, 66, 67

scup, 147, *147–48*

sea herring, 200n8

seascapes, 70–73, 74, 76, 159–62, *162*, *163*

Second Beach at Newport (Whittredge), 161–62, *163*

Senter, Oramel, 137, 156

Sewall, Samuel, 39–40

sharpshooters, 60

ships. *See* vessels; *specific vessels*

Smith, John, 15, 17, 18, 19

Smith, Nathan, 113

Smith, Nathaniel, 106

soils: during colonial period, 21, 22, 28, 29; at end of 18th century, 47–48; explorers' descriptions of, 16–17; formation of, 9–11, *10*

Southwick, J. M. K., 129
Spindle, Isaiah, 97
sports fishing, 164, 165–66, 172
Squanto, 22–23
Standish, Myles, 36
stationary shore fishing gear. *See* pound nets/
    pound fishing; weirs/weir fishing
Stein, Roger B., 71
Steinberg, Theodore, 181n3
Stewart, Prince M., 170
Stilgoe, John, 15
Storer, Humphrey, 68–69
Study of Fairhaven Waterfront (Bradford),
    79–80, *80*
subsistence fishing, 3, 38, 40, 105
Swift, William, 46

Tallman, Benjamin, 115–16
technology: and bait fisheries, 64–67, 90–91;
    and cod fisheries, 61–63, *63*, 191–92n17;
    hook improvements, 57–58; and mackerel
    fisheries, 57–60, *58*, *59*
terrestrial ecosystem: Bradford on, 23; explor-
    ers' descriptions, 16–17; management dur-
    ing colonial period, 25; and population
    growth, 52, 69–70; relationship to coastal
    ecosystem, 24–25, 49
Thoreau, Henry David, 82–87
Tisquantum, 22–23
toll bait, 65–66
tourism: antebellum, 154; and art, 82, 157–59,
    163–64, 203n42; and coastline manage-
    ment, 172–73; emergence as major industry,
    182n4; first, 47; and fishing industry, 154,
    155–57, 172, 182n4; and late 19th-century
    attack on pound fishing, 164, 165–66,
    169–70, 171–72; post-Civil war develop-
    ment, 155–64; reconnecting with rural past,
    157–58, 203n38; as traditional Cape Cod
    industry, 175; and weir fishing, 164
trade: export commodities, 26–27, 31–33, 34,
    39–40, 41, 56; regional, 69–70
traps. *See* pound nets/pound fishing
Travels in New York and New England
    (Dwight), 28
trophic levels, 145–46, *147*, 201nn13–14
True, Frederick, 149, 151

Truro, 48, 49, 63, 70, 138
tub trawls, 62–63, *63*, 66, 67, 191–92n17

United Nations Educational, Scientific, and
    Cultural Organization (UNESCO), 176

van Beest, Albert, 77, 78–79, 81
vegetation, described by explorers, 16–17
vessels: in art, *62*, 72–73, 74–75, *76*; bait rooms,
    67; for mackerel fishing, 59–60. *See also*
    specific vessels
Vickers, Daniel, 181n3
Vincent, Daniel, 166

Wampanoag, 7–8, 13, 14
War of 1812, 56
wealth as comparative, 50–52
weirs/weir fishing: Baird proposals, 135,
    199n48; and baitfish, 96–97; and congres-
    sional inquiry, 127–35; expansion after
    Baird recommendations, 138–39, 140–45,
    142, *144*, 200–201nn8–9; and fishermen's
    relationship to fish, 112; as future fish stock
    preserver, 176–77; hook-and-line fisher-
    men's campaigns against, 111, 113–27; late
    19th-century attack against, 164–72; mar-
    kets, 4; as monopoly, 165; overview, 3; and
    recreational tourist interests, 164. *See also*
    pound nets/pound fishing
Wellfleet: in art, 75, 77; employment in fisher-
    ies, 63; increasing reliance on sea, 49;
    mackereling, 60; population decline in lat-
    ter half of 19th century, 151; railroad station,
    101; regulation of inshore fisheries, 92–93
West Indies trade, 39–40, 41
Westport, 116
Whitman, Levi, 49
Whittredge, Thomas Worthington, 160,
    161–62, *163*
Wianno, 155
Wing, Daniel, 39
Winslow, Edward, 20, 21, 22, 24
Wood, William, 24–25
Woods Hole, 101, 146–47, *148*

Yarmouth, 47, 153
Yarmouthport, 101

11/12/21 - Is there any way to understand what step in the process this proper picture may represent?